From
SILICON VALLEY
to SWAZILAND

How One Couple Found Purpose and Adventure in an Encore Career

RICK & WENDY WALLEIGH

From Silicon Valley to Swaziland: How One Couple Found Purpose and Adventure in an Encore Career

Published by Wheatmark®
1760 East River Road, Suite 145, Tucson, Arizona 85718 USA
www.wheatmark.com

ISBN: 978-1-62787-185-3 (paperback)
ISBN: 978-1-62787-186-0 (ebook)
LCCN: 2014954651

To our children, Adrian and Diana,
who are already working to make
the world a better place.

Acknowledgements

$\mathcal{M}$any people have contributed their support to us over the seven years that we worked to publish this book, and we would like to give them at least some small level of recognition and thanks.

First must come all of the people we worked with in Swaziland and Kenya, both TechnoServe employees and participants in the TechnoServe projects. Some are mentioned by name (real or pseudonym) in the book, and others are unfortunately too numerous to mention. We were new to international development and they informed, coached, and interpreted for us so that our work could be useful.

Next, we'd like to thank our friends and colleagues who read our book at various stages of refinement and provided feedback to make it better, including Holly Marvin, Holly Krueger, Tim McLellan, and Simon Winter. We are especially grateful to Bruce McNamer, George Schutter, Leslie Johnston, Debra Dunn, and Ron Boring for giving us feedback and writing endorsements.

In the professional arena, Arielle Eckstut was a great editor and coach, and Lori Leavitt and Grael Norton have been our able guides throughout the publishing process.

Thanks to all. Without them, this book would not have happened.

Contents

Swaziland

Swaziland

San Francisco to Mbabane

*A*s the twin-engine turboprop climbed out of Oliver Tambo airport, we could see the densely packed slums surrounding Johannesburg, but the urban landscape quickly disappeared. It was winter in the southern hemisphere, and the flat terrain below was dry and brown. The land was chopped up into tiny plots for farming, most of them fallow. They looked rather sad, as farmland does when nothing is growing. The flight from Johannesburg to Matsapha Airport near Manzini, Swaziland, takes less than an hour, but this was our fourth flight since leaving San Francisco. We had been traveling for thirty-six hours, including two overnight legs.

The journey from San Francisco to Manzini, Swaziland, is just about the longest possible trip on earth. In addition to contending with the long flights, we had to manage our carry-on luggage through the multiple airport transits. Since we were staying for nearly six months, we brought a lot of luggage. The airlines allow you to check two bags per person, so we had four large suitcases weighing the maximum of fifty pounds each. In packing, we had allocated them fairly—that is, three for Wendy and one for me. She wasn't going to Africa without a sufficient wardrobe and a six-month supply of her favorite beauty aids and toiletries.

However, throughout the trip, Wendy was a real trouper. Since two hundred pounds of luggage was not a sufficient allowance for all of our stuff, we also maximized our carry-ons. For carry-ons, the airline allowances are by size, not weight. Consequently, we each carried a thirty-five-pound duffel and a fifteen-pound computer bag. These were heavy for me, and my shoulders ached, but as we slogged through our last transit, I wasn't sure if Wendy was going to make it. Going through the terminal at Oliver Tambo, she looked as if she was about ready to drop. I helped some, and she pulled through bravely. Later, we saw the rough, red welts she had from the shoulder straps, but they cleared up in a few days.

As our flight approached Swaziland, the topography changed again. We began to see a few small mountains. They looked like the foothills in California, but craggier. When it rains in California, the foothills are covered with green grass. In late spring, the rains stop and the land turns light brown as the vegetation dies. In California PR terms, the hills turn "golden." They're really dead brown, like straw, but can still be beautiful in a rugged, natural way. In Swaziland, it rains in the summer and the winters are dry. The approaching hills looked comfortably familiar, like California with the dry, straw-brown grass contrasting with the black rock and the red dirt.

As we approached Matsapha International Airport, I wasn't nervous or even excited. I was mostly curious and definitely fatigued. On landing and deplaning, the airport felt welcoming and comfortable in a cute and informal way. Since Matsapha has the only paved runway in Swaziland, it is an international airport by default. It had the smallest commercial airline terminal I had ever seen, particularly at an international airport. The terminal had one door for arrivals and one door for departures. Separating the two doors was a pleasant little garden, about ten feet square, of local flora surrounded by carefully positioned rocks. Someone had taken time and effort to make it attractive, and it worked. We entered the arrivals door and passed through immigration and customs in a space the size of our living room at home.

Outside the terminal, Kiki, the driver from TechnoServe, was waiting for us with a warm, smiling face, and we were very glad to see him. With very few people awaiting the arrival of our flight, it wasn't hard for us to pick out Kiki. And as we were the only non-Africans on the flight, it wasn't hard for him to identify us.

We loaded up our luggage and set off for Mbabane (pronounced by humming the *m* and then saying "buh-bahn"), the capital of Swaziland and our home for the next six months, about a half hour away. Our first destination was the TechnoServe office where we would be working. The office was on the second floor of a small, modern shopping mall in the center of Mbabane (population 90,000). The TechnoServe office had been open only since February, but was already becoming crowded. We met fourteen people, but there were nearly twenty names on a whiteboard that showed everyone's location throughout the day. Among our future colleagues, only Leslie, our country director and boss, plus three other volunteers had come from the United States. Leslie had worked for TechnoServe in Mozambique for several years prior to Swaziland. Everyone else was from Swaziland. Some were full-time employees and some were interns, but everyone was young, most of them younger than our two children. After we met our coworkers, we got local cell phones and then bought a few groceries so we could exist until Monday.

Having spent two overnights on airplanes and having endured a nine-hour time change, we got tired very quickly, so we were driven to our lodgings about four miles outside of Mbabane. We were delighted to see the quaint little cottage where we would be living. Our cottage and several others were located on the grounds of a Christian retreat center along with a small conference facility and a chapel. The cottages were widely spaced and surrounded by large eucalyptus trees. Our front door exited to a patio overlooking a deep valley with mostly forest on the opposite side. Once again, we could imagine we were in the foothills of California, except for the thatched roofs on the cottages.

Later, as we ate dinner, we discussed our first impressions. From what we had seen, Swaziland was definitely a developing country. However, it seemed cleaner, neater, and sometimes more modern than many others we had visited. Especially in the center of Mbabane, where there was a shopping plaza dating from the early nineties and two small malls that were newer, we felt the ambiance of a small working-class city in the United States or Canada. It wasn't an exotic environment from an African novel or a movie. The city streets were better maintained than in some U.S. cities, and the road from the airport to Mbabane was a four-lane divided highway. While the cars were not extravagant, they were not all old and run-down as they are in many developing countries; and they seemed to be plentiful. However, contrasting with the pleasant, if not inspired, architecture of the shopping area was a huge concrete skeleton of an abandoned multistory building that dominated the hill above the city. I was sure that there was a story of speculation and probably corruption behind the giant edifice because it looked as if it had been abandoned, partially constructed, many years earlier. I wasn't judging, and I hadn't drawn any immediate comprehensive conclusions; I was just trying to take in the comparisons and contrasts to begin the mental processing.

My other immediate impression as we walked around Mbabane was of a disproportionately youthful population. Since we were walking around a shopping plaza at 4:00 p.m., the youthful crowd could have been just what would be expected at a shopping mall at 4:00 p.m. anywhere in the world. However, I couldn't help but think about the AIDS epidemic that was ravaging Swaziland, worse than any other country in the world, and producing an average life expectancy of only thirty-two years. Maybe it was what a society looks like when AIDS kills a huge proportion of the adults and produces a generation of orphans.

How Did We Get Here?

*I*t's hard to know when the idea started for me. Maybe it had been percolating since I read a biography of Dr. Albert Schweitzer when I was a child. Or maybe it only started a few years ago as I became one of the frontline baby boomers contemplating what I wanted to do in "retirement," whatever that means anymore. I had always admired Albert Schweitzer, who gave up a great life in Europe to be a doctor in a remote region of Africa. However, I hadn't been so moved that I wanted to be a hero and give up all the worldly pleasures of a good life. I wanted a good career and the rewards that went with it.

Now was different. We had been fortunate in our lives and careers. We weren't rich, but we had enough saved that we didn't need to focus on maximizing our income. Also, our children seemed on their way to careers of their own. One was in medical school and the other nearly finished with law school. So when I left my last high-tech job, I evaluated our finances and decided that I'd finished my primary career, but I wasn't ready to stop working. For a number of years, Wendy and I had periodically discussed what we would do next as we contemplated wrapping up our primary careers. Neither of us wanted to be heroic, but we both wanted to "give something back." We both wanted to be working on something of obvious benefit to society.

Wendy had taken the first step in this direction. Four years earlier, she was feeling frustrated and unsatisfied selling just one more new technology product. So she left her career as a director of marketing in the high-tech industry where she had spent her career. She took time off to contemplate and explore what she wanted to do next. As she thought about her interests and how she might contribute to society, she narrowed her focus to three major themes: youth (especially young women), education, and entrepreneurship. Her next step was to network and explore for potential opportunities that could satisfy these interests. After a lot of lunches and coffee sessions, a friend suggested that she might want to join the board of directors of Junior Achievement (JA) in Silicon Valley as a part-time activity while she continued to explore. The focus of Junior Achievement is teaching young people the life and business skills they will need to thrive in our free market economy. So it aligned precisely with Wendy's interests, but it wasn't a full-time activity.

Wendy joined the Junior Achievement board and immediately assessed that JA needed help with marketing. There was no marketing plan, so Wendy set out to create one. She did extensive interviews with the executive director, the staff, donors, and other stakeholders and developed a marketing plan that would allow JA to increase their revenue and the number of students that they could serve. The executive director loved the plan and convinced the executive committee of the board that she needed someone to implement it. She wanted to hire Wendy as a full-time employee. The executive director got her approval and approached Wendy, who was excited, but a little surprised and definitely hesitant. The position sounded great, but Wendy had been expecting to take more time off. In the end, the opportunity was too good a fit to pass up, and Wendy agreed to start in a part-time role that quickly evolved to full-time.

Wendy became JA's vice president of marketing, and several months later, when the vice president of development left, Wendy became vice president of marketing and development. She was paid half of her former salary, and she still worked long hours, but she felt she was doing it for a better reason. In addition to teaching kids about the free enterprise system and how to be successful in business, Junior Achievement encourages young people to stay in school, study hard, and to see themselves as future entrepreneurs or businesspeople. It was a great fit with Wendy's interests and allowed her to use her skills and experience to benefit society.

While Wendy was at Junior Achievement, I was still pursuing my career in the high-tech industry, but I knew it wouldn't be for many years. It had been a very enjoyable, challenging, and rewarding career. I had been a partner in a large consulting firm, a senior vice president at a start-up and a general manager in a software company, but I was ready for a major change. I thought a lot about what might come next. As with the millions of baby boomers who will soon reach the traditional retirement age in good health, I knew that I could easily live another thirty years, and I knew that I would have a lot of time to fill. I didn't play golf, which can fill more time than any other human activity I know of, so I had to think of something else.

I knew I wanted to contribute something back to society, and I knew I wanted something that would excite me, but I wasn't sure what it would be. My first thought was to become a paramedic and support relief efforts after global disasters. It sounded exciting and heroic, but it would have meant a year of training and then being away from Wendy for extended periods of time. I realized that I needed a more disciplined approach to my search. I bought *What Color Is Your Parachute?* and followed the instructions and exercises for a "life-changing job hunt." In one exercise, I decided the person that I would most like to be was Kofi Annan because he worked to achieve world peace. I decided I wanted to work on world peace, and I knew I could use my skills and experience to do it.

It may not seem obvious as to how experience in management consulting and managing high-tech companies can directly contribute to world peace. However, a few years earlier, I had read Tom Friedman's *The Lexus and the Olive Tree*, and in my opinion, he had defined the path to world peace. Paraphrasing, with apologies, his idea was to get everyone doing business with each other to generate economic benefits for all parties. Once people got significant benefits from doing business with each other and developed strong stakes in preserving society, they wouldn't go to war against each other because they would understand how devastating it would be to their lives. In other words, the idea is to create enough economic incentives not to go to war that they offset the many other causes that push people to war. It all seemed very logical to me—create economic development to decrease the possibility of war and, along the way, reduce poverty.

I wasn't so naive to think that this was an easy path to solving all the world's problems, but I do believe that one person can make a difference. My philosophy is to light one candle rather than curse the darkness. When confronting difficult or undesirable situations, I hate feeling hopeless. I always look for a solution, and the solutions to difficult problems are often complex and difficult themselves. If I was going to pursue this path, I didn't want to be simple-minded or foolish. I really wanted to know what the experts said about how to foster economic development. If I was going to put a lot of effort into something, I wanted to be contributing in the most productive way.

So my next step was to study. I read over twenty books related to international economic development. Some were academic; some were inspirational. Some were very hopeful, others just the opposite as they recounted all the mistakes that continue to be made in the name of trying to help poor people and developing countries. As I read the books, I continued to focus my direction, but I didn't find anything that made me change my course.

The first thing that I learned from all my reading is that the experts don't have a clear, consistent recipe for successful economic development. However, as I read, I became convinced that building private enterprise was the best way to achieve sustainable success. There are too many stories of grand government schemes costing hundreds of millions of dollars that have failed to make a difference or just failed outright. Also, with large government projects, there are too many people who can benefit whether the project is successful or not. Naturally, this includes the graft that is endemic throughout the world, but it also includes all of the people who get an income from contracting to do the work whether the work generates real benefits or not. But for independent businesses, there will ultimately be a success or a failure, and it is not hard to measure the successes and keep score. You can keep doing the things that work and stop investing in the things that don't. Independent business development also promotes freer societies as we've seen in many developing countries, such as South Korea and even China. Once again, don't get me wrong. I know that there has been a lot of exploitation of people and resources by business. However, on balance, free-market economic development is good, and independent businesses with some government regulation are the ways to make it happen.

Fortunately for me, and probably not coincidentally, I had a lot of experience in private business. I knew how to help businesses solve problems, and I knew how to help businesses grow. So my skills aligned with where I saw the best opportunity to contribute. I had theoretical convergence, but I had no idea as to where to apply my theoretical solution. I didn't know if any real-life organization doing international development needed my skills. I also had no experience in international development or the whole nonprofit arena, and I didn't even know most of the major players in the field.

I needed to do more research, so I went to the web, and I started networking in person. On the web, I started researching the larger organizations that I had heard of such as CARE and Heifer. I also read about the Peace Corps, USAID (United States Agency for International Development), and various agencies within the United Nations. I asked all of my friends who they knew who might be in the field, and I went through the alumni directories of MIT and Harvard Business School to find fellow alums who worked in international development. As I talked to all of these people, I asked them for additional contacts. I eventually talked to over eighty different people about what I wanted to do. Some were in government, some in academia, some in large nonprofits or NGOs (nongovernmental organizations), and many were in smaller NGOs. They all gave me ideas about organizations that might be of interest to me. Then I researched those organizations on the web and made contact to find out more. Thank goodness for the Internet.

After making contact, I visited a number of organizations where I thought I had relevant skills and experience and interviewed for potential job openings. Although people were impressed with my background and experience in business, I kept hearing the same refrain, "But you have no experience in international development or even the nonprofit arena." There was a terrible mismatch. Without the international development background, no organization was going to hire me into a senior-level position despite all of my business experience and accomplishments. On the other hand, it made no sense for the organizations, or to me, to hire me into an entry-level position. It was a frustrating dilemma.

As I spoke to knowledgeable people in the international development field and explained to them specifically what I wanted to do, a number of them recommended that I talk to an organization called TechnoServe. TechnoServe's tagline was "Business Solutions to Poverty," and their mission was to grow businesses that could provide livelihoods for the poor. It sounded like a good match, and so I contacted them.

TechnoServe was located in Washington DC, and I was going back to the DC area for Thanksgiving, so I arranged to meet with Bruce, TechnoServe's CEO for an informational interview. With TechnoServe's approach to international development, my business background was highly relevant. However, I knew that my lack of international development experience would still be an issue, so I explained to Bruce the challenge that I had been having with other organizations. Bruce had a solution immediately. He agreed with the position taken by other organizations, but he also saw that I had important qualifications and experience. He said that with my background in business, it would only take a year or two of international development experience for me to develop the credibility I would need for a senior-level position in an NGO. And he had a solution for where to get the experience.

TechnoServe had a volunteer consultant program wherein people with business skills volunteered on TechnoServe projects to provide business insight. TechnoServe provided housing and twenty-five dollars per day for food and incidentals. Participants in the program were called "volcons" (volunteer consultants), and most were young people in their twenties or early thirties who had worked for prominent consulting organizations. Many of the volcons worked at TechnoServe for three to six months right before or right after getting their MBAs. Obviously, Wendy and I were older, but that also meant we had a lot more business experience. We could also devote a longer period of time to an assignment. I told Bruce that the opportunity sounded interesting and that I would discuss it with Wendy.

While I was doing all of my research, Wendy was still working for Junior Achievement. She wasn't quite ready to leave her job, but she knew the time would be soon. Since we would eventually be undertaking our international venture together, I had continued to discuss my thoughts with her, and she was supportive. She had always wanted to try living in another country but had mostly been thinking about locales like London, Paris, or Hong Kong. Living in a developing country hadn't really crossed her mind, but she was brave and willing to try a new adventure. Since she was still working, she was happy to have me do all the research and planning. One time, as we were discussing my latest findings and thoughts while I was preparing dinner in our kitchen (she was working full-time and I wasn't), she told me to choose where we would go and she would go along.

She said, "I have just four requirements for any place where we will live: First, there can be no flying bullets. Second, the name of the country must not end in 'stan.' Also, there must be flush toilets, and there must be hot showers."

I had no problem with these minimal restrictions since I knew by focusing on business, that we wouldn't be living in a mud hut in a rural village. As I continued my discussions with Wendy, I told TechnoServe that we would be interested in the volcon program, but just not yet. Seven months later, Wendy was finally ready to leave Junior Achievement, and I called TechnoServe to tell them that we were ready to take on overseas volunteer roles. They told us they would send out our résumés to their local country directors to see if there were any opportunities that would fit our backgrounds. Within two days, we heard back from Leslie, TechnoServe's country director in Swaziland. She had started up TechnoServe's new program in Swaziland just a few months earlier and was still recruiting staff. She was very excited about our skills and background and explained that she had openings that would be a perfect fit for each of us. She also thought we could help her immensely.

The primary focus of the Swaziland operation was to help small businesses to be successful and create jobs and economic growth. For this focus, my management consulting experience was very attractive because most of Leslie's staff would be consulting to small businesses. My background was particularly attractive because I had been a consultant for many years and most of her staff members were very young. Although they were smart, they had limited experience, and Leslie thought that I could be a mentor to them. Another objective of the Swazi operation was to set up a program of youth training in business skills and entrepreneurship. With her recent work in Junior Achievement, Wendy was a perfect fit for this initiative. Leslie wanted us to fly to Swaziland immediately. We weren't ready to take off immediately, but in less than a month, we were on a plane. After all the research and waiting for Wendy to be ready, everything seemed to happen very quickly. We just packed our bags and moved to Africa without a very clear idea of where we were going or exactly what we would be doing. We did limit our initial commitment to less than six months, just in case, but our friends were still amazed. For us, it wasn't that difficult to commit. We were confident that we could survive for six months. More importantly, we knew that we would be working for a social benefit, and that the whole experience would be an adventure.

Settling in

Familiar Work in an Unfamiliar Environment

*O*n our first morning in Swaziland, we both suffered from serious jet lag caused by the nine-hour time difference from California. We had essentially switched night and day. I got up in the middle of the night to read for two hours before returning to bed, and we both slept in until 10:30 a.m. After breakfast, we weren't sure what to do. While we were in a beautiful setting, we were basically trapped because there was nowhere to easily walk, and we didn't have a car. We had been told that the conference center had a workout facility, so we asked for the key. We walked to what turned out to be a one-room cottage with a few dumbbells and an all-purpose exercise machine with missing parts. We hadn't expected much, and so we weren't disappointed, but we never went back. We exercised briefly with a set of elastic tubes that I had brought from home, and both of us tired really quickly.

We didn't have Internet access at our cottage, but we had heard that we could get on and check our e-mail at the Mountain Inn, a very pleasant sixty-two-room hotel at the top of the Malagwane grade overlooking the valley below. Many years earlier, the family who owned the Emafini Christian Center where we were staying had purchased the Mountain Inn when it was a famous brothel and converted it. Liz, our landlady and the matriarch of the family, volunteered to drive us up the two miles to the inn.

As we arrived at the Mountain Inn, we breathed a sigh of relief after the quick trip up the Malagwane grade, a very steep and winding section of the highway to Mbabane. The Malagwane grade would never exist on a four-lane highway in the United States. It was too steep and had excessively sharp curves. The speed limit was ostensibly 60 kph (36 mph), but as we learned from experience, no one drove that speed. Drivers in the powerful Mercedes and BMWs that could climb the grade without downshifting would roar up the hill at 120 kph (over 70 mph). (These people, often members of parliament or government officials, were known locally as members of the MBenzi tribe, even if they drove BMWs.) But in addition to the MBenzis, the grade was always sprinkled with massive, over-loaded trucks going 20 kph (12 mph). I later had many chances to drive up the grade and personally experience the excitement and danger! The dual challenges were to not slam into the slow trucks as I came up rapidly from behind and to not get hit in the rear by a fast car as I passed the slow trucks, all the while maneuvering around the sharp curves. Every trip up or down the grade was an adventure, and soon it became our daily commute.

On our second morning, Sunday, we got up late again, still struggling with oppressive jet lag. We had breakfast at 11:30 a.m., so we decided that it was our lunch as well. While I was lounging in the living room with a book, I got another indication of the local similarity with California. As I looked out of the glass French doors, I noticed a large plume of smoke from the forest across the valley. I didn't panic immediately, but I knew the brush was dry and the thought of California forest fires came to mind. I had observed that we were surrounded by tall eucalyptus trees, and I remembered that they burn easily and very hot. I began thinking about what I would pack if we had to evacuate in a hurry. I went outside to survey the situation. At the base of the huge smoke plume, I could see some low flames in the brush. There was no fire higher up in the trees themselves, so I decided not to get too excited. I would just watch calmly and patiently. I figured that if there was an emergency, someone would warn us.

I went back to my reading but got up periodically to observe the fire. While the smoke plume remained huge, the fire didn't seem to be moving. After a while, Liz drove by. She was obviously observing the situation as well. I flagged her down and asked if we should be concerned. While visibly showing some concern, Liz said that we shouldn't worry. If the fire did start moving our way, she felt the fire breaks on their property would stop it before it became threatening. She also indicated that her son Patrick would certainly be the first to raise an alarm since his house would be the first to be in danger, especially considering his thatch roof. Her primary concern seemed to be with the environmental impact that all the smoke was having. She said that the fire was probably started by locals seeking honey from beehives. Evidently, their tactics consist of generating smoke to get the bees to leave their hive so that the honey can be removed without interference. Liz was upset not only with the impact that these methods generate, but also that the honey seekers don't always put out their fires.

I returned to reading and began to speculate what work would be like when we started in the morning. After two weekend days, we were very content with our surroundings. We felt as if we were on vacation in a small cabin in a California state park. The small stove in the kitchen required a match to light the bottled gas, and there was no dishwasher. There was, however, a clothes washer and dryer. We decided to give them a try. Although the controls on the washer had unfamiliar symbols, we pretty much figured it out. We put in the clothes and the detergent, and when we pushed one of the buttons, it started. Unfortunately, I came back later to find the floor flooded. After investigating, I determined that the drain hose from the washer had come out of the drain pipe and irrigated the floor. I went over to Liz's house to get a mop and then got up all the water. At least we knew the floor was really clean.

Wendy had been quietly working on her computer in the kitchen, periodically staring out of the window through the steel bars that prevented burglary. At one point she detected a slight shadow and lifted her head to see a vervet monkey calmly sitting on the window ledge outside the bars. He stuck his hand through the bars and reached around a bit, but he couldn't reach anything of interest. (The bars were configured to prevent nonhuman burglary as well.) After the two stared at each other for a while, the monkey calmly left. It was just a brief encounter but was one of the many small clues that reminded us that we weren't in California. As we settled in over the next few weeks, we frequently saw families of monkeys playing among the eucalyptus off to the side of our house and occasionally in the mulberry tree in our front yard. It was almost like a visit to the zoo every day.

On Monday, we started work, and the first thing we saw when we went to the office was the morning paper. The front-page story, complete with picture, was about a woman who was seriously burned in an outhouse explosion. As the very detailed article explained, evidently someone had been using gasoline to clean grease off some car parts. After completing the cleaning, the excess solvent and dissolved grease had been thrown down the local outhouse. Shortly thereafter the unsuspecting woman had sat down to do her business, and while sitting, lit up a cigarette and threw the match down the hole. The resulting explosion did extensive damage to the outhouse and seriously burned the woman in some sensitive areas. However, she was expected to fully recover. That was the major national news story in Swaziland that day.

We learned that the flavor of Monday's front-page story was typical, and Tuesday's front page didn't disappoint as it combined human interest with politics. It was about the speaker of Parliament and his speech on the sexual performance of Swazi men. Swaziland had the world's highest rate of AIDS with its resulting mortality. The death rate from AIDS was of great concern to the government since it typically killed young adults in their most economically productive years and often left orphans behind. It was well known that the major cause of the AIDS epidemic in Swaziland was multiple concurrent partners engaging in unprotected sex. The parliament was debating whether they could do anything to remedy this situation and reduce the rate of AIDS. At this point, the speaker of the Parliament arose and gave an impassioned speech. He said that the major problem was that too many Swazi men did not know how to sexually satisfy their wives. Consequently, the women were seeking satisfaction with other partners and causing the AIDS problem. He exhorted Swazi men to do a better job of satisfying their wives and keeping them at home. We learned that stories like these or features on domestic violence and corruption frequently grabbed the daily headlines because Swaziland did not play a major role in geopolitics. For us, the novelty of reading the local tabloids quickly wore off.

Getting down to work, we spent our first week getting started on our primary projects. Wendy began working with Atiba, a TechnoServe colleague, to create a School-Age Youth Entrepreneurship (SAYE) program to inspire a pool of school-age (teens and early twenties) Swazis to become entrepreneurs. The primary activities within the program would be to introduce these youth to the business world and the skills necessary to create a business. Although the government, banks, and the local offices of a few international corporations provided good jobs for some of the best students, the country had 50 percent unemployment, and many people felt that they had to leave for South Africa to find a decent job. The hope was that with business knowledge and especially entrepreneurship skills, young Swazis might find or even create economic opportunity in their own country. Wendy was a perfect fit for the role, and Leslie was happy to have someone with Wendy's prior experience in Junior Achievement.

For their first activity, Atiba and Wendy met with several groups in rural and urban areas to understand how to leverage any existing youth-oriented business/entrepreneurship activities, especially the already-established "pre-voc" (prevocational or school-to-work) pilot schools. Their experience in visiting two of the "pre-voc" schools and meeting with some of the graduates quickly convinced them that this was a "big aid" experiment that had failed.

The pre-voc program had supposedly been catalyzed by Mozambicans' migration to Swaziland during their civil war. These refugees came with nothing, but many started their own tiny businesses and over time began to hire Swazis. Seeing the immigrant Mozambicans hiring Swazis made the Swazi government very uncomfortable, and so they decided that their students needed better classes in entrepreneurship. They received a big grant from the Africa Development Bank. Farm machinery, farm animals, new labs, and classrooms were purchased and placed in sixteen pilot schools across the country. After only a few meetings, it was clear to Wendy and Atiba that the "pre-voc" programs had significant problems. Among the obvious problems were the four large tractors that were purchased for training students but never delivered to the high schools and the minimal animal husbandry that could be taught because the animals at many schools were exclusively female.

According to the teachers, the program had been imposed

on them and the schools from above, inadequately marketed to parents and teachers, and implemented with minimal teacher training. Also angering parents and teachers was the lack of impact measurement or additional certification for students who completed the program. The pre-voc program originators also improperly set expectations by promising but then not delivering financial support for graduated pre-voc students to start businesses.

As Wendy and Atiba continued their research, another visit was hosted by a native Swazi who had graduated from Colorado State University and then earned a master's degree from Colorado School of Mines before returning to Swaziland. Five years earlier, his village's young boys had banded together to explore how to create businesses so that they could become employed. As expected of many group efforts, less than 20 percent of the students did more than 80 percent of the work on the initial bean-growing project, but the project still achieved a $100 profit. Five years later, the profit had not been used, no other businesses had been started, and the bean-growing success had not been sustained. It was clear that the youth did not understand how to create a viable business. The young men were still living at home with no income source of their own. Although some of the young men had once displayed initiative, the Swazi host for the visit felt that most of the young people lacked motivation.

The next meeting occurred between TechnoServe and LULOTE, a training firm that TechnoServe had identified as a potential local partner. Everyone in the meeting agreed that the pre-voc education was not adequately preparing students for entrepreneurship and was unlikely to become the foundation for TechnoServe's planned youth program. They also discussed other possibilities. No one knew of any existing program in Swaziland that actually provided hands-on learning about business such as how businesses start and how the money system works. Any advice for small businesses and the few entrepreneurs in the country was offered only by paid consultants. Even UNISWA (the University of Swaziland) only offered theoretical courses on business without any experiential content. From her prior experience, Wendy knew that Junior Achievement had established successful programs in multiple African countries as well as in numerous developing countries in Eastern Europe, Asia, and Latin America. After further discussion, there was agreement that Junior Achievement would be the best platform on which to build the Swazi youth program. Wendy was assigned to make the initial inquiries to Junior Achievement about starting a new country program in Swaziland. For her first step, she arranged for Atiba, Leslie, and herself to meet with the director of the JA South Africa office in Johannesburg. On the same trip, they also planned to visit a one-stop business center, cofounded and cofunded by multiple financial and consulting organizations, that helped budding entrepreneurs in Johannesburg to get information and the support they would need to start and operate businesses.

Later, the combined TechnoServe and LULOTE team met with the chief inspector in the Ministry of Education and four of his key staff to validate their findings on the pre-voc program. The role of the chief inspector is to monitor the quality of secondary education across Swaziland. The discussion was frank, and despite some finger-pointing at teachers and the poor marketing of the program, the inspectors seemed to agree that the pre-voc program was not successful and unlikely to change without a major overhaul. Additionally distracting to the inspector's staff was a concurrent initiative to implement the new International General Certificate for Secondary Education (IGCSE) based on the British education model. The ministry seemed to look to TechnoServe and LULOTE as experts to help solve their problems, and the team did agree to come back to them with some possible strategies.

While Wendy was starting on the youth program, I learned that my focus would be on working with specific entrepreneurs who needed help creating or growing businesses, consistent with TechnoServe's local mandate. In many countries, TechnoServe worked primarily with smallholder farmers and agro-processing companies since 80 percent of the world's poor were farmers. However, in Swaziland, the focus was on helping people to start or grow small and medium enterprises in any industry, which could also include agriculture. Since the program in Swaziland was new, we had a two-pronged approach. We accepted requests for help from anyone with reasonable business prospects while at the same time we broadly researched the local economy to see what industries or agricultural sectors in Swaziland might be able to become reasonably competitive.

My first two clients had come to TechnoServe for help. Prior to my arrival, they both had met briefly with Leslie and dropped off their business plans. I spent my first week familiarizing myself with their plans before meeting with them in person. The first one that I studied was MPE Timbers. Their plan was to pressure-treat wooden poles with preservatives. Pressure treating allows electric and telephone utilities to put poles into the ground where they resist rotting and destructive insects for many years. Swaziland didn't have a high-quality pole treatment company, but they had lots of raw timber for poles. A large portion of Swaziland is covered with commercial forests, also known as timber plantations. As we later drove through these areas, we saw miles and miles of straight trees growing in straight rows at regular spacing. It was obvious that Mother Nature had some help in creating these forests.

Swaziland's electric utility company was conducting a program of rural electrification using imported pressure-treated poles. With seemingly ready access to raw material and no local competition, our entrepreneurs, Brian and Robert, had seen a business opportunity. They had found a used pressure-treating facility that was for sale, so they put in some of their own money, recruited some investors, took out a loan from the local development agency, and started a company. The loan was secured by the equipment to be purchased, but also personally guaranteed. As Brian and Robert surveyed their market and access to further capital, they heard nothing but good news. Their business plans showed high profitability and a very quick payback on their investment, especially for large utility poles, which were in high demand as both Swaziland and South Africa expanded their electrical transmission grids. The used equipment that the entrepreneurs had located was larger and more expensive to purchase and install than what they had originally planned, but it would allow them to treat large utility poles, so they expanded their plans for the factory and moved forward with confidence. As they installed the equipment and constructed the required buildings for the plant, their cash began to run low, and they sought additional financing. Although the climate for investment had seemed very bright before, it suddenly became dark, and they could not get funds. They tried many sources, but although they were complimented on their business plans, every institution turned them down.

After much searching, they were introduced to a local investor who said that money would be no problem and agreed to give them what they needed. They verbally agreed on a disbursement schedule, and the pole plant again started moving toward production. Very quickly, the investor said that he was having problems collecting amounts due him from government projects, and he could not deliver cash in the amounts and on the agreed to schedule. Although the investor ultimately gave our entrepreneurs 80 percent of what he had initially promised, they again ran out of cash, having only performed test runs at the plant with no significant sales.

MPE Timbers had come to TechnoServe to help them find

financing for a project that still looked very favorable on paper;
although the estimates of the capital required were now triple
what they had been originally. We all agreed that our review and
recommendations on the project might lend it sufficient credibility to get a better chance at funding. I felt the whole story
was strange because it had been six years since the company
had been formed and over four years since they had taken out
the original loan. This was a different business world for me.
I was accustomed to the pace of Silicon Valley where things
happen fast, and when you run out of money, you sell the furniture, vacate the premises, and move on to your next job within
a few months. If this was such a good business, why hadn't it
succeeded? Or if it wasn't, why hadn't it been put out of its
misery? This was a very different animal, and I was intrigued
to figure out what could and should be done.

As I asked questions around the office, I learned that from
the perspective of local economic development, everyone was
enthusiastic about this project and still wanted it to succeed. It
would provide over two hundred jobs in Swaziland, including
harvesting the timber. It would also provide the local utilities
with home-grown poles at a much lower cost. It looked great
on paper. I thought maybe I could apply my consulting experience to understand the situation and create a potential solution.

As I puzzled over MPE, I read the business plan from my
second client. He wanted to start a bottled water company. A
group of college students had done a study for him of the local
bottled water market and found that there were approximately
eight companies competing, including Coke and Nestle. They
also found wide discrepancies in the prices that these companies charged and consequently concluded that the price that is
charged doesn't matter much to consumers. Our entrepreneur
thought he would be able to capture 20 percent of the market.
He owned some land with a well that would be his source of
water and had analyzed what equipment a bottling plant would

need and what it would cost to purchase and operate it. He had committed to putting up 15 percent of the total investment himself and was looking to borrow the other 85 percent. Because this was already a large amount of money, he decided that he couldn't afford to set up his own distribution capability, so he planned to subcontract it.

In business school, we occasionally got cases like these, often on exams. They were great vehicles for demonstrating everything you knew about an area of business because there were so many things that you could explain were wrong and why. Sometimes after discussing a case in class, the professor told us what had happened to the company. With this type of case, we always hoped it wasn't the one exception in a million that was successful despite violating every known business principle. I don't remember a single case that surprised us. I knew the right answer for my client. My challenge was how to tell him in a credible and empathetic way.

In discussing this with my junior colleague, Mpendulo (again, hum the *m*, then "pen-du-lo" with long vowel sounds for the *u* and the *o*), I explained that the only way that this business could succeed would be to establish a unique brand that addressed a specific niche and to do this with very little money available for advertising (against Coke and Nestle). Obviously tongue in cheek, I suggested that we start a rumor that this water would either heal very sick people or increase male potency. Those were the only ways I could think of to make this business successful. More seriously, we set about collecting information that would clearly demonstrate the futility to our client.

For both Wendy and me, the first week of work was intense as we jumped into our new assignments, and the days went by quickly. To our surprise, after only one week of work, we got a three-day weekend. Saturday was declared a national holiday in Swaziland because it was the birthday of the prior king, Sobhuza II ("So-bu-za" with long vowel sounds for the *o* and *u*, short for the *a*). As with many holidays in Swaziland, the holiday declaration seemed to come at the last minute and to be a surprise, even though Sobhuza II's birthday was well known. Sobhuza II was the father of the current king, Mswati III, and the longest reigning monarch in any country in history. (It must have been his eighty wives who kept him healthy). Leslie decided that it would be unfair to celebrate a holiday on a Saturday, so she closed the office on Monday and gave us all a three-day weekend. Not bad for our first week on the job. We rented a car and drove to Kruger Park in South Africa for three days of big game viewing.

Back at work on Tuesday, Mpendulo and I met with the man who wanted to start a bottled water company. He was a very pleasant, gray-haired gentleman, probably not much older than me. He was retired but had a BS degree from Penn State University in agricultural mechanization, which had been his specialty throughout his career. Based on his idea and a good source of clean water, he had hired one consultant to write a business plan for the bottled water business and another consultant from the beverage industry to develop a set of specifications for a bottling plant.

However hopeful, our entrepreneur had very little in the way of ideas as to how he would compete with the large companies that were already in the market. He thought that he might be able to get preferences from local merchants because his would be a local Swazi company. He had talked to a number of retailers, although not the large ones, who had been encouraging, but all told him to come back when he had actual product to sell. He indicated that local hotels already had deals with existing water companies, but he thought he could break into this market if he formed a partnership with Tibiyo, the Royal Swazi company, that had investments and influence in many businesses throughout Swaziland. He hadn't yet talked to Tibiyo in the two years that he had been pursuing his idea. He had talked to a large multinational food products company with a local presence about doing his distribution. In the discussions with the large multinational, the local manager had indicated a possible interest in sourcing private labeled water from him. However, the manager who had been encouraging had now been transferred to another location and the new manager didn't show as much interest. When asked how he intended to promote his product, which we thought would be critical to any possible success, our entrepreneur had a one-word answer, *advertising.*

Mpendulo and I also inquired about the planned capacity of his plant and the size of the Swazi market. His planned capacity was roughly 60 percent of the total Swazi market, but he hoped to export to Mozambique and South Africa.

While any potential investor in the United States would have quickly dismissed this proposal, TechnoServe was trying to encourage entrepreneurship in a developing country. We needed to put in the extra effort to explore any possibility. I was also new to Swaziland and didn't want to alienate anyone. This meant that I needed to thoroughly research a proposal before giving someone the bad news that their idea just wasn't justifiable. So Mpendulo and I planned our investigation.

Smelling the Roses

Exploring Our Surroundings and Understanding the Culture

$\mathcal{M}$y opinion is that when you've finished your primary career and you're working in your next phase, there is more time to smell the roses, and you should take it. Whether you're still working for pay or volunteering, you've made most of the money you're going to make in your lifetime, and you've had most of the career advancement. At this point in your life, you don't need to work sixty to seventy hours per week. Forty hours of serious hard work (or less if it's a part-time role) is just fine. For many of us who have aggressively pursued our careers for thirty years or more, this is a revelation and a challenge. But if we can take this principle to heart, work can be positively pleasurable.

When we limit the amount of time we devote to our job, we can have much more time for exploring, understanding, and appreciating our environment, especially if we're living in another culture. This can be incredibly good fun as well as mentally stimulating. And it will help you live a longer, healthier life. Gerontologists tell us that challenging ourselves later in life with new experiences, situations, and learning will keep us more mentally sharp and physically fit than a routine without these. Wendy and I wanted to work hard for a cause, but we also wanted to take advantage of our situation and take in all that we could of the culture and sights that surrounded us. We wanted to make our time in Africa an adventure. We wanted to explore. We wanted to experience the idiosyncrasies of the local environment and culture. So we did.

At the end of only two weeks, Wendy and I knew that we really needed to have a car, so we rented one for the duration of our stay. It gave us necessary flexibility on what we could do and when, including going to the Mountain Inn at any time to use Skype and call the United States. We also had a lot more freedom to visit the local highlights. Even though we were paying for the car, our combined $50 daily stipend went pretty far in Swaziland, and we were spending much less money than we would have been in the United States. Although we now had a car, Wendy had been sick all week, so we didn't immediately take a big trip, but we did visit the Swazi Cultural Center, primarily a reconstructed Swazi village from the nineteenth century.

Historically, the Swazi culture was male dominated (many would say that it remains so today), and polygamy was traditional. Today, few Swazi men, other than the king, have multiple wives, but some still do. In the past, polygamy was the rule rather than the exception. Men were allowed as many wives as they could afford to marry and support. The first expense was the traditional present to the future wife's parents; seventeen cattle if the woman was a virgin. Discounts were negotiated for nonvirgins, and if the couple already had a child together, it was definite proof. After marriage, each wife had her own two huts, one for sleeping and one for cooking. The husband could decide which wife he wanted to sleep with each night. He also had his own separate hut if he wanted peace and quiet. (Some traditions die hard: Although polygamy was no longer common in Swaziland, less formal relationships continued. As mentioned earlier, unprotected sex with multiple concurrent partners was a major reason that Swaziland had the highest rate of AIDS in the world.)

After the tour of the village, we watched a performance of Swazi dancing and singing. The dancing was more athletic than most traditional dancing Wendy and I had seen in other countries, and the singing had great rhythm with multipart harmony. The performance wrapped up with a traditional rendition of "The Lion Sleeps Tonight," which was written by a Swazi.

Later Saturday evening, we observed a slice of current culture in Swaziland. We had been invited to go with people from our office to a local country club for dinner and a wine auction. We had no idea what to expect, but we looked forward to the opportunity to socialize with our coworkers. The country club was some distance away from Mbabane in a more rural area. Strangely, it was located adjacent to a very large canning plant for fruits and vegetables. We pulled into the dirt parking area and walked with our friends to the clubhouse.

Immediately, when we entered the clubhouse, I felt as if I was in an Elks Lodge or an American Legion Hall in a rural United States community. The floor was concrete; the ceiling was acoustical tile with commercial-style fluorescent lights. There was a fireplace that gave some ambiance, but it was overwhelmed by the rest of the slightly down-at-the-heels décor. The room was filled with tables covered with paper tablecloths and surrounded by folding chairs. The decorating committee had actually done a very nice job dressing up these tables with attractive centerpieces made of local fruits and accessories. We arrived early, so we went into the bar where a self-serve wine tasting was in progress.

The bar had similar décor except the ceiling was lower, presumably to make it cozier. We sampled a number of wines from South Africa as more people arrived. When we went back into the main dining hall, most of the tables were full, and we were immediately struck by the sea of whiteness. To put this into perspective, when walking around Mbabane, the population we saw was over 99 percent nonwhite. In fact, my experience had been that, walking down the street, white people had a tendency to stare at each other with the implied questions of, "I wonder who that is and why they are here?" At the country club dinner, the couple of mixed race background at our table had the only nonwhite faces in the room.

With further observation, the crowd seemed to fit the American Legion theme. There was a lot of white hair as well as white skin. Most people were in their fifties through seventies and looked like farmers or perhaps small businessmen from a rural community. We were in our late fifties as well, but the idea that "sixty is the new forty" hadn't made it to Swaziland. Some of the women were nicely dressed and obviously paid attention to their appearance. However, a lot of the men had significant bellies that projected well beyond their belts. I did see two younger men, perhaps in their thirties, apparently trying to dress cool and sophisticated. They both had on informal jackets over wide open-collar shirts with pushed-up sleeves. I think the idea was to simulate the Miami Vice look, but it came off as a rumpled imitation of a style that had long been out of fashion.

My thoughts were obviously biased by the sophisticated Silicon Valley environment we had left just two weeks earlier. However, I couldn't help but think that these people were probably Afrikaners who had migrated from South Africa with all the negative implications from the history of apartheid. Of course, when looking at me, I think most people in Swaziland guessed that I was from South Africa as well. So we all have our prejudices. I was told at a later date that most of the whites in Swaziland aren't actually from South Africa but instead came directly from Europe. All of these people whom I had observed were probably very nice, hardworking individuals who had contributed to the economy of Swaziland. I just couldn't ignore the stark contrasts with both Silicon Valley and the general population of Swaziland, and I felt very uncomfortable.

After we sat down at our table, the auctioneer for the evening took the podium. He was an elderly gentleman, portly, and dressed in a white shirt with a string tie. He took command and told us that the wine auction would be completed before dinner was served. We had mild trepidation since the only food on the table was bread and a small cheese plate garnished with a few vegetables. We had no idea! There were one hundred lots of wine that were auctioned off, and it took forever. I thought people would start passing out from hunger, but the auctioneer went on and on. Finally, after fifty lots, he took a break, but this only meant that dinner was further postponed. Dinner was served after 10:00 p.m. When we finally got to eat it, it was a pleasant pedestrian meal, well-done beef with mixed vegetables, potatoes, and a decent dessert.

During dinner, I got the opportunity to talk to the husband of one of my coworkers. He had a position of responsibility with the largest local bank. As we talked about the older age of the crowd at the auction, he said that seeing this demographic had become more common in the native Swazi population as well. The cause was the AIDS epidemic that was still killing off a huge proportion of Swaziland's young adults despite the omnipresent cautionary billboards and readily available condoms. His bank had encouraged many of their retired employees to come back to work because so many of their productive younger workers had been lost to AIDS. From a larger perspective, there was serious concern that the Swazi population was evolving to a distribution with many children and adolescents (including many orphans) and a number of people over forty, but with a "hole" in the twenty to forty age group. The implications for both the business community and the society in general were ominous.

Although the AIDS epidemic threatened the country long-term, the weather had a more immediate impact on us. In general, the weather since we arrived had been very pleasant. It had been similar to northern California weather in the early spring with daytime temperatures usually approaching 70°Fahrenheit. The nights had been cool, around 50°F, which isn't bad if your house is centrally heated, but ours wasn't. Our cottage had small, relatively ineffective space heaters in two of the rooms. They definitely didn't heat the house and really didn't seem to make a difference if they were on or off. So the nights were very cold. Although we were used to having our own sleeping space in a queen-sized bed at home, compressing ourselves together in a double bed under a sheet, a blanket, the bed cover, and a quilt seemed a reasonable compromise to keep warm.

After a few weeks, the weather began to get a little warmer. Not a lot, but it was noticeable. It had definitely gotten just a little warmer at night, and on some mornings, I hadn't worn a jacket to work. It had just turned to August, which is the equivalent of February in northern California. And like California in February, some days were actually warm if you went out in the midday and soaked in the radiant heat from the sun.

With the relatively mild and temperate weather lulling us into a sense of pleasant complacency, we weren't prepared for the occasional intensity of Swaziland's storms. Then we had two nights of fury. The first night, we had an amazing storm. It wasn't a hurricane, but it came close. At dusk, the wind came up. I had never experienced wind so strong without rain. It was intense. I don't think the winds got over seventy-five miles per hour, but I imagine it blew at fifty or sixty and carried on for several hours. Then it started to rain. The most intense rainstorms I ever experienced had always been in the tropics, but this was just as severe. The intense rain and wind continued for several hours. We could hardly sleep. Throughout the night, Wendy and I kept thinking about the forest of eucalyptus trees right next to our cottage, hoping they wouldn't fall on us. Later, the rain stopped, but the wind kept up all night long. The early morning was calm and gave way to a beautiful day with perfectly clear air and not a cloud in the sky. Our view over the Ezulwini Valley was beautiful. We understood why it is called the Valley of Heaven.

With the previous night's weather behind us, we went to the office. Unfortunately, we heard from the business advisor in charge of horticulture that one of her clients had his crop of baby vegetables wiped out by a hailstorm. She had visited his farm and taken pictures. The hail had been severe and had accumulated so much that it looked like snow on the ground. The localized hail didn't cause widespread devastation, but it had totally destroyed our farmer's crop, causing a twenty-thousand-dollar loss. Crop insurance was so expensive in Swaziland that it essentially didn't exist, so individual farmers paid the price for the whims of nature.

The rest of our day was uneventful, and Wendy and I left the office around 6:00 p.m. The wind picked up, just like the night before. As we drove the few miles to our cottage, we began to notice that the street and traffic lights were out. We hoped that it didn't affect our house but expected to come home to darkness. Although all the way home there were no lights on the main road, as soon as we turned into the Emafini complex, we could see glimmers of light in the distance. We had hope. As we drove over the top of the hill on our dirt and rock road, we could see the exterior lights from our cottage. We were happy. And when we scrambled into the house and closed the door, we felt we had achieved our refuge.

I began to cook dinner (while we were in Africa, I did all the cooking as Wendy created a website to keep our friends and family up to date on all of our activities) while Wendy packed for her planned trip to Johannesburg with Atiba and Leslie in the morning. The wind was really blowing again. No rain, but tree branches were being broken and blown about. And the constant roar was like a wind tunnel. The lights flickered. The television was intermittent as the reception of the satellite dish was interrupted. Just as I finished cooking and was putting dinner on the plates, the power died for good. We had dinner by candlelight. Actually, we had the modern version of dinner by candlelight and LED. Our son, who is an outdoor equipment aficionado, had convinced us to pack battery-operated LED headlamps. So we used these with the candles for dinner. How very strange; the eerie, sterile, high-tech beams from LEDs combined with the primitive, warm glow of candles. The novelty of the candlelight dinner wore off quickly.

The previous night, the winds weren't hurricane force, but this night, I'm sure they were. They roared all night, making it impossible to stay asleep. As the wind ripped branches off the trees and smashed them against the windows, it sounded as if the panes would shatter. I worried as to what I would do if they did. Periodically, I was able to doze off until a particularly loud crash against a window would wake me again. Luckily, the windows never broke, and we survived the night.

In the morning we surveyed the damage, and it was significant. Trees were uprooted and lying everywhere. Our cottage had relatively minimal damage although a piece of the roof had been ripped off and blown away. Large branches and a broken tree, twelve inches in diameter, had fallen within ten feet of our bedroom. Our closest neighbor had a two-foot diameter tree uprooted within six feet of his house, and he had major roof damage. The exit road from our Emafini compound was blocked by a large fallen tree. We called the office to get a ride to work, but we had to climb over downed trees and branches, with Wendy's suitcase, to get to the main road where our driver could pick us up.

Fortunately, our shower worked. We had hot water and electricity from the Emafini backup generator. Others in the office had been without power and water for two days. On the road to work, most of the traffic lights were out. Everyone who had gotten into the office had a story to tell about downed trees, blocked roads and detours, and our office Internet was down. Wendy's trip to Johannesburg was delayed to make sure the roads were passable. We were informed that the roads were passable, but Johannesburg had gotten a rare snowfall overnight. With every bit of warm clothing she had, Wendy finally set out with her colleagues.

The weather remained cold, and the winds continued for a third night. They were not as severe as the night before, but there were more trees down when I got up the next morning. Electricity and water remained off in many areas. Once again, people in the office had lots of stories: going to hotels for showers, being given a bucket of water to wash up, etc. I continued to be fortunate. (Wendy was still in Johannesburg.) Our compound had a generator for electricity, which also powered the water pumps. For the most part, I had electricity and water pressure. However, the previous night, as I had been reading and debating with myself as to when to go to bed, they shut off the generator, the lights went out, and I had my answer. In the morning while getting ready for work, I heard a strange sound from the toilet, which turned out to be the water in the tank draining back into the pipe because the pumps had quit. I hadn't taken a shower and was not looking forward to going to work unshaven and unshowered. However, within fifteen minutes, the water pressure came back. I shaved first, just in case, because the effects of being unshaven are more obvious than being unshowered. I showered as well, but did it quickly and didn't soap too much of my body at once in case the water disappeared again.

Wendy's trip to Johannesburg was a big success. She and her colleagues were able to witness a very successful JA program operating in an adjacent African country. They were also able to observe a highly effective and heavily utilized business center for entrepreneurs. Following her trip, Wendy contacted JA International's Africa director to begin discussions on starting JA in Swaziland. From the conversation, she learned that JA had operated in Swaziland ten years earlier but had been shut down due to financial irregularities. However, JA was willing to re-start the program with the backing of an organization like TechnoServe. Since TechnoServe did not have the people resources to start up the program alone and eventually wanted to turn the program over totally to a local partner, LULOTE was chosen to be the local sponsor. With these developments, the School-Aged Youth Entrepreneurship (SAYE) program began to take shape.

Wendy's trip to Johannesburg was a big business success, but it didn't help her sickness, so Leslie recommended a local doctor, and Wendy finally went to see him. The doctor was an interesting chap. He was probably in his midseventies and seemed to practice very informally, as would have been done sixty years ago in the United States. His offices and equipment also looked as if they may have been new fifty years ago or more. I saw a baby scale that was the exact model my mother had used to weigh me. The doctor was originally from England but had immigrated to Swaziland many years ago. He was pleasant and seemed to know what he was doing. He diagnosed Wendy with bronchitis and prescribed antibiotics and cough medicine, which his assistant dispensed. Wendy paid the total bill for medicine and the doctor's visit. It was about $40 cash. No insurance, no co-pays, no submission of the physician's bill to the insurance company for reimbursement, partial payment, and subsequent billing to the patient for the remainder with computers printing out a paper trail at every step. It's too bad the doctor supported only himself and his office staff. If he had been working in the United States, he could have charged five times as much and supported a legion of administrators and clerks at multiple insurance companies and intermediaries. Sometimes the simple old ways work just fine.

The medicine seemed to help, and Wendy's condition improved. She had a follow-up visit with the doctor, and I went along because we both needed a specific signed certificate from a doctor to get our work permits/visas. Even though we had signed letters from our doctor in the United States that indicated we had been recently examined and found to be in good health, we still needed to have this specific Swazi government form signed by a doctor. The form that the doctor signed certifies that he has examined us and that we are not "idiots, mentally defective, deaf, dumb and/or blind." Everyone has a good laugh over the form, but the government requires them anyway. This doctor signed a lot of them.

Although the medicine seemed to help Wendy's condition to improve, it may not have been the only source of benefit. Wendy's cough was really nasty-sounding, and it could be heard by anyone in the vicinity when she coughed. After her visit to the doctor, she happened to cough while she was in the restroom for our office building. A woman came up to her and said, "You must get rid of that cough."

Wendy said, "I know. I just came from the doctor."

The woman said, "No, I mean I can help. I have the healing touch from Jesus. Let me help you." The woman then proceeded to put her hands on Wendy and prayed for a few minutes. No results were immediately obvious, but Wendy continued to get better. We could never be certain as to the real source of her improved health.

Start-Up Challenges

$\mathcal{F}$rom many years working in business, and especially Silicon Valley, I've learned that for a start-up business to be successful, the stars of marketing, production, and finance have to align; and before starting a business, this possibility should be confirmed through research and analysis. Mpendulo and I were taking a step by step approach to prove this was possible for MPE and at the same compiling evidence that it would never work for bottled water. We confirmed that there was a strong demand for high-quality pressure-treated poles in Swaziland of the type our client could potentially supply, but first we had to get them some funding so they could go into business. For our water-bottling client, we did further research, which continued to confirm my initial impression that it would be a very bad idea to start a new bottled water company.

Part of the bottled water research was an interview with the professor whose students had done the initial industry analysis. Their paper had been more of an undergraduate class project rather than a report done under the professor's supervision, which helped to explain the quality of the conclusions. The study concluded that marketing and distribution were the keys to success in the bottled water industry, which were right on, but the rest of the findings, including that a new company could compete in this environment were very naive.

Mpendulo and I also wanted to follow up on our client's idea to work with Tibiyo, so we scheduled an interview with a woman working in their new business development department. I still haven't figured it all out, but there are huge overlaps and very gray boundaries among what belongs to the king, his company Tibiyo, the government and the country. Thuli was intelligent, thoughtful, and articulate. She had previously worked for the World Bank outside of Swaziland but had decided to come home. She had given our objective a lot of thought and had several ideas as to how Tibiyo could use private-labeled water from a local source. Although her ideas were good, they were small volumes, and she knew it. She also was concerned about the viability of a new bottled water company because she had been involved in evaluating the potential for a similar company in Lesotho. The opportunity had seemed promising and the company had been funded, but it had always struggled. She referred me to some contacts at the company who would be willing to tell us about their challenges.

Our next step was to evaluate the market from the perspective of the only local supermarket where we got very clear feedback from the manager. Without any prompting, essentially his first words were, "I don't want another supplier of bottled water. I have too many now, and I'm reducing the number of brands that I carry."

As we talked to this major potential customer, I thought about the business school professors who teach introductory marketing and the authors who write books on starting new companies. Everyone who understands business success emphasizes the need to focus on the customer. Who are the customers? Why do they need your product? Where will they buy your product? Why will they choose yours over the competition? Throughout my business career, I had seen the importance of this type of customer focus reinforced many times over, and I have always believed that the customer is right. They have the money; you're trying to get it. And if they aren't willing to part with it, then your business is out of luck. In other words, it doesn't matter if you have a great source of pure water and a beautiful bottling plant. If no one wants to buy your product, you're bankrupt. Actually, you'll probably never get that far. If there is any rationale in the organizations that might provide funds, they'll never give you the money to build that beautiful bottling plant. We needed to check a few more sources, but I had already started to think about how to present the sad truth to our client.

Wendy was also staying busy. Although her primary objective was to establish the youth program, her mandate was to work more broadly on promoting entrepreneurship. Under this mandate, a specific objective was to work with Atiba to develop the TechnoServe Business Place for Emerging Entrepreneurs. This was envisioned to be a one-stop "gateway" to help people start small businesses, similar to the business place they had observed in Johannesburg. Resources were envisioned to include a reference library, Internet access with several computers, skill and knowledge assessment tools, in-person advisors for initial guidance, and senior consultants for more technical advice. Wendy was familiar with this concept because it is similar to a program operated in many major U.S. cities by the Small Business Administration and SCORE (Service Corps of Retired Executives).

However, finding a location, operational methodology, and funding model in order to establish a one-stop business center in Swaziland proved to be a major challenge. South Africa's Black Empowerment initiative provided an umbrella for the concepts and funders to come together to create their center. No such movement or financial backing existed in Swaziland. TechnoServe had limited funds to initiate a center, so it clearly needed multiple partners to establish and sustain it. Additionally, determining exactly where to locate a center and exactly the right services were major issues as well. The next steps were much less clear for this project.

However, at this time, UNISWA (University of Swaziland) was also thinking of establishing a regional business resource center, but they had not gotten beyond the conceptual stage. They were struggling with what this new institute would do, the kind of programs to run within it, and how to fund it. After research, discussions and evaluating the alternatives for a business resource center, Leslie, Atiba, and Wendy agreed that the best way forward would be to partner with UNISWA and either locate a center on their campus or adjacent to the campus in Manzini.

Seeking a potential site for the business place, Wendy and Atiba drove the one-hour drive to Manzini, the largest Swazi city (over one hundred thousand people). Although it was larger than Mbabane, it was not the government capital and was not as well-kept. Its downtown was pretty old, dilapidated, and polluted from all the buses, cars, and kombis (small vans used as local buses); but it was the easiest city to reach from all parts of Swaziland.

Consistent with partnering with UNISWA, Wendy and Atiba first explored the campus as they looked for potential colocation sites. Then they visited Mavuso Trading Center outside Manzini, a large convention-type complex built by the government/king that was meant to promote Swaziland by hosting business fairs. In its first three years of existence, it had been fully booked for only two weeks per year. The remainder of the time, it went mostly vacant with occasional social, sports, and business events; another grandiose idea on which a lot of money had been wasted. Not seeing any opportunities in university or government space, they also visited a number of commercial buildings. No one offered anything but retail rental pricing, some even above market rates. Wendy and Atiba were very dejected that no one wanted to help them and give back to the community. Since USAID, the primary donor for TechnoServe's work in Swaziland was only willing to pay for a percentage of this business gateway, Wendy knew that she really had her work cut out for her.

As Mpendulo and I continued to collect data on the market for bottled water, one useful visit was to the country general manager for an Italian multinational food company that focused on dairy products. When asked about bottled water, he indicated that they had tried bottling and marketing their own line of water several years prior. They had abandoned it. He was sympathetic to our cause but said he wanted no part in the marketing or sales of bottled water. He was willing to discuss simple distribution of any products we had to offer because he had a fleet of trucks for distribution and carrying more products could reduce his costs per unit. However, he didn't think that we could even sell bottled water to the major grocery retailers since they already had too many brands on their shelves. He knew the business, and his thoughts confirmed what we already knew.

Another interesting visit was to a real estate broker who was selling a water bottling plant complete with its own source of water. Mpendulo, my junior colleague, had called this broker to find out some business information on the property that was for sale. The young woman with whom he talked said that we would have to meet with the owner of the brokerage business. I'm sure they thought we might be potential buyers.

The owner of the brokerage business was a well-known mini-tycoon in Swaziland. He owned a number of businesses and had a reputation for being successful with everything he touched. His background was Asian, but he had lived in Swaziland since he was quite young. He was impressive to meet. He was a well-groomed, fast-talking, articulate, energetic businessman; and what a salesman! He told us how wonderful the water business was, how he had gotten numerous contracts to export water, how they had established a brand, how important water is for health, and how they had just been too distracted by his other businesses to aggressively pursue their bottled water business. That's why they were selling this modern, high-capacity, stainless steel water bottling plant with its own source of pure clean water. We declined the offer to visit the plant, thanked him very much, and left with a different message than the one he wanted to sell. We knew that if the business had been a good one, he would have continued it himself or at least sold it as a going concern to get a higher price.

We also talked, by phone, to the bottled water company in Lesotho, another small country in southern Africa about twice the size of Swaziland. This company had been started a number of years ago with a lot of hope, fanfare, and the expectation that they would bottle water for export to Mozambique, Botswana, etc. They were operating at 12 percent of capacity and selling only in Lesotho.

Based on our research, and an informal conversation Mpendulo had with our client, we knew it was time to give him the bad news. We would not be helping him if we delayed giving the message. The sooner he dropped this idea, the sooner that he could possibly move on to something else. And maybe in our discussion with him we could give him some insight that would help him to better evaluate his next venture. I put together a short PowerPoint presentation that described the issues with his idea and the research we had done to back up our position. However, I thought it would be best for Mpendulo to give the actual presentation. In addition to making it easier for our client to accept our advice, coming from another Swazi, I thought this would be a good development opportunity for Mpendulo. Even though I wouldn't be giving the presentation, I anticipated the experience with dread. The man was so nice and so optimistic. I hoped he wouldn't take it too hard.

When our client came in, there was a conflict for the only conference room, so the three of us had to meet around Mpendulo's desk. Mpendulo walked our client through the presentation. He explained the logic of business competition and what it takes to be successful. He explained our research and why a new bottled water company without some unique approach could not be successful. Our client listened carefully and silently. Mpendulo was very empathic and soft in his delivery. At the end, our client reiterated his original idea and why he had thought it would be a good one. He thanked us for our help and told us he would have to think about all we had told him. Then he left, obviously very disappointed. We felt bad too, but there was no value in wasting resources—his or ours—time, or money on a business that would ultimately fail. We needed to help people discover and develop businesses that would be successful.

Concurrently, we worked on MPE Timbers, making some progress, but not nearly as much as hoped. We brought the principals from the company, Brian and Robert, into our office for a multihour meeting, hoping to get some good financial start-up numbers from them so we could start doing our analysis. Unfortunately, the numbers they had were too general. They might have been right, but they had no support. Also, expenses for the first year had been estimated and then spread evenly across the months. We really needed to know what would be spent at the beginning, then as they ramped up, and finally what would be the steady state. When starting a business (and later as well) cash flow is critical! There was some grumbling about doing more detailed work, but we emphasized that if they were lending money, they would want to know where it was going. So Brian agreed to get us numbers by the following week.

Later the same week, we had an exciting development. We met with an investor, Dave, who was potentially interested in putting money into MPE Timbers. He had already been a successful lawyer and investor in Swaziland. He had been talking to TechnoServe about another opportunity and then got referred to us. Dave had been involved with the timber industry before and was interested in doing more value-added activities to timber in Swaziland. At the time, Swaziland was exporting a lot of raw timber and importing wood products. It seemed to all of us that this situation created multiple business opportunities. Brian was coming back to our offices the next week, so we planned to introduce him to Dave.

The following week was an interesting one for clients. On Monday, Brian drove over from Johannesburg to meet in our office, so we included Dave. The meeting was friendly and both parties were interested in talking about Dave's possible investment. I was in another meeting when Brian and Dave were introduced and started talking, so at first, Brian thought this was a chance meeting. Later I assured him that it wasn't chance. Although there was some luck involved with our initial identification of Dave as a possible investor, I told Brian that I had already spent considerable time with Dave to introduce him to the project.

We all knew that we were just starting a long process of courtship and negotiation before a deal could be worked out, or not. However, we did get into serious discussions on some issues such as ownership. At the end of the discussion, we agreed that the next step would be getting numbers from Brian so that we could do our analysis and see what worked financially. Then we would familiarize Dave with the whole business, have him visit the actual plant, and ultimately get Dave to figure out his conditions for a deal.

Throughout the week, I worked with Dave to familiarize him with the economics and the possibilities of the business while giving him a chance to bounce his ideas off me. His wife, Fiona, also got involved, especially looking at the numbers that had been developed so far. By the end of the week, Dave had come up with the conditions for his interest. After looking at everything, Dave saw the proposition as high risk. I would have called it medium risk, but since the business had run out of cash twice and it was Dave's money, we called it high risk. In return for the risk, Dave wanted the possibility of high return while minimizing his risks in other areas, including potential problems with disgruntled shareholders. Since a lot of Dave's law career had been in pursuing shareholder suits, he knew the pitfalls. Consequently, he wanted 100 percent share ownership. We knew that this would be a tough hurdle to overcome, but Dave was interested in structuring attractive ongoing incentive arrangements for the existing shareholders to persuade them to give up their shares. He had a number of other conditions, but this was the most challenging. I planned to present it to Brian and Robert and to see what their level of interest would be.

Brian was supposed to have new start-up numbers to me by Wednesday at the latest, but I didn't have them Friday morning, so I called him. As mentioned, Brian lived in Johannesburg, which was known for its high crime rate. His wife had been a victim. Although she had survived, she was very shaken up. The mugging happened when she went to her sister's house to check the progress on her sister's new kitchen. Her sister and husband had gone out of town, but the workmen were supposed to continue their work. When Brian's wife walked into the house, she was grabbed, roughed up, tied up, and put on the floor with the workmen who had already been tied up. The thieves then continued their robbery. No one was critically injured, but there was some physical trauma, a lot of emotional trauma, and some dealing with the police. I was very willing to wait for the financial numbers, and I wasn't going to Johannesburg (other than the airport) unless absolutely necessary.

My colleagues heard that I had time to take on more responsibility, so this same week I picked up partial responsibility for two additional clients. One company was in the business of installing thatched roofs on houses but wanted to get into making products, such as roll-up blinds, out of thatch. This idea immediately sent up red flags for me because the only obvious connection between these two businesses was the raw material, which is usually not a good justification. I immediately had trepidation about what my new clients were thinking, but the proposed business could potentially employ a significant number of rural women in collecting the thatch, in weaving it, and also in the final assembly process. So I agreed to try to help them. The other new client was a six-month-old baking company that was making a traditional Swazi cornbread product. The thatch company wanted our help in starting up their new business and the baking company wanted our help in figuring out how to be profitable and get additional financing. With these additions, I was busy.

I paid a visit to the bakery company, Tasty Meals. The founder Phiwa (pee-wah) was a warm, energetic, and very likable young man in his mid-thirties. He was a native Swazi but had attended Colorado State University, in civil engineering, and was quite intelligent. He had thought a lot about his business, both before and after founding, and had done some analysis of his financials and his marketing. Although his analysis and insight were not up to what I would expect from a thoughtful U.S. MBA (masters in business administration graduate), they were much better than what I had seen to date in Swaziland. He also had a woman working for him as basically the COO (chief operating officer) of the company. Nolwazi had a degree in business, and from our brief meeting, I could tell that she understood both marketing and financial concepts and had some good marketing insights. However, she was nine months pregnant and on maternity leave. Since she was bored waiting around at home, she came into work and joined us for our meeting.

In starting the company, Phiwa had seen a market opportunity to produce and sell a traditional Swazi cornbread called mealie bread, made from green mealies and typically served with emasi (soured milk). In southern Africa, mealie just means sweet corn, which most Africans call maize, and green mealies just means fresh corn. Although the name was not appealing to us, it was the type of treat that grandma would make for the family when fresh corn was in season, and Swazis associated it with home and family. Mealie bread required careful, time-consuming preparation, and was not produced or sold commercially. Phiwa thought that busy families would be interested in purchasing this traditional product commercially, so he started the business.

Although our first meeting was primarily introductory, we went over some analysis and ideas. Based on his prior month's costs, I calculated his breakeven, which was about twice as many loaves as he was currently selling. While his margins were below what would be expected in the specialty bakery business, 45 percent versus 60 percent, a small price increase would have put them right in line. Whether or not he increased his price, Phiwa needed to focus on increasing sales. We discussed a lot of approaches to doing this, with emphasis on broader distribution and a "push" marketing strategy using merchandising materials with the retailers and at the point of sale. We all knew that trying to create broad consumer demand that would "pull" the product through the distribution channels and the retail outlets was totally unreasonable because of the cost of the advertising that would have been required. Nolwazi had some excellent ideas for marketing, but they would have required investment in promotional materials, and since Phiwa had already exhausted his savings and his borrowing limit, his options were very limited. And he was continuing to lose money.

That's why he needed our help. I thought it might already

be too late, but I really liked Phiwa's entrepreneurial spirit, his intelligence, and his friendly personality. And he was creating jobs for poor women in both food preparation and sales. I was excited to try and help. We quickly met again, and I began my analysis and consulting. I knew the company had to increase sales to get to a breakeven point, so we started talking about where and how they sell their product. I had lots of questions to lead us through a disciplined analysis, but the discussion jumped all around. Phiwa and Nolwazi had lots of stories as to where they were selling, where they weren't, what had been successful, and what hadn't. They also had lots of ideas as to how to improve, but they didn't have a logical step by step plan as to what to do, how, and when. After our discussion, Tasty Meals still didn't have a plan, but I realized how much time it would probably take to help them create one.

As we continued to talk about the many marketing and sales activities that could increase sales above breakeven levels, Phiwa, our entrepreneur, went off on another tangent. However, this one turned out to be critical. Sales weren't his only problem. It would have been foolish to spend money to increase his demand because he was having trouble purchasing enough green mealies to consistently support his current sales. So developing a reliable year-round supply of maize was critical to his survival. Because of the tremendous seasonality in availability and price of fresh maize, he thought growing his own might be the only way to assure a continuous supply at a reasonable price. However, even if this could work, it would take three to four months from planting to a first harvest, another challenge. I was beginning to feel that I didn't have enough fingers to plug all the holes in the dike.

Moving from sales and marketing to finance, I learned that Phiwa had recently gotten a R150,000 ($21,500) overdraft facility (line of credit) for working capital. He had planned to use this for marketing activities to increase sales. However, he had a lot of past due bills when the loan came through, and now he'd used R140,000 out of the R150,000 available. I calculated that he was losing about R20,000 per month. So in summary: Our entrepreneur was selling about half the volume he needed to break even. He couldn't increase sales because he couldn't find enough raw ingredients, but he probably couldn't pay for them anyway. And he would run out of money in less than a month. I knew how to help a lot of businesses in a lot of situations, and I knew I could help our friend to figure out a solid business plan, but I wasn't a miracle worker and didn't have money to lend.

A week later, I met again with Phiwa and his partner, Sifo, the owners of Tasty Meals and told them that I didn't lend money and didn't grow mealies, so I couldn't help them with their short-term problem. I was trying to give the situation a little humor, but they already understood how grave the short-term situation was, and they recognized that they would have to deal with it. This gave me some relief. So we sat down and started to discuss a business plan that could lead to success in the longer term and possibly financing, which would be absolutely necessary. The two primary areas that needed to be addressed were sales/marketing and sourcing of mealies. Since you can't sell something you don't have, we started with the sourcing strategy.

The major problem with sourcing was that the mealie bread product requires fresh corn (green mealies), which was only available at an attractive price during four months of the year. During these four months, farmers throughout the country have had the right combination of rain and warm weather to grow lots of fresh mealies. Since the supply is high, the price is low. However, during the rest of the year, as the weather gets colder, there is less land at a low altitude to be warm enough to grow the mealies. In addition, at that time of year, the land has to be irrigated because it doesn't rain. Naturally, the supply goes down and the price goes up. In their business planning, our entrepreneurs had used an average year-round price that was double what farmers charged in the plentiful season. They thought that this would be sufficient, but it wasn't, and it also neglected other logistical problems. Unfortunately, in the coldest season, the price of green mealies could be four times its low price. Moreover, the farmers with irrigated land that is warm year round don't harvest corn in the plentiful season. They only plant it when they know it will be scarce and command a high price. So Tasty Meals couldn't pay these farmers an average price for a year-round supply. They had tried a number of approaches to contract for a consistent year-round maize supply at a reasonable price but hadn't been successful. The farmers liked the higher prices in the plentiful season but, when the mealies were scarce, didn't want to part with their crops at a price lower than what they could get from other buyers. It's one of those things that looked good on paper but didn't work in the real world, a good example of how entrepreneurs get educated.

We created a lot of scenarios and did a lot of analysis to reinforce the conclusion that the entrepreneurs had already reached: They had to grow their own mealies for eight months of the year. We even calculated exactly how much land they would need based on the yield per acre and the number of loaves they would sell. Our cost projections said that the business could be profitable, but it would depend on the price paid for renting the land. So their next action item was to look for irrigated land in the Lowveldt (lowland area) where it would be warm year round and hope that the rental price would fit into our model. Then all they would have to do (on the supply side) would be to reliably grow the mealies, a challenge for any farmer, much less, two civil engineers.

By the time we finished these calculations, we had spent four hours analyzing the supply problem and our brains hurt.

It had actually been a very productive session. Because the two principals in Tasty Meals were both engineers, they understood the concepts and the importance of analysis and were quite facile with numbers. It was actually a pleasure working with them. However, creating business models was not as hard as trying to reconcile the models with the real world, and that was the next step on the supply side. If they couldn't operate like the models, mealie bread couldn't be profitable on a year-round basis, and Tasty Meals would have to be radically changed to survive. And that was just the supply side. Our next meeting would be about marketing and sales where the engineers had much less knowledge.

My second new client was Linopp, the company that wanted to start a business manufacturing products from thatch (grass). Linopp had arranged for me to go with them to a defunct factory in South Africa that had made thatch roof tiles thinking that they might want to go into that business. I had scheduled Kiki, the TechnoServe driver, to pick us up at the office at 7:00 a.m. to go to Carolina, South Africa, about an hour and a half from Mbabane. My primary client contact, Jabulile, arrived on time, but his colleague arrived about a half hour late, something I experienced a lot in Africa. Some of this can be blamed on the lack of reliable transportation, but a lot of it is just custom and culture (which can be incredibly frustrating for a Silicon Valley transplant committed to the pursuit of productivity). Our passenger gave a friendly apology for his lateness and the fact that we had been sitting around waiting for him, but he didn't seem to be hurrying as he casually bought himself a newspaper for the ride.

Our plan was to drive to a settlement in Carolina where we would pick up a man who had the keys to the shuttered factory and would show us around. He had been the foreman when the factory was operating. We drove to the border and passed through immigration. As we drove into South Africa, the land became flatter, and we passed miles and miles of rolling brown grass fields mixed with timber plantations.

When we got to Carolina, we pulled off the road into what I can only describe as a small settlement. It was more than one house, but much too small to be a town. It was surrounded by a barbed-wire fence, and we entered through a gate comprised of only barbed wire strands held in place by sticks. We drove along two tracks in the dirt and pulled up in front of a house with a young woman sitting in front. This house was one of two in the settlement constructed of brick with metal roofs. The other buildings, arranged in no particular pattern, were all wattle and daub (sticks and mud) in various states of disrepair. Some looked inhabited, others did not. Many were too dilapidated to be inhabitable. Perhaps some were for animals as were the many barbed-wire pens and corrals, also in various states of disrepair.

It turned out that the man we were supposed to meet was not around. However, the young woman sitting in front of the house was his daughter, and she communicated to my fellow passengers that she could get the key and go with us to the factory. She went into the house and returned with the key and a woman who was apparently her mother. After some discussion back and forth in Siswati and Zulu (which are mutually intelligible), the mother evidently agreed to let her daughter show us the factory. However, as her daughter was about to climb into the car, her mother called out to her one more time. The mother seemed to be concerned. There was a brief exchange, and the girl reached into her pocket and handed her mother a cell phone. Then we drove to the factory less than a mile away.

The factory was not expansive. It was more like a large workshop. The building was brick with multipane metal-framed windows. It was exactly the same type of construction seen in many abandoned factories in the United States. However, no one had begun throwing rocks through these window panes. Inside, some of the equipment and half-finished products were still on hand and collecting dirt. From the remains of the simple manufacturing equipment that was used, I could deduce the process. Basically, stalks of thatch, about eighteen inches long, were packed side by side into a metal frame. The tips of the thatch that protruded were covered with a piece of fiberglass tape and then dipped into a viscous resin. When they passed through an oven, the resin hardened like solid rubber and held the thatch together to become a roof tile.

Building similar equipment and manufacturing similar tiles would not have been hard. Perhaps even this factory was for sale. However, as I told my client later, we didn't know anything about the market. I had researched some sites on the web that sold thatch roof tiles in the United States, UK, and Australia. However, none of us had any idea of the size of the market, the prices paid to the factories, or what the competition would be like. I explained to Jabulile that we had to look at the sales and marketing side of the business as well as production. He agreed to do some research on the market before I saw him again in two weeks. I suggested that he try to contact wholesalers who might buy the products.

When we next met with the people from Linopp, they wanted to know what my plan was for their new business. I was taken aback. I explained to them that it wasn't TechnoServe's role or responsibility to independently create a business for them. I explained that we would give them a lot of help, coaching, and even do a lot of the writing up of a business plan, but that it had to be their plan. They needed to do the research and make the decisions around what they thought could work and how they wanted to approach the market. They seemed surprised and left shortly thereafter. They hadn't done any market research, and I never heard from them again.

Observations and Lessons Learned, So Far

*A*fter working with Swazi businesses for just a short time, I came to a conclusion, not surprising in retrospect. Economic development is hard and can proceed very slowly. Any entrepreneur in the United States knows how difficult it can be to start a new business, and that's within a highly developed business ecology. In Africa, it's much harder.

I quickly came to another conclusion. The Swazi business community had a tremendous lack of entrepreneurial sophistication. On one hand, the majority of people had no idea how to start a business beyond subsistence agriculture or simple retailing, and there were few resources to help them. On the other hand, there were educated people who believed that because they had an idea and were willing to make a small investment that they could hire a consultant to write a business plan that would make them worthy of major outside investment. Clearly we were literally and figuratively at the other end of the world from Silicon Valley with its large venture capital community and cadre of experienced entrepreneurs.

In spite of these challenges, I'd learned a lot and had concluded that I could contribute a lot. Although the businesses I was working with in Swaziland were much smaller and simpler than those I had consulted to in Silicon Valley, the basic principles were the same, and the fundamental requirement for understanding what to do was still basic business analysis. Although TechnoServe's objective in Swaziland was to encourage people to be entrepreneurial and start businesses, I knew we also needed to help people understand what it really takes. Most people had no concept of how hard successful entrepreneurs have to work or the upfront analysis and thinking that are required for a successful business. Coming from Silicon Valley, I had seen some wildly successful ventures and many that were not. I knew that although there was always an element of chance, most of the successful ventures were rigorously thought out in advance and had to go through a tough review process before receiving venture capital. And once the company began operating, the work hours were extreme and the pressure intense.

The hopeful entrepreneurs in Swaziland had never had the benefit of learning the requirements for starting a new business from observing a highly developed entrepreneurial culture and the role models it generates. More problematical was that they didn't have a good grasp of some of the basic disciplines. They especially lacked understanding of marketing (other than advertising) and finance. Production was much more familiar and more tangible so that when most people thought about starting a business, they thought about production first. Then after they'd done exhaustive analysis on hiring, training, constructing a factory, costing the product, etc., they would give only a brief explanation of how they would sell it. They didn't spend a lot of time analyzing who would buy the product, why customers would buy, what the competing products were, how much the customers would be willing to pay, etc. All of these are basic marketing questions that a new company must answer well if it is to succeed. But these were unfamiliar concepts to most of the people I worked with.

So I worked with my clients to answer these questions. We couldn't just do comparative research using databases available on the web or reports from research firms. In most cases, we did our marketing research by directly interviewing potential customers. In the case of MPE and the potential bottled water company, it was pretty easy because there were so few large customers. In the case of Tasty Meals, we sent saleswomen throughout the country to interview hundreds of small shop owners. I also encouraged the other consultants in our office to think about sales and marketing first with their clients. My point was that if you don't know how you will sell your product and why people will buy it, then it is a waste of time to do detailed analysis on how it will be produced. This was hard for most people because marketing and sales were so much less tangible and familiar than production, but we made good progress.

The other concept that potential entrepreneurs really struggled with was how to finance a business. Although some people didn't know that financing could be available, the larger problem was that others thought that just because they had a business idea that capital would magically be given to them. Also, there was a very limited understanding of the different characteristics of equity and debt. It seemed that equity capital generally wasn't available, and no one wanted it anyway because they would have to give up a large percentage of their ownership. Many people seemed to think that just because they had a good business plan, a bank should love to loan them 80–90 percent of the necessary capital and expect only prime plus a few percentage points in return. I wasn't dejected or discouraged; I was just learning what needed to be done and trying to figure out my approach. As I had always told my junior colleagues in management consulting when they complained how difficult some of our assignments were, "If it was easy, they wouldn't need us."

Even with a good understanding of finance, finding investment capital was still a problem. Although some entrepreneurs could qualify for loans under special programs with relaxed credit terms or guarantees, few lenders would provide 100 percent of the capital required to start a business. Existing companies who wanted to expand were often highly leveraged already so experienced the same problem. For both of these, some equity capital was required before additional loans could be obtained. However, since most of TechnoServe's potential clients were not wealthy, they did not have the necessary investment capital to start a business. Further, very little equity capital was available for investment in the Swazi market. This was particularly true for the types of businesses that were TechnoServe's clients. Most were in agribusiness and would be characterized as high risk, moderate return ventures, which made them unattractive to strictly commercial investors looking for the highest returns and the lowest risk.

For our clients in Swaziland, TechnoServe wanted to bridge this gap and fortunately had some available funding that could be used for direct investment in small and medium enterprises. For deserving ventures, funds could be used as the required equity portion of the necessary financing. Presumably, with this equity, businesses could qualify for additional loan financing so that the impact of the equity funds would be leveraged. However, if funds were to be used in this way, TechnoServe had to address a lot of issues and make several critical decisions. Since I was the only person in the office with experience in financial analysis, Leslie asked me to develop a discussion document on the potential for TechnoServe Swaziland to provide a small amount of funding directly to some of our clients who could not access financing in any other way. She asked me to identify and describe the issues, develop an initial proposal, and then circulate the document for comments and discussion.

The first issue was the one I always addressed first during my management consulting career, "What is our objective?" Specifically, TechnoServe's overall objective was to overcome the obstacle of the inadequate supply of equity capital for businesses that could provide jobs or other economic opportunities for the poor. In more detail, we wanted TechnoServe's clients to be using this equity to allow them to access (not replace) other sources of funding, which would allow them to grow their businesses, hire more people, and generally put more money into the economy.

Getting the strategic objectives defined was a good first step, but my next step was to specifically define the financial objectives for our pool of funds. In commercial financing, this is easy. The main objective is obvious: to earn a high return on the investments (with appropriate consideration of risk). In economic development finance, the strategic objectives take precedence and influence the financial ones. This leads to some very nontraditional thinking and challenges in balancing competing objectives.

The range of potential financial objectives in development finance extends from purely commercial returns to giving direct grants, i.e., from getting a high return on investment to getting no return and giving away (losing) all the money. A purely commercial approach to a pool of development projects would require high projected returns (including taking a high percentage of ownership and a large amount of collateral) to offset the expected losses from the high risks. Direct grants are at the other end of the spectrum and would have no expectation of recovering any of the money invested. Although both of these approaches are widely used, from my perspective, they both seemed extreme for the proposed TechnoServe direct funding. The commercial approach provided nothing new to the market and was unreasonable given the nature of the companies that TechnoServe would be supporting. The direct grant approach is simple and straightforward but would have been much less productive in terms of social return on investment since there was no potential for investment funds to be recycled. In addition, grants (giving away money) always set a bad precedent because they destroy the proper market incentives and can encourage dependency.

The approach I proposed was to provide subordinated investment funds at very low rates, recognizing that, over time, the yields on these funds would probably not offset the losses associated with the high risks of these investments. In other words, the pool of funds available for investment would probably disappear over time, but hopefully, it would be a slow process; and the investment funds could be recycled several times before they were completely gone. Although the expectation was that from a portfolio perspective, some investments would fail and that over time a below-market return would not compensate for high risk, every individual investment would be made with a reasonable prospect that it would be repaid. Expecting to lose all of your invested capital, albeit slowly, is a very nontraditional way of thinking about investing. I preferred to call it innovative. I even suggested we start a major marketing campaign calling the concept, "Lose Money Slowly," but it didn't catch on. I was better at finance than marketing.

The thinking got even more interesting as I contemplated the form of investments to make. Since the objective of the TechnoServe financing was to allow businesses to access bank loans, the banks had to perceive the TechnoServe investment as common equity or something very similar so there would be no question as to who got the assets if a business went bankrupt. In a commercial environment, TechnoServe's high risk would be compensated for by the possibility of a high return. A similarly situated private investor would demand ownership of a large percentage of the business in the hopes that it would be successful and generate large returns. However, TechnoServe didn't want the responsibility of owning any of the business. In other words, TechnoServe wanted to take on a high risk with the probability of a low return. Strange as this sounds, it was probably the only way to accomplish the strategic objective without just giving the money away. Where was Alice in Wonderland when I needed her to explain things?

More Exploring and Cultural Immersion

An Aborted Trip, a Braai, a Wedding, the Reed Dance, and South Africa

At the end of the week we were going to Maputo, Mozambique, a city known for its crime (seemingly less violent than Johannesburg). Evidently, robberies of individuals on the street were somewhat common, so we were told that it was advisable to carry two wallets, one of which you could give up readily. Although robbery could happen, the most pervasive crime was the theft of headlights, side mirrors, and windshields from parked cars. We heard that this was so common that people went to extreme measures to prevent it. Perhaps it was an urban legend, but it was rumored that some people had been known to crack their own headlights, mirrors, or windshields just to make them unattractive to thieves. People also had metal strips welded across their headlights to prevent theft. Evidently, this was quite effective against theft but made it really difficult to replace a defective headlight.

Other than the minor issue of crime, Maputo was supposed to be a very interesting city with beautiful beaches. The weather wasn't suitable for sunbathing, but we were looking forward to staring at the ocean and walking on the beaches. Then on Monday, we'd visit the TechnoServe office in Maputo to get some insight into the programs in Mozambique.

We didn't make it to Maputo. We did try, really hard. We got up at 7:00 a.m., very early for us on a Saturday, and left the cottage before 8:30. We had packed carefully to make sure we had all the right clothes and everything else we would need for crossing the border and staying in Maputo. I had heard the border crossing was more challenging than going into South Africa, but I didn't know how challenging it was going to be. People had told me that you had to have your blue book (car registration) with you and you had to fill out extra paperwork relating to your car (designed to reduce smuggling of stolen cars) on both sides of the border. Since we had a rental car, we didn't have our registration, but I made sure to take our contract and the form that showed we had switched cars since we first signed the contract.

The drive up to the border was less than two hours and very pleasant as we went through the Lowveldt for the first time and saw the endless sugarcane fields. We also enjoyed the sign warning pedestrians and cyclists against lions and elephants as the road passed through the Hlane (Schl-ah-nee) game reserve.

At the border, we parked our car and went inside the immigration and customs building. We filled out two immigration forms, handed them to the officer, and she stamped our passports, all without any written instructions or speaking. When we drove to the actual border gate, we discovered that we also needed a 654 customs form, so we went back inside. The 654 form required a lot of detail on the car: make, model, year, registration number, engine number, etc. I filled it out to the best of my ability. As the customs officer reviewed the form and was about to sign it, she remarked that I hadn't included the engine number for the car. I said it was a rental, and I didn't know the number. I didn't want to crawl around the engine compartment and assumed that this would get me off. Boy was I wrong! The customs officer had a concerned look on her face and went to speak to someone else in the glass-enclosed area behind the counter. She came back and asked us to follow her as she came out from behind the counter. She said she was going to try and get someone to help us. I didn't know why we needed help. Wendy and I walked over to the area near the border gate, and she spoke to a middle-aged gentleman who seemed to be the manager. He asked for our rental contract. He showed me, at the bottom of the contract, the section that says the car is prohibited from going to Kenya, Angola, Mozambique, and several other countries. He said we would need a written waiver from the rental car company, and he offered to call them for us. I gave him the number, and he went back inside.

A short while later, he came back out and said that Avis wanted to speak with us. I assumed that they just wanted to verify that the car was really in our possession before faxing the waiver. Wrong again! The woman I talked to in Swaziland said that waivers could only be granted by their main office in South Africa, and it was closed until Monday. I asked to speak to her supervisor. She said the supervisor would not be in until Monday, and even if she were available, she could not grant the waiver. She said she was sorry but pointed out that my contract did say that I couldn't take the car into Mozambique. I agreed that the contract indicated that, but that nobody had pointed it out to me when I rented the car. (Okay, I should have read the whole thing, but does anyone who has rented hundreds of cars over the years read the whole contract? I did pay very close attention to the rates, which had been incorrect and needed fixing, when I first got the car. Maybe that can be my excuse for not looking more carefully at the rest of the contract.) There was no alternative but to turn around and head back to Mbabane, which we did.

I was incredibly frustrated. Usually in the United States,

when I'd encountered similar situations, I was able to speak to a supervisor or a manager who understood my problem, wanted to help solve it, and had the authority to work something out, even if it involved me paying an extra fee, etc. Not here. There was no way out, and no one to speak to. I felt helpless, and I was also angry at myself for not having looked at the contract thus having to share the blame. I just wanted to leave and hurried Wendy into the car. As we were leaving, she asked if we had to do anything about immigration. I didn't want to be bothered with one more thing, and I said I didn't think so. So we left. However, as I was driving back and continued to stew, I remembered that the immigration officer did slide our passports through the computer. I wondered if that would show that we had left the country and never returned. Would it give us a problem the next time we wanted to leave the country? Would they think we slipped back into the country illegally? I grumbled to myself about the whole situation all the way home.

On the way home, as a diversion, we decided to stop off at the Swazi Sun Hotel and Spa in the Ezulwini Valley to have lunch and check out the spa. In California, Wendy periodically liked having massages, and she had heard that this spa was good and reasonably priced. The hotel was located next to a very green golf course, which was in sharp contrast to the surrounding brown and red terrain. The large gates, like the outside of the imposing hotel, were white, giving a strong colonial feel to the place. We walked through the elegant and formal lobby to the poolside bar, which was serving lunch. Although the pool and surroundings were more modern than colonial, the whole ambiance was of white wealth. And even though some of the guests were of color, I speculated that thirty years ago, it was a very pleasant, refined retreat where white South Africans could indulge themselves in relaxation, gambling, and sometimes other vices not readily available in South Africa. It was still a beautiful resort, and although the gambling was less of a novelty, it was supposedly still a great place to spend a weekend with your mistress.

After leaving the spa, we went home to pick up my computer and head to the Mountain Inn so I could send e-mails to cancel our hotel reservations in Maputo along with my Monday meeting in the TechnoServe Maputo office. We bought steaks and a bottle of wine for dinner. The steaks were good, but they weren't the fresh seafood we were expecting by the ocean in Maputo. And the wine was bad; we threw half of it away. Overall, we had survived, and it wasn't a tragedy, but I still worried whether we were in the country legally.

On Sunday, since we hadn't gone to Maputo, we had the opportunity to go to a small going-away braai (Afrikaans for *barbecue*) for one of the TechnoServe employees. She was going back to the United States to attend the Kennedy School of Government at Harvard. Braais are very popular in Swaziland. This one was held at Mlilwane (hum the M-lil-wahney), a small game reserve close to Mbabane, that was mostly limited to various members of the antelope family but also had warthogs and hippos. When we arrived, the warthogs were plentiful and running free through the camp.

I hadn't had a lot of up close and personal experience with warthogs, so I didn't know how meek or aggressive they might be. Consequently, I was a little nervous as a large warthog began poking his tusked snout into some of our food, right next to where I was standing. In the United States, the only animals I've ever confronted to protect picnic food have been aggressive birds, so I didn't exactly know what to do. Initially, I made some mild shooing noises and gestures but was ignored. Not wanting to appear too timid to the rest of the group, I gathered my courage and lunged aggressively toward the warthog; fortunately, he backed away because I don't know what I would have done if he hadn't.

Later, we saw a number of people congregated by a short stone wall adjacent to a small lake, so we went to see what was happening. Immediately on the other side of the three-foot-high wall was a gigantic hippo. We could easily have reached out and touched him. We didn't think touching would be advisable (hippos look cute but kill more people than any other animal in Africa), but we did enjoy looking close up. The hippo was probably the size of Wendy's Volkswagen at home. He seemed calm, perhaps even a little dejected as it appeared that he had a cold. Both his nose and eyes seemed to be runny, and we felt sorry for him. We felt for him even more because some of the young warthogs who were also in the area seemed to be taunting him. The young warthogs would approach the hippo's head and attempt to kick dirt in his face. When the hippo turned and bared his teeth, the warthogs would quickly retreat, but then they would come back and try again. Naughty boys trying to show off, I'm sure.

As we sat and watched this scene continue to play out, six more hippos, both babies and adults, emerged from the swampy pool and joined our friend on the shore behind the wall. They seemed to be eating a bit and socializing with each other. A number of warthogs were also eating and socializing in the same area. It was a very cute pageant. After watching for a while, we decided to go. As we were leaving, we took a better look at the low wall that had separated us from the hippos. It continued on for about twenty feet, but then it ended, and there was nothing to keep these gigantic animals from going around the ends!

On Monday, our office manager called the Ministry of Immigration about our little mix-up at the Mozambique border and was told that we would just have to explain the next time we were passing through immigration on our way out of the country. I hoped that it would work.

On Tuesday, as we drove up the Malagwane grade to work,

we were reminded as to how treacherous it was. As we rounded the last sharp curve before Mbabane, we had to slow because of all the cars, including police, on the edge of the road. A number of people were standing and staring over the sharp cliff. The missing section of guardrail gave a big clue as to what had happened. In the next day's paper, we read that a woman had been driving up the grade, rounded one of the sharp curves, and almost hit the center divider. She overreacted, whipping the steering wheel in the other direction, sending her car through the guardrail and over the cliff. Her car flipped at least once and plunged over three hundred feet down where it came to rest upright. The woman, who had been protected by her seat belt and airbag, was able to climb out of the car and had only minor injuries. A passing motorist had climbed down to help and handed the woman a cell phone. She called her husband to tell him that she'd had a minor accident on her way to work. When the husband arrived at the scene, he said he nearly had a heart attack. Needless to say, the car was a total wreck, and the woman was very lucky to be alive. The crash was the headline in Wednesday's paper, a welcome change from the usual stories of political corruption and family violence.

The following Saturday, one of the business advisors in our office, Sonnyboy, was getting married, and a number of us from the office had been invited. Seven of us drove in two cars to a small rural town about an hour and a half north of Mbabane. Most of the drive was on tar (paved) roads, but as we neared the town, we turned on to a good dirt road for the last few kilometers. As we drove among the homes and small farms, I remarked that this was the scenery of a developing country, not like what we saw every day in Mbabane. The wedding was to be held in the auditorium of the local high school. We pulled into the high school grounds and parked with the other cars on the grass. It felt like a movie scene of a small town in the rural Unite States preparing for a hometown football game. We walked through the high school grounds, which were quite extensive, to reach the auditorium. The high school construction seemed simple and uninspired but functional and solid. The floors were smooth poured concrete, the walls concrete block, and the roofs galvanized steel. The auditorium had a high ceiling with exposed wooden trusses holding up the corrugated metal roof. It was not large, seating approximately two hundred people in molded plastic chairs. However, one side wall opened with large doors to an anteroom that sat a hundred more. Both rooms were full.

Because we had heard that these events never start on time, we had arrived later than most and were lucky that the people in the other car had saved us seats in the main hall. We sat down as the preliminaries were starting not knowing what to expect, except that it would be a long service. Just to clarify, this was a Swazi-Christian wedding. The Swazi traditional wedding would be the next day and would be only for the family. The service started with singing by what was called a choir but was more gospel ensemble than traditional choir. There were six singers with microphones and amplification. They were accompanied by an electronic keyboard with built-in electronic background rhythms. Two very large speakers flanked the group. Their music sounded familiar but was not exactly like anything I'd heard before. It sounded like American gospel combined with the type of African music recorded by Paul Simon. It had the same effect as American gospel. Most people in the audience joined in the singing, and many stood up to sway with the music. The entire three-and-a-half-hour service was filled with music. After every scripture reading, prayer or speech there was at least a choral response and usually a more formal "Musical Item" as described in the program. As with the preliminaries, these performances by the choral group were usually joined by the rest of the congregation. The songs were familiar to everyone because as people joined in, they not only knew the lyrics but were singing in multipart harmony. The effect was wonderful. It gave a great feeling of warmth and togetherness. We felt very happy to be there and not at all awkward to be the only white faces in the crowd.

After the preliminary singing, the wedding began with the procession of the wedding party down the aisle. But this was not a traditional procession and "The Wedding March" was nowhere to be heard. There were five bridesmaids beautifully attired in lavender satin dresses accompanied by five grooms-men in black suits with white shirts and lavender neckties. They paired up at the rear door of the auditorium and then each couple did what I would call a "disco-stroll" down the aisle to music with an appropriate beat. Each pair took several minutes to dance down the aisle. After they had all reached the front of the room, the groom appeared. He was dressed in a white, four-button suit with a black shirt and a gold tie. He stood out like an eighties Motown rock star. He waited in the aisle to greet the bride as she was escorted down the aisle by her brother. The bride wore white. It was a beautiful (aren't they always?) traditional wedding dress. Once meant to symbolize virginity, nowadays all U.S. brides wear white. Apparently, this is also the custom in Swaziland since the bride and groom had a three-year-old son together and appeared to be pregnant with another.

Besides the singing, the remainder of the three and a half hours was comprised of evangelical-type prayers, a rousing sermon, ceremonies, and laudatory speeches by friends, relatives, and multiple ministers. It would have been more interesting to us if it hadn't all been in Siswati, which we didn't understand since everyone in our workplace spoke English. Occasionally a word or two of English was spoken to describe the next event, and we were able to figure out where we were in the program. Most of the time, we were clueless. We got occasional help from the Swazis in our group when we were supposed to do something. One of these explanations came near the end of the service. Music started playing, and we were told that we were expected to give a donation. I looked for the offering plates to begin making their way through the crowd. But no. This was a different type of donation and a different process. This donation was for the newly married couple, and it was to be placed in a container at the front of the hall. The music that began to play had a good beat for dancing, and that's what we did. Essentially all of us in the congregation got up and danced our way to the front of the room to drop our donation in the box. Then we each danced our way back to our seats, all the time keeping to the beat of the music. It was joyful, somewhat controlled, chaos.

Shortly thereafter, the ceremony ended, and we followed the wedding party as they exited the auditorium and proceeded to where a late lunch was to be served. Since we had actually received an invitation to the wedding, we were among the "invited" guests and got to eat a sit-down lunch with the wedding party and family in one of the high school classrooms. The other three hundred plus guests had to queue up outside to go through a cafeteria line to receive their lunch served takeaway style in a Styrofoam container. Of course this isn't bad if you haven't actually been invited to the wedding. We learned that in the Swazi culture, when you have a wedding, you should assume that the whole village or congregation (or both) will attend, and you must prepare to feed everyone who attends. This can make planning very difficult, but they seemed to have plenty of food for over three hundred people.

The meal after the ceremony was very short, and it was just a meal. There were no other activities. After the long service, much of which had been joyous and beautiful, even if we didn't understand it, the lack of a reception or party of some sort was a letdown. It felt like all the joy had disappeared with the end of the wedding, and now everyone went back to the daily basics, starting with just getting a meal.

Our exposure to the culture of Swaziland continued during the following week with preparations for the Reed Dance. The Reed Dance or Umhlanga (pronounced phonetically, but the "hl" sound is guttural and tough to get right) is one of the two most important Swazi festivals of the year and is written up as a "don't-miss" event in all of the travel books. During the festival, which lasts several days, up to forty thousand young women from throughout the country come to the king's lands in Ezulwini Valley. Here they gather reeds to take to the queen mother's residence and repair her kraal (technically refers to a cattle pen similar to corral but often used to mean the entire homestead). On the next to last day of the festival, they present the reeds to the queen mother in an elaborate ceremony. On the last day of the festival, the young maidens parade and dance before the king and queen mother. Historically this was done so the king could choose an additional wife from among the crowd. In current custom, we were told that if the king wants another wife, he chooses ahead of time. And unlike his father, the current king wasn't choosing a new wife every year. The current king had only fifteen wives whereas his father had more than eighty. Also traditionally, the young women would parade and dance completely naked, but modern ideas have impinged on this practice and now the women are at least somewhat clothed on the bottom. Most, however, do participate topless.

Although Wendy was not enthusiastic about the idea, I definitely wanted to see the event. The men in the office strongly encouraged us and suggested that we should attend in traditional Swazi costume. With some hesitation, we agreed and went out with Mkhululi (hum the *m* then "kuh-loo-lee"), another business advisor from our office, to purchase our attire. The important pieces in the traditional male outfit are as follows: a colorful necklace of fine beadwork in one of several traditional patterns; a long bright cloth wrapped around the torso and knotted to cover the right shoulder; two sarong-type skirts worn on top of each other, not at all matching the top cloth, knotted around the waist to expose the right leg; and a furry loincloth worn over the skirts. My loincloth consisted of two impala hindquarters, which meant that there was a tail bump suggestively protruding from the front, probably purposeful. At least I didn't have to wear the traditional male underclothing. Evidently, this consists of a hollowed out gourd tied on with a leather thong. I'll leave the specifics to the imagination, but just thinking about it made me uncomfortable.

Mkhululi had graciously agreed to go with us to the celebration, and so we agreed on a time to meet at his house on Monday. We had to make all of our arrangements early in the week because we both had busy schedules with clients on Thursday and Friday.

Even though Monday was a holiday, we got up early. We wanted to make sure we had time to shower, put on our native costumes, and drive to Mkhululi's house in time for the festival. We had no idea as to what to anticipate in terms of crowds or how difficult it would be to park. As we were finishing up the struggle to properly attire ourselves, making comparisons to various pictures in the newspaper, magazines, and guidebooks, I got a phone call. It was Mkhululi.

He said, "I have bad news. I called my father this morning to borrow some of his traditional clothing. He asked me what I needed it for. I said that I needed it to go to the Umhlanga. He said, 'Sorry, but the ceremony was yesterday.' I said, 'But today is the holiday.' He said that today was the holiday only because it was Monday, but the celebration was yesterday. I am so, so sorry."

My heart sank. We were all dressed up. It wasn't a fortune, but we had spent several hundred dollars to look authentic. We were lucky enough to be in Swaziland just at the time of the Umhlanga, and we had missed it. I couldn't be mad at Mkhululi because he had helped us with the clothing and had volunteered to escort us to the event. Around the office, we had mentioned that we were going on Monday, and no one had said anything. I didn't know what to do. Mkhululi suggested that we go to the king's lands where the thousands of young women were camping and the festival was held just to see if there were any activities planned for today. Based on our experience over the last two months, this made a lot of sense. In Swaziland, schedules for things like this were not well specified or publicized in advance. Somehow, people just kind of knew or found out. In fact, the specific date of the Umhlanga was only decided and publicized a few weeks prior. It's not clear how the date is determined. If it were based on the sun or the moon, it certainly could be calculated years in advance, but it's not. I guess that helps it retain some of the mystery, and more importantly, someone gets to retain his sense of importance because he gets to determine the date.

Not to look entirely stupid, we changed back into our regular clothes and drove to Mkhululi's house. Mkhululi had just moved into his new house. While he was at work, his wife had done most of the moving and furniture arranging. She was exhausted and needed some sleep, so Mkhululi brought his one-year-old daughter along with us as we drove the few miles to the king's lands. As we got close to the main festival site, we began to see lots of young women and the temporary infrastructure necessary to support them. It looked like the aftermath of a parade, the packing up of the circus, or the end of a Girl Scout camporee with some significant differences. As we approached, we crossed a small river on a one-lane bridge. Along the river banks, we could see dozens of young women washing their clothes and bathing. Those that were bathing were completely naked and seemed very comfortable with that fact. The Girl Scouts would not have approved.

We continued driving through the bustling crowds of young women and eventually arrived at a makeshift parking lot outside the gates to the king's residence. A number of cars were parked, and there was a gaggle of police officers chatting among themselves. Mkhululi got out and approached one of the officers to find out if anything official was happening that day. He came back to the car and brought good news. Yesterday had been the ceremonial presentation of the reeds to the Queen Mother. However, today was scheduled for the parade and dancing for the king! We hadn't missed it! The activities would start at 2:00 p.m. We would come back, and we wouldn't even worry that the start was probably quoted in "Africa time." It didn't matter that we would have to sit and wait for a while; we were going to see the Reed Dance. We took Mkhululi back to his house and agreed to come back at 1:30 p.m.

After a few errands, lunch, and changing back into our traditional clothes, we drove back to Mkhululi's house. His wife Katy was awake and would go with us to the Reed Dance along with their young daughter. Mkhululi had given us some coaching on our attire so now my two skirts were held up by knotting the ends of the cloth together rather than with safety pins, as had been the case this morning. The cloth around my torso still relied on the safety pins.

We piled into two cars and headed for the stadium at the king's residence. As we approached, we had the same feeling that we'd had at Sonnyboy's wedding, like arriving for an important high school football game in a small town, except here the crowds were bigger. We parked in crooked rows in a field next to the stadium and walked along the long fence to the stadium entrance. The metal detector we walked through at the entrance was something I'd never seen at a football game, but the feeling was still similar. The stadium had seats for probably five thousand spectators, but the parade ground in the center was over three times the size of a normal football field. The stands on the near side, next to the king's reviewing area were full, so we had to walk around the entire field to get to the open seats. As we were walking, we went past thousands of half-naked young women lined up for their parade. We tried not to stare at them, and they tried not to stare too much at us. However, they were looking at us a lot. We definitely stood out. Out of probably four thousand spectators, we were among the less than 1 percent who were white and were probably the only white family in traditional dress. Did I say we stood out? And did I say that Mkhululi paraded us in front of most of the spectators in the stadium before we chose our seats?

Although we felt conspicuous, there was a friendly sensation coming from everyone who was looking at us. The people made us feel that we had made the right decision to dress traditionally. And we felt proud about how we looked. In fact, we got help on looking even better. As we were walking to our seats, two young men came up to us and said that they appreciated our dressing traditionally, but that we hadn't gotten the outfits quite right. They would help us. I had the most serious problem. Although my top wrap covered the correct shoulder, I was using safety pins, which is taboo. The young men showed me how to knot the cloth so that it was properly held in place without pins. We thanked them, took some pictures, and then went on to our seats.

After the arrival of the queen mother and then the king, the actual events began, which weren't spectacular. It was not like the closing ceremonies at the Olympics. It was just forty thousand half-naked young women, dressed in costume, divided into local groups, parading in formation around the stadium and then stopping to dance in front of the king. In recent years, the ceremony had attracted more very young girls, and the first group in the parade was comprised of toddlers with their chaperones trying to keep them in order. The second group was comprised of members of the royal family. After that, a knowledgeable Swazi citizen could probably tell the groups apart based on their home towns, but they began to all look the same to me. After a few thousand pairs of naked breasts, the novelty wears off. It was a unique cultural event, and I'm very glad I attended, but I won't need to go back again right away. Mkhululi hadn't been in ten years.

Later, when we discussed our experience with our friends and colleagues, we heard a surprising range of opinions on the Reed Dance festivities. Most of the Swazi men and some of the women thought that it was an important part of Swazi tradition and should be preserved. However, most of the women we knew (educated and city-dwelling) thought that it was demeaning to women and was just one example of how the Swazi culture and society were still male-dominated and oppressive to women. Mkhululi said his daughter would definitely participate as soon as she was older, but Katy said that wasn't going to happen. It reflected the general Swaziland condition, a small country with strong and proud traditions (including a powerful king) confronting the modern world.

We didn't stay to see all of the sections of young women parade in front of the king or the singing that followed. As we were leaving, a fashionable, attractive woman asked us to pose for a picture. An adolescent, who might have been her daughter, joined us in the photo. We thought nothing of it until we heard later that it was in the local newspaper. The caption under our picture congratulated whoever had helped the tourists to dress so authentically.

On Tuesday, we continued our short vacation and went to Cape Town. Any flight out of Swaziland is expensive, so we drove the four-plus hours to the Johannesburg airport to save over $600. We later learned that the shortest route on the map is not the shortest route in time; we saw a lot of small towns along our drive. We also saw the settlements (shantytowns/ slums) near the Johannesburg and later the Cape Town airports. These were the remains of apartheid when black Africans were forced to live in "townships" on the outskirts of major cities. When apartheid went away, the residents of these townships could legally move elsewhere. However, that didn't mean that they could afford to move elsewhere, so these communities remain. Evidently, they were slowly being upgraded with sewers, running water, and electricity; but this was, of course, very expensive for the government and was taking a long time. Today, the living conditions in the former townships remain a source of terrible frustration for millions of South Africans.

Within these communities, each individual dwelling (politically correct euphemism for shack, hovel, etc.) may be no worse than those in the poor communities in Swaziland, but the impression is very different. In these settlements, there are thousands and thousands of tiny makeshift dwellings packed tightly together housing hundreds of thousands of people. Some of the South African settlements are larger than the largest cities in Swaziland, and several together would contain more than Swaziland's total population. Today, some of these former townships offer tours and overnight stays, but we had seen enough from a distance. Even from a distance, it makes a visceral impression that you don't easily forget. I was angry at the former apartheid government and its supporters who had forced the residents into these conditions, and I tried not to despair about how difficult it will be to get everyone out of these settlements. I frequently had to remind myself that major change comes step by step and that lots of little steps add up over time.

After an uneventful flight, we drove to our Cape Town hotel and only got slightly lost along the way. Our hotel was in a community called Bantry Bay and, as might be expected, had a very nice ocean view. This part of the coast, near the tip of the continent, is a mixture of cliffs and small beaches. Our hotel was perched on a steep slope that rises up to Lion's Head, one of the distinctive mountains surrounding Cape Town. After unpacking, we went out for dinner along the Victoria and

Albert Wharf, a beautifully developed, modern, tourist, and shopping area.

Cape Town is called the mother city of South Africa because it was the original European settlement. It is also southern Africa's most attractive and cosmopolitan city. With its wonderful geography, some people think it is one of the most beautiful cities in the world. Many people will also tell you that it feels much more like Europe than Africa. One of the reasons for this is that in Cape Town, "Africans" are not the majority, and the population is much more racially diverse than other African cities. However, I need to explain this statement and the quotes around Africans. It has to do with approaches to racial classification and previous discrimination.

Historically in the United States, anyone with any African ancestors was referred to as colored, Negro, black, or African-American with all of these terms being synonymous but acceptable in different eras. Even people who had mostly white ancestors were categorized (and often discriminated against) using one of these terms. The rules of racial discrimination were different in South Africa. Instead of having basically two racial groups, black and white, South Africa has historically had three: white, black or African, and a third group called colored. The whites were pure white; the Africans were pure black; and the coloreds comprised everyone in between, including people of Asian as well as mixed-race background. Because of the history of the various races that came or were forcibly brought to Cape Town, and because of a generally more liberal populace, Cape Town has a high percentage colored population. In Cape Town, coloreds, not "Africans" comprise the majority. Cape Town's cultural diversity plus the long history make it a very interesting city. For example, one of the sights we visited was the Jewish museum. This modern facility employs a wide variety of exhibits and media to chronicle the history of the Jews in South Africa, including their contributions to the community and the economy and their opposition to apartheid. In fact, it was a Jewish firm that gave Nelson Mandela his first job as a lawyer.

In addition to Cape Town's historical, cultural, and topographical sights, e.g., Table Mountain, there is also the Cape Peninsula to visit. This is the peninsula that goes from the city of Cape Town down to the Cape of Good Hope. Cape Town has many similarities with San Francisco, e.g., water on three sides, hills/mountains, cool weather, and fog. The Cape Peninsula has a lot of similarities with the Monterey and Big Sur areas and makes for a nice oceans-hugging drive. If you start down the peninsula on the west, you're driving along the Atlantic, and if you come back up on the east, you're driving along the Indian Ocean. Even though the Cape of Good Hope is not really the most southern point in Africa, it is the most southwestern point and still considered the dividing line between the Atlantic and Indian Oceans.

Right next to the Cape of Good Hope is Cape Point, a little farther south but not as far west. At Cape Point, you can walk or ride a funicular up to the top of the point for a great view. When we arrived, we were told that the funicular was closed for maintenance, and we would have to walk. Overhearing some other tourists, we quickly realized that there was no maintenance going on. The funicular was closed because it was being held for Vladimir Putin, the president of Russia, who was visiting South Africa. As we neared the end of our climb up the walkway to the top, we saw the cavalcade of flashing lights coming down the road to Cape Point. Soon after, Vladimir Putin emerged from the top of the funicular, surrounded by guards and attendants. He was the shortest person in the group, but also the most intimidating. His steely visage was complemented by his wardrobe and muscular physique. He was dressed in a dark sport jacket and slacks with a black turtleneck that gave him the ominous look of a mafia don. Although he is short, you wouldn't want to pick a fight with him. He has the build of a martial arts instructor and probably the skill as well. He looked briefly at the view, got back into the funicular with his entourage, and quickly the cavalcade left. We walked back down to our car and drove back up the east side of the cape, visiting a colony of "jackass" penguins along the way. Although now properly called African penguins, their braying sound makes it obvious how they got their name.

Business Finance and Other Challenges

*B*efore our short vacation, Mpendulo and I had visited the Swaziland Investment Development Company (SIDC) to confirm their position on MPE Timbers. In our previous meeting, they had said that there could be money available to invest in a restructured company, but it wasn't clear to me how much and under what conditions. SIDC had mentioned their interest in a new partner and some new management, but once again, it wasn't clear as to how firm these interests were. Although we had found Dave, a possible new equity investor for MPE, Brian wanted to pursue the alternative of getting funding only from SIDC. If this could work, the existing shareholders could preserve their equity. If not, bringing in Dave would mean that existing shareholders, while receiving some compensation, would lose all their equity in the company.

The meeting with SIDC clearly answered my questions. I had prepared a long list of questions to gently probe our contact about their interests and direction. It wasn't necessary. After answering my first question, Mr. Dlamini (slur the "d-luh-mee-nee," the ancestral name of a large portion of the Swazi population) elaborated that SIDC was not interested in getting deeper into difficulty with MPE. They wanted a way to reengineer the situation and turn it into a favorable investment. To them, this meant getting an equity infusion from a new partner, preferably someone from the industry who would take an active role in management. If these conditions were satisfied, then SIDC might be willing to make an additional investment but only in a restructured company with high prospects for success. It was a short but pleasant meeting. All of our questions were clearly answered, and we knew what our path had to be going forward.

On our way back to the office, I planned my phone call to Brian. I had to make the situation clear, but I wanted to retain a sense of optimism and generate enthusiasm for working with Dave. I really thought Dave would be a good partner and would deal fairly with the existing stakeholders, giving them a chance to recoup their investments and make some money.

The call with Brian was long, as expected, but it went well. As often happened when conversing with Brian, I spent a lot of time listening as he recapped six years of plans, dashed hopes, struggles, and excuses for failures. However, after hearing how the meeting went with SIDC, Brian quickly grasped that he was not in a good negotiating position. Basically, he knew that Dave was his only hope for salvaging anything from MPE. So we began talking about what Dave's conditions would be and what Brian would want out of the deal. As we talked, a scenario emerged that could be agreeable and beneficial to all sides. Both Brian and Dave believed that Brian could contribute a lot in getting the plant and the company running. However, after many years of working for himself, Brian was not interested in a long-term management position in a company where he didn't own significant equity. Instead, he suggested the possibility of setting up his own sales company in South Africa selling treated poles coming from Dave's plant. This type of scenario could fit with Dave's preferred mode of operation, which was to have arrangements with independent responsibility, risk, and rewards but also including incentives for mutual success. Brian agreed to talk to Robert and explain the situation to him. I agreed to meet with Dave and explain their interest in moving forward. At the end of the day, I was feeling good that we had some direction and perhaps even momentum.

I continued to crank through some more numbers for MPE. Although not an Excel wizard, I could put together some pretty good spreadsheets. At least they clearly showed the important factors and consequences of various scenarios. I even graphed the cash flows over time resulting from alternative decisions. I wanted to make it as easy as possible to see what the choices were and what the outcomes could be. I also wanted to make it easy to see the effects of changing assumptions. My primary beneficiary was intended to be Dave. He's a lawyer with a great intuitive sense of business, but not a numbers person. I wanted him to understand and be comfortable with the story the numbers told.

I met with Dave later in the day. I brought him up to speed on events and loaded him up with spreadsheets to review. I suggested to Dave that the next step would be to get all of the relevant parties together for a one-to-two-day meeting to begin working through the details of a start-up plan and a deal. He agreed, and I asked Mpendulo to schedule the meeting for two weeks in the future. Although I knew most of the work was still ahead, I was feeling good that we at least had a strategy. As I later told Wendy, "Although there are still 101 tactics that have to go right, at least we have a direction." On Monday, after returning from Cape Town, I learned that Mpendulo had scheduled the two-day meeting among Brian and Robert from MPE Timbers and Dave to start on Tuesday but that it had been postponed until Wednesday because Robert and Brian had uncovered two new prospective investors, and one was actually visiting the treatment plant site that day. I was shocked that two potential investors had suddenly emerged, so I called Brian to see what was going on. Evidently, Brian and Robert had been talking more about Dave's initial conditions for a deal, specifically that Dave would end up with 100 percent ownership, and they really didn't want to agree to it. Independent of how much they might be compensated, they wanted to retain at least some ownership. Something in their discussion must have motivated them to try harder, and somehow they discovered their new financing candidates. One was the investment arm of a trade union group in South Africa. Robert had gone to college with one of the officers. The other was the Investment Development Corporation (IDC) of South Africa to whom Brian had been introduced by a friend of a friend.

Brian indicated that Robert had already taken his friend, from the South African trade union group, to see the plant and would probably want to stop by our office and talk with us in the afternoon. They were both still planning to meet with us the next day. Later, Robert did bring his friend to our office and wanted me to present my assessment of the project to them. This was something that I wasn't really prepared to do. Since we had only one prospective investor, I hadn't seen the need to pull together a formal report; although I had done a lot of the necessary financial analysis. So we met in our conference room, and I talked informally about the attractive characteristics of the project and said that I was working on the formal report. This seemed to be enough for today, but it was clear that I had to start some serious writing.

These developments totally changed the nature of the meeting that we needed to have the next day. I called Dave and asked him to come to the office tomorrow afternoon. Mpendulo and I would meet with just Brian and Robert in the morning. We still needed to get a lot of details on the start-up plan, but we also needed to plot out how they wanted to approach the various investors.

On Wednesday, it became very obvious that I had to quickly

issue TechnoServe's version of the MPE business plan and funding request. Brian had met with the representative of IDC of South Africa, and he was also interested in getting our report. I committed to getting out the report by the end of the next week, which meant finishing it early in the week so that it could go through internal reviews and revisions. I also needed additional information from Brian to finalize some of my financial numbers. He committed to deliver it the next day.

Throughout the morning meeting with Brian and Robert, Mpendulo and I got our questions answered on the start-up plans. In the afternoon, we brought Dave in to talk about our original topic, the conditions for a deal. Dave was still opposed to less than 100 percent ownership, but he said that he would be willing to consider some shareholding for Brian and Robert, if he didn't have to invest too much. The higher his necessary investment, the less he was willing to consider other shareholders. So everyone wanted to see my report and particularly the financial analysis that showed the required investment under various scenarios. We also discussed the most important risks remaining to start up the company. In addition to resolving the various sources of financing and ownership, the major risk was that MPE had not secured a sufficient long-term supply of poles (timber). There were lots of forests in close proximity to the MPE plant, but MPE had to get a commitment from one or more of them to supply poles. Robert agreed to work on this, and Dave said he would look into it as well with his contacts in the industry. Without the commitment for a supply of poles, I agreed with Dave that the risk of the deal was unreasonably high.

Overall, we had some good meetings. We weren't moving ahead as quickly as I had hoped, but there was activity, and it was generally positive. I would write my report. Brian and Robert would show it to the new potential investors, I would send it to Dave, and then we'd go from there. Assuming that one of the investors would commit to the funding, we still had to resolve all of the other issues, which weren't trivial. Several of the issues were deal killers if they remained unresolved, but I was hopeful. Once we got a lead investor, I thought the rest would be possible, but certainly not easy.

The following week, I finished the MPE Business Plan and Funding Request and sent it to Leslie for review and approval. To simplify my task, I had decided not to duplicate the materials that MPE had already produced that went into depth on the market and the particulars of their business. I focused on the big strategic and other critical areas, foremost, on the financial requirements and opportunity. Once the business got going, it could generate great profits, but in the short-term it would require a lot of capital, and there were still a number of serious risks. I put all of this into my document and hoped I hadn't skewed it too far in one direction or the other.

Two days later, I incorporated comments from Leslie and Mpendulo and sent the document as a draft to Brian and Dave. Brian sent the report on to Robert and both of them planned to meet with the investors from South Africa the next day. Later Brian called and said he thought the document was fine as written, so I gave him permission to take "DRAFT" off the document and to present it to the interested investors.

On Sunday, Brian called to let me know that he would be going to England that evening to check on the health of his mother, who was in her eighties and diabetic. He had gotten a call from his sister requesting that he come visit and help make decisions about his mother's condition and care. His mother had been living independently but had been having difficulty with her health and taking care of things in general. It was time to have her move to a retirement home.

Brian also wanted to let me know that the meeting with the union investors had gone well and that activities should continue whether or not he was able to return quickly from

England. In three weeks, the union representatives would be coming to Swaziland to visit the plant and to meet with us in our offices. They wanted to hear an outside opinion on the project. I told Brian not to worry. We would be ready, and we would take care of them. Again, I felt a great sense of responsibility and wanted to present the situation appropriately. I wanted the deal to go through because it would generate jobs and economic growth, but I wasn't supposed to be a salesman. The business could be very profitable, but that wasn't guaranteed, and there were serious risks. I wanted to be enthusiastic but very factual, so began planning my presentation.

Finally the date for my MPE performance arrived. Robert had brought the trade union representatives from South Africa to our Swaziland office to hear the project overview. I think they understood my unusual position. Although I was promoting the project, I had the credibility of a third party. They evidently trusted that I could maintain the proper balance between the two roles. The conflict of interest was obvious, except that I would not benefit personally from a deal. Given that, I guess they saw that I could maintain my integrity.

Overall, the session went well, but it wasn't easy. I didn't really know the roles and responsibilities of the people who I presented to, but I think they were probably from the governing board of the union rather than investment professionals. They were intelligent and knowledgeable, but they weren't financial experts and a lot of my presentation was about the financial aspects of the project. When contemplating an investment of nearly a million U.S. dollars, it was important that they understood all the aspects of the investment, both the business itself and the financial aspects of the deal. Robert had explained a lot about the business basics and the union team had already visited the mothballed MPE facility. My role was primarily to explain that we thought this business had good market and profit opportunity and what the required investment and expected financial returns could be. I also needed to back up my opinions with our analysis.

I had done some very thorough analysis, showing alternative scenarios for different rates of plant expansion and various financing approaches with different mixes of debt and equity. Although somewhat challenging, this was basic financial analysis and consequently the easy part. I knew what I was talking about but struggled with how to explain it and not make people's eyes glaze over or put them to sleep. This was always a challenge in my consulting career. After doing extensive analysis on a company's operations and coming up with many detailed findings and recommendations, how do you boil it all down into a crisp presentation that senior executives will listen to while sitting still.

The fact that this presentation was mostly about finance, an esoteric topic for many people, made it especially challenging. Most people, even some experienced business people, don't understand why a company that will be profitable from day one needs financing. They don't understand the difference between profits and cash flow. They don't understand why an increase in an asset like accounts receivable can make a business run out of cash. The problem was that understanding all of these was important to understanding the MPE investment. A business can be very profitable, but if its customers don't pay their bills for two months, the business will need a lot of cash (financing) to operate. I tried explaining all of these things, and in the end, it went very well, but I felt a lot of pressure throughout because the MPE team was depending on me. And this was with a very friendly audience. Fortunately, they wanted to understand, and in the end, I thought they did. The next step was just waiting as they discussed the opportunity with their colleagues and bosses, who would make the final decision.

While I was waiting on MPE, I focused on Tasty Meals. Before going to the Reed Dance and Cape Town, I had met with

Phiwa who had brought me up to date on his progress. He was in the process of securing several small plots of land to grow Tasty Meal's own maize. The plots were numerous and small because Phiwa had to be opportunistic to rent good land at an attractive price. We worked on Tasty Meals's requirements, month by month, for planting and harvesting, and they looked promising. The bad news was still that once they planted the maize, it couldn't be harvested for at least three (maybe four) months. The good news was that after the maize began producing, they didn't need that many hectares of growing land to get them into the plentiful season. This would limit the expense but was still money that Phiwa and Tasty Meals didn't have.

After spending most of our time on the supply, we talked about increasing sales. I told them what the sales and marketing plan would have to look like, and we began to explore ideas about increasing sales. I reemphasized that an important part of our activity had to be going from ideas to developing a real plan that would be actually used when mealies became available.

When we got back from Cape Town, Sonnyboy was also back from his honeymoon, so we visited Tasty Meals together. The first thing we heard from Phiwa was that absolutely no mealies were available at any reasonable price, so they had shut down production. Although they had been able to tentatively contract to rent land to grow their own maize (and pay at harvest), they had no money to pay for seed, fertilizer, etc. They were trying to tap all of their friends for short-term, high-interest loans, but so far they hadn't been successful.

One great thing about Phiwa was that he could put aside these short-term, critical concerns and focus on the long-term business plan with the confidence that somehow the business would be successful. Maybe it came from growing up in Africa and achieving personal success in the past despite tremendous odds. I didn't know what he was feeling inside. Despite the fact that his business was about to die and he was going to lose all of his investment and the collateral he had pledged against the loan, outside he seemed relatively relaxed and was able to focus on the analysis and planning. I admired his attitude and fortitude. It reminded me of some of the dedicated entrepreneurs I have seen in Silicon Valley.

I continued to work on the sales and marketing plan with Phiwa and one of his salesladies, emphasizing that they had to be very specific about where the sales were coming from and how they would make them happen. They had to justify the future sales numbers based on extrapolating their experience to date. Numbers in a spreadsheet without support were not going to be acceptable, especially since the business had never achieved breakeven volume. I explained that their first deliverable had to be a detailed spreadsheet of all the sales through the various channels with supporting backup that showed why they were confident in their estimates. Tasty Meals's second deliverable had to be the marketing plan that supported the sales numbers. If they needed signs to support sales in small shops, it had to be in the marketing plan. If they needed specialized racks and displays for the supermarkets, it had to be in the marketing plan. And there had to be a person and date assigned to get things done. The less money available, the better a plan has to be. Tasty Meals had no money available, and getting more would be difficult, so we had to have an excellent plan. They realized that they had a lot of work ahead.

When I met again with Tasty Meals, they confirmed that they could rent enough land to supply themselves with mealies year round, but they still didn't have any money to commit to planting. In the good news category, they had made great progress on the sales plan. Several women who had been selling the mealie bread were visiting shops throughout the country to evaluate their sales opportunities. Then the women were projecting sales for each store, based on their prior experience with similar stores and their conversations with the owners. The numbers were good with solid logic behind them. More importantly, the projections would generate a good profit for the business, and the women weren't finished. They felt they needed another week to go through all the possibilities in the whole country. The short-term news was negative, but there was hope in the long-term. Phiwa took us out to lunch, and we briefly forgot about the threat that was looming over him.

Later that evening, we met with a food-processing expert who had come from the United States to meet with a number of bakeries. Many bakeries had problems with their products drying out and going stale. This expert was recommending the use of defatted soy flour to help extend shelf life. Shelf life had been a problem for Tasty Meals as well, so we thought the consultant might have some ideas. As he explained to us, Tasty Meals didn't have a problem with their product drying out and becoming stale. Tasty Meal's problem was that the product was moist and would readily allow the growth of mold. Although Tasty Meals had tried various preservatives in the recipe, nothing seemed to work in concentrations that didn't spoil the taste. The expert suggested that a dilute solution of preservative could be sprayed on the outside of the product rather than mixing it into the batter. In this way, the preservative would go only where it was needed, on the outside of the product, and it would be so dilute as to not impact taste. We all thanked the consultant, and Phiwa committed to trying it out. This would make it easier to sell the product in smaller shops and in more remote areas that would have slower turnover and less frequent deliveries.

As I tried to help my individual clients, I kept thinking about the whole office and how we could quickly make a visible impact. From my business school and consulting days, I remembered the standard mantra of strategy—focus. My perception was that our office had not been focused on a limited number of industries to support. This was understandable since the Swaziland office was new and hadn't yet had time to do a complete analysis of which industries had the most promise. However, I thought that we had done enough analysis of enough sectors that we could at least begin to focus. I volunteered to facilitate an off-site planning session with the intent of focusing our efforts and getting tangible results quicker. This was an activity I had done many times in my career as a management consultant, and I felt quite comfortable taking the initiative. I also felt that it would be a team-building exercise for the business advisors as they shared their activities and plans with each other.

The objective for the full-day session was to position all of our existing and potential projects (representing subindustries) into a two-by-two matrix based on the magnitude of the benefits that the project would produce and the speed at which those benefits could be achieved. Then we would concentrate our resources on the projects that would deliver the most benefits quickly. Since we didn't think that there would be many projects with large and rapid benefits, we also decided to pursue a portfolio of other projects. Some of these projects would produce very large benefits but might take three to four years to achieve. Other projects would generate smaller benefits but could be accomplished quickly. We would choose a few of each.

At the end of the day, we had categorized all of our projects. We had decided which ones we would pursue and which ones we wouldn't. We had also determined the levels and types of resources we would need to pursue these projects and agreed on some hiring plans. Overall, it was a really good day. Next, the business advisors needed to develop their more detailed plans and decide what benefits they would commit to delivering and the timeframe for achieving the results. But none of this was imposed from above. It was generated by the business advisors themselves, and consequently was more motivating. I felt good about the day, and even if we didn't see radically different results right away, I felt that it gave us more focus and the results would come.

TechnoServe in Maputo, Johannesburg, and Nairobi

$\mathcal{W}$e spent the next weekend and the following Monday in Maputo, Mozambique. Leslie and her husband, Stuart, had a one-year-old son, Charlie. Since they had lived most of the past four years in Mozambique, they decided to have Charlie's birthday party in Maputo with friends. We decided to ride along and avoid the $300 charge for a special waiver to take our rental car into Mozambique. We also decided to avoid the chance that our car would be vandalized in Maputo and that we would have to pay the hefty deductible on the insurance. The drive to Mozambique was pleasant and seemed quick because there were four of us chatting. We went through a new, less trafficked border post and there was no one in line at immigration. The best part was that our unused visas from our previous attempt to go to Maputo were still effective, so we didn't have to pay again.

Much of the drive was through lightly populated areas, especially in Mozambique. The small settlements we saw in the rural parts of Mozambique appeared cute and quaint. The grass houses looked neat and clean, almost like dioramas in a museum. The appearance and the warm emotion they generated in us were deceiving. These houses weren't built with grass and other natural materials because they make a great house. The people living in them didn't have anything else. These people were much poorer than those living in the awful-looking shacks in the South African townships, but who can say that one or the other is better off? The people in rural Mozambique probably didn't worry too much about crime, and they lived amidst pleasant scenery. On the other hand, they probably didn't have good access to schooling and had little hope that they or their children would ever have a better existence. The daily struggle in the townships was probably much more threatening, but at least the people in the townships had some small chance that things could get better for them or ultimately their children. I was very thankful that I wasn't in either place.

As we drove through the outskirts of Maputo, we began to see the informal settlements that surround the city, just like Johannesburg or Cape Town. Somehow they didn't seem quite as bad or as big, but they were still upsetting. As we got into the major part of Maputo, we began to understand the mixed messages that we had gotten about the city. Leslie and Stuart had commented about the lovely beach area with its fish market and ocean views. Maputo also has movie theatres, interesting restaurants, and nightclubs, which are limited or nonexistent in Swaziland. But we had also heard lots of stories about the crime and the decay in the city. Through the weekend, these competing themes dominated our feelings.

On the way into the city, we stopped for a nice cup of Portuguese coffee. However, in choosing where to get our coffee, the primary criterion was being able to closely observe and protect our parked car. As we arrived at the home of Leslie and Stuart's friends, where the party would be, their security guard led us through the gate in the high fence, topped with barbed wire, which surrounded their house and garden. As we went through the yard and into the house, we passed the large diesel generator that was used when the power went off. There were no overt threats or serious inconveniences, just little hints from the surroundings that we were in a very different place.

On Sunday, Wendy and I walked around the more interesting parts of the city, some of which were in the older and more run-down sections. The area right around city hall was actually quite attractive and clean, but only a few blocks away, the sidewalks deteriorated and so did the buildings. Some were just broken shells that looked like they were bombed out twenty years ago and were now just strewn with trash. We thought that these buildings might actually have been bombed out during the long civil war. However, we were told that the civil war never actually reached Maputo. These crumbling hulks were just the result of poor construction, neglect, and urban decay.

Although we were walking a recommended route from the guidebook, Wendy and I frequently felt uncomfortable. The good news and the bad news was that in almost every block, there was at least one building with a security guard standing outside. These guards provided a deterrent to petty burglars, but not to serious criminals. We heard several stories of people being robbed by thugs with guns while an unarmed security guard could only watch. In defense of the city, our feelings were probably worse because it was Sunday, and there were few people around many of the areas we traversed. And we didn't feel hassled by aggressive panhandlers or hawkers. However, we did have a locally provided map with clearly marked "NO GO" areas on it, which we carefully avoided.

After probably a four-mile walk through the downtown area, we decided it was time to go back to our modern hotel overlooking the beach. We had already decided to go to a famous fish restaurant farther up the coast for dinner. When we emerged from the five-mile cab ride, we were underwhelmed by the décor of the famous restaurant, to say the least. The interior had concrete floors and furniture of 1940s diner style.

It seemed clean but was definitely without ambiance. At first, we took a table outside on the open porch, but when a thunderstorm began, we quickly moved inside. The wonderful food made up for the lack of décor. We both had the biggest prawns we've ever seen in our lives. I had four with tails about ten inches long. They were simply and delightfully prepared, and it was like eating four small lobsters. On the menu, they were only quoted at "market price," and so we panicked when the waiter told us that each plate would be a million metacais. I quickly did the math and realized that they would be expensive, but less than $40 per plate. It was a great meal, and on the cab ride back to the hotel, we got to watch a spectacular lightning show over the Indian Ocean.

The cab, like all of the ones we took in Maputo, was pretty run-down. And it seemed that all cabbies drove around on empty. I think they bought gas only when they got a fare, and once our driver actually had to stop at a gas station immediately after he picked us up. When we arrived back at the hotel, I wanted to tip the cabbie, but only had the exact change or a larger bill that was three times the fare. I asked him if he could change the larger bill. He checked his cash and all that he had was the fare that I had given him on the trip to the restaurant. I pulled out my exact fare and Wendy was able to dig through her cash and find enough for a decent tip, but it gave us an idea of how much he was earning.

On Monday morning, we visited the TechnoServe office in Maputo and met with Jake, the country director. Jake had been the country director since TechnoServe started in Mozambique nine years earlier, and he had overseen some outstanding projects. TechnoServe had played an important role in revitalizing Mozambique's cashew industry, and they had begun to develop the domestic poultry sector. Jake was excellent in articulating the TechnoServe approach to development and of giving examples of how it had been carried out in Mozambique. It was really great to hear the success story of a mature office. In Swaziland, TechnoServe had only been operating for seven months and so couldn't demonstrate a lot of results. I was always asking why we couldn't focus more and get results quicker, but then I'd remind myself that development is really hard and often takes time. Sometimes it felt like pushing a rope, but the Mozambique story was reassuring. After our meeting with Jake, the driver from the Maputo office took us to the border, and Kiki, the driver from the Swaziland office picked us up and drove us back to Mbabane.

Maputo was interesting and energizing, sometimes for good reasons, sometimes because we were nervous or concerned. It definitely had features, like a social scene, that made it attractive to volunteers in their twenties and early thirties, but we were definitely more comfortable going back to our much-less-exciting life in safe and predictable Mbabane.

Only a week and a half later, I visited the TechnoServe offices in Johannesburg, South Africa, and Nairobi, Kenya. Seeing the TechnoServe Maputo office had been wonderful, and I wanted to observe more mature offices. It was a good week to go because Wendy was going to Nairobi for a Junior Achievement pan-Africa conference, and from Swaziland, you had to go through Johannesburg to fly to Nairobi. We flew together to Johannesburg and met in Nairobi to fly home to Swaziland.

Though Johannesburg was the headquarters for TechnoServe in South Africa and the regional African headquarters office as well, it was not a big office. It had four full-time employees, two part-timers, and a volunteer. Most of TechnoServe's employees worked in the field, very remote from Johannesburg. The office was in an attractive area of the city and was surrounded by a ten-foot wall with a massive electronic gate. This type of protection was common and perceived as necessary for homes and small office buildings in Johannesburg. In fact, most walls surrounding homes and buildings were topped with either rolls of barbed wire or an electric fence. The TechnoServe office wall did not have this, and maybe that's why it had experienced four break-ins within the last month. The office was moving to a different location in the near future.

Both Johannesburg and Nairobi were known for their crime, and it continues today. It is usually in the background as an offset to the attraction of living in a large city with all of its excitement and amenities. Only occasionally, when a friend gets robbed or carjacked, does it reach top of mind. Usually, it just stays in the subconscious as you remember to lock your car doors, hide your computer, and keep cash separate from the credit cards and passport that you really don't want to give away if robbed. However, I thought this tension seemed to wear on people. Maybe some people got used to the fear or ignored it, but I thought for most people, it just created a higher baseline of stress as they went about their normal activities. They also seemed to frequently question whether this was really how and where they wanted to live. It was funny how fans of both Nairobi and Johannesburg thought that their city was only somewhat dangerous but were afraid to venture out in the counterpart. Fans of each side insisted that the other city was much more dangerous. In fact, one young woman told me how civilized robberies were in Nairobi. If you cooperated and handed over your money, you had nothing to fear. However, she didn't trust that a robbery would go so smoothly in Johannesburg.

During my visit to the Johannesburg office, I got an opportunity to talk informally with Simon, TechnoServe's vice president for Africa and his one regional director, Sandra. Among the topics I discussed with them was how difficult economic development is. I understood this from a theoretical level from all my research and reading, none of which provided a simple recipe for success. But this discussion was very practical, tangible, and real. We talked at both the macro and personal levels. At the macro level, many people are aware of the vast amounts of money and human resources that have been put into development projects. Post–World War II Germany and Japan have generated economic miracles from devastation while much of Africa is worse off than fifty years ago. Many development efforts have been successful, but many more have not. The development professionals have learned a lot of expensive lessons but were getting better at it. Even when development works, it can proceed very slowly. Simon and Sandra agreed that sometimes it felt like trying to run through deep water. This was very hard for aggressive, business-oriented people who wanted to demonstrate that they could produce results, and quickly. Specifically, I talked about my concern that I wouldn't be able to point to any fully completed project when I left Swaziland at the end of my tenure. Simon and Sandra, who admitted to having similar feelings earlier in their careers, assured me that, at some future time, my work would produce tangible results.

At the same time, I could see how challenging development work had continued to be for them. The regional executives, like many others at TechnoServe, had spent time in the commercial sector, and some of the nonprofit practices really wore on them. TechnoServe had been very successful in recent years as donors recognized the wisdom of the TechnoServe approach. This had meant rapid growth in funding and programs. But donors always want their money to go directly to the beneficiaries of programs, not what they perceive as overhead. Donors also want precise accounting to show that funds are segregated and their funds go directly to achieve their objectives. This isn't unreasonable; it's just hard and requires overhead. Consequently, there's always a strain on the infrastructure and the management team, which have to be lean, particularly during a period of growth. I had seen this before, especially in consulting firms and the rapidly growing high-technology companies that had been my management consulting clients. TechnoServe's particular challenge was that it was essentially a rapidly-growing, non-profit, consulting firm. The strain on the regional executives was obvious.

It was also obvious that all of the really competent expats in development kept asking themselves if this is what they really wanted to do. Most had experience in the private sector and constantly wondered if they should go back and instantly double their salaries. They wondered if they would ever be able to move back to their home countries and afford to buy a house. They wondered if their current location was the right place to raise children of school-age. They wondered because there were big consequences to all of these decisions, no matter which choices they made. I empathized with them and felt very lucky to have the freedom to choose what I wanted to do without the huge consequences. Of course, my freedom only came because I was much older and at a different stage in my life and career.

My visit to the Johannesburg office was positive overall, but it forced me to do a lot of hard thinking and introspection. On the other hand, the visit to the Kenya office was positively joyful. The Kenya office had been open since 1973 and could point to a long record of significant impact. The office had grown rapidly over the past year and had nearly forty professionals. Among their recent successful creations were three major dairy hubs with cooling tanks. These hubs collected small quantities of milk from thousands of farmers who owned only a few cows each. The milk was tested and then held in a cooling tank until a large truck from a major dairy processor could pick it up. As with many TechnoServe projects, the dairy hubs connected smallholder farmers to commercial markets, allowing them to create a steady income. The hubs also allowed farmers with a steady record of milk deliveries to establish credit for purchases such as seed, veterinary services, and school fees. The Kenya office also had great projects in other sectors, such as bananas.

Donors were asking them to replicate their Kenyan success in Uganda. Working with the Kenyan Ministry for Youth, the Kenya team was developing a business plan competition that might generate ten thousand entries. The Kenyan office staff was energetic and motivated. I was excited and had a great time sharing experiences.

Junior Achievement

$\mathcal{A}$s we flew back to Swaziland together, Wendy and I discussed her progress and plans for Junior Achievement (JA) and her experience at the conference. I already knew that she had achieved a very solid milestone before leaving Swaziland. The JA vice president for Africa had sent out an e-mail to JA Worldwide that the Democratic Republic of Congo would be the ninth JA member nation in Africa, and Swaziland and Gambia had become JA affiliates with plans for eventual full membership. TechnoServe would build the capacity of LULOTE to become responsible for the School-Age Youth Entrepreneurship (SAYE) program for sixteen to twenty-four-year-olds. Together, they planned to pilot *JA Economics for Success* and the *JA Company* programs within a few months then add *JA Job Shadowing* and *JA Service Learning* the following year and maybe a *JA Company* student competition in year three. Within five years, the plan was to serve over 7,500 SAYE students.

While the notice was very inspirational, the steps between the JA vice president of Africa's announcement and the actual pilot of the first training classes required many, many hours of detailed efforts before Wendy and I left Swaziland. Although there was general agreement on what would happen, Wendy had to use all of her project management and relationship skills to work with the multiple divisions within JA to receive, customize, and reproduce the classroom materials that would be required.

In the end, Wendy was able to customize and locally print some of the JA materials that had been received electronically. However, several heavy boxes of student workbooks and other classroom handouts had to be transported in Leslie's luggage as she returned from a visit to the United States. In addition to preparing the materials, Wendy also had to train the local trainers who would be delivering the classes and had never seen JA materials before. I was going to help with the training, and at least I had previously volunteered to teach a couple of JA programs in the United States so had a clue where she was leading the trainees.

The JA conference in Nairobi was an energizing experience for Wendy and a diversion from her flurry of activity in Swaziland. As is usually the case, the people were the highlight. She felt privileged to spend time with the twenty other JA country managers and staff. She said that the challenges these people were overcoming daily to make an impact on their countries made the stresses of JA United States and her own challenges in Swaziland seem quite small. She described many of the individuals starting with Phil and Robert from Zimbabwe whose humor kept their whole group laughing for three days and who had made JA successful despite their political environment (a very positive attitude and a sense of humor must be necessities to survive in Zimbabwe). Then she went on to describe Jules, a great dancer from the Democratic Republic of the Congo, who had to start up JA despite the uncertainty of upcoming elections and ongoing violence throughout the country. Then there was Luciano from Angola who would need all of his pastoral skills and spiritual perspective for starting up JA in a country coming out of many years of instability. Quiet and shy Teddy from Zambia had persisted over the previous few years to serve a few hundred JA students annually when many others would have given up.

At their JA Africa "graduation," the two women from Nigeria, Franca and Kunbi, dressed in traditional costumes including the wrapped headgear and put everyone in a festive mood. At the conclusion of the conference, each participant received a tongue-in-cheek award that was announced by the person whose last name preceded theirs in the alphabet. Wendy's award was announced by John Wali from Kenya (sounds the same as Walleigh, but there's no familial relationship or resemblance). The Swazi participants from TechnoServe and LULOTE bonded with their peers who greatly respected their initiative. It was a good start for the Swaziland JA program. Wendy said that the conference was typical of many JA events she had attended—very long, intense, and satisfying despite 8:00 a.m. to 9:00 or 10:00 p.m. daily schedules. She was inspired from her three days with JA colleagues from all over Africa who shared their passion and energy despite political instability, HIV/AIDS, and global neglect. It was very humbling for her to know what these JA people had survived while retaining their energy and commitment. She also felt that everyone learned a lot from each other and that there really was hope for the future of Africa with people like these.

Back in Swaziland, with the inspiration from her African peers still fresh, we continued our JA activities the very next weekend. On Saturday, Wendy and I, along with five additional volunteer trainers from TechnoServe and our Swazi partner LULOTE, simultaneously taught the first JA classes in Swaziland in three different locations. The *JA Economics for Success* was chosen as the first class to be taught. With this introductory course as a pilot, Wendy and her colleagues could gauge what class content was appropriate for each age group, how long the sessions needed to be, and how to help prepare the JA volunteer teachers.

Fortunately, Wendy and I had previously taught this class in the United States so it was adapting the material to the new culture and training teachers who had never observed, never mind taught, the classes that were challenging. In one example of how Wendy had to rewrite the content, one module teaches young people in the United States the dangers of spending too much money on their credit cards and building up large balances. In Swaziland, credit cards for young people were almost nonexistent and the students couldn't understand how people could be so foolish as to spend large amounts of money they didn't have. (Who says U.S. society is more advanced than Africa?) In all, over one hundred sixteen- to eighteen-year-old students from nine secondary schools learned how to assess their skills, interests, and values; make informed choices and decisions; and to appreciate the consequences. We piloted the *JA Economics for Success* on three sequential Saturday mornings in multiple locations to benchmark the capabilities of students from rural and urban areas and public and parochial schools. The first class consisted of playing a game to have a successful career with realistic simulation of choices about schooling and spending money. All of the volunteers enjoyed themselves, and it seemed as though the kids did too. It was great to see that teenagers are similar all over the world.

Over the next few weeks, Wendy kept busy with the SAYE (School-Age Youth Entrepreneurship) youth program. In addition to choosing, modifying, and piloting the curriculum, Wendy was asked to help pursue donor funding to support the program long-term. She called on her sales and marketing skills from her corporate days as well as her fund-raising experience from JA Silicon Valley, where she had led the staff to annually raise U.S. $1 million through grants, events, and donor solicitation. Through a few published lists of businesses and financial, civil, and other institutions as well as online research and colleague information, Wendy created a potential donor list to start targeting. In her remaining time in Swaziland, she helped create a presentation to appeal to business donors then began to set up appointments for Leslie and herself in both Swaziland and South Africa where most of the multinationals were head-quartered.

Wendy also arranged and facilitated the final session of *JA Economics for Success*, which was especially interesting for us because it included three local guest speakers. The first was Mrs. Gamedze, the executive director of LULOTE and a Swazi senator, chairman of the SwaziBank board of directors and on the board of multiple other institutions. Wendy had become very impressed with her and her passion toward developing youth. She spoke from her heart to the thirty-plus young people about growing up poor but aiming to get a diploma to teach business classes in secondary school. She went on to graduate from university, eventually received a master's degree in Scotland, took courses in the United States, and now runs an NGO among her other duties.

The second speaker ran a local enterprise, Gone Rural, which had been nominated for global recognition by the BBC (British Broadcasting Corporation). Her staff worked with nearly seven hundred rural women who gathered weaving grass, sold it for dying to Gone Rural, who sold it back to the women to weave into home-ware products that will sell well because of Gone Rural's coaching on design, color, and quality. Gone Rural would then buy these finished products back from the women to sell in their shops. Gone Rural's president was a white Swazi by birth and commitment, who talked frankly to the students about her business's global competition. She emphasized that whatever business they start, these young people will need to keep ahead of global competitors who copy designs and then manufacture and sell products at lower prices.

The third and final speaker was a former employee of Mrs. Gamedze at LULOTE who now owns and operates a supermarket in the nearby city of Malkerns and a café in Manzini. He talked partly in Siswati so we didn't understand everything, but he grew up in poverty and at one point raised his many siblings for a few years on his own while his mother was very ill. He really connected with the kids as he talked about his interrupted education, chaotic life, and persistence toward achieving his goals. One young woman asked what kept him going, and he said his Catholic faith. In a country that is 90-plus percent Christian, I'm sure that resonated. When she arranged the session, Wendy knew that these three speakers would have a much greater impact than anything she or I could have said. They did, and they powerfully reinforced the concepts we had taught in the previous JA program sessions.

Our Emafini cottage with our backyard swing was a retreat from nearby bustling Mbabane, Swaziland.

Performers demonstrate the Swazi Tribal Wedding Dance at the Swaziland Cultural Center near Mbabane, Swaziland.

Sad, sick hippo hangs out at the stone wall (with a nearby opening!) a few feet in front of us at Mlilwane Park, Swaziland.

Rick is assisted in getting redressed as a proper Swazi man before we attend the Reed Dance in Swaziland.

Men from the royal Dlamini family attend the Reed Dance.

A royal Dlamini family princess—indicated by the red feathers in her hair—relaxes with her mobile phone before she marches in the Reed Dance in Swaziland.

Nearly 40,000 young women parade before King Mswati III of Swaziland during the Reed Dance, in hopes of being chosen to be his next wife.

Incomplete and abandoned buildings contribute to an eerie feeling in the downtown area of Maputo, Mozambique.

Rick stops along typically littered sidewalk near a colorful car, in Maputo, Mozambique.

During the Junior Achievement pilot, a LULOTE staffer teaches one part of the JA Personal Economics program to Swazi high schoolers in Manzini, Swaziland.

High school girls discuss a team activity during the pilot of the JA Personal Economics program in Manzini, Swaziland.

High school boys work on an individual activity during the pilot of the JA Personal Economics program in Manzini, Swaziland.

At our Emafini cottage, Rick stands next to our car with a few now-shrunken hailstones which destroyed the windshield, blew out the back window, dented the car and broke both rear view mirrors during our last week in Swaziland.

Businesswoman of the Year Award Dinner

$\mathcal{T}$he big event of the next week was the Swaziland Businesswoman of the Year Award dinner. This was an annual award that had been initiated the previous year. TechnoServe had purchased a table's worth of tickets, so ten of us from the office attended. In many ways, it was like all the award dinners for many causes that Wendy and I have attended in the past. On the other hand, it had its own Swaziland peculiarities.

Wendy was an expert in running this type of event. She didn't enjoy doing it, but she was an expert. She had run many events for Junior Achievement in Silicon Valley over the previous four years, including the annual awards dinner for over five hundred people. The organizers of the Swazi event could have used her help. One of her first rules was to plan the schedule very tightly and then force people, especially speakers, to adhere to it. This is a principle that the Oscar Awards finally adopted when it started to appear that the ceremonies would run completely overnight. A second principle was to limit the number of speakers to only those you must have. She used these principles to keep the events to a reasonable length and to keep the audience somewhat attentive.

The organizers for this dinner didn't adhere to either of these principles. The opening remarks by the mistress of ceremonies were followed by welcoming speeches from each of the two major sponsors. Then there were speeches by the acting prime minister, the minister of Industry and Employment, and finally the keynote speech by the businesswoman of the year from South Africa. All of these speeches preceded the presentation of the profiles of the candidates, and all of the above preceded the main course. Dinner was served at 10:00 p.m.!

In partial defense of the speakers, one of the reasons that any speech had to be so long was the Swazi custom of recognizing and honoring all of the attending dignitaries at the beginning of each speech. Not to do this was considered very bad form, and if you overlook someone, you may have made a powerful enemy for life. Consequently, each speech began, "Honorable acting prime minister, honorable minister of Industry and Employment, global chairman of sponsor number one, African chairman of sponsor number one, Swaziland managing director of sponsor number one, managing director of sponsor number two (fortunately, they were a local company and didn't have visiting chairmen), members of parliament, members of the diplomatic corps, captains of industry, etc., ladies and gentlemen." This only added to the tedium of the speeches and the restlessness of the audience. A few times, the audience had to be quieted down so the speaker could actually be heard.

However, no one had to be quieted when the minister of Industry and Employment was speaking. He was a dynamic, engaging personality, and he used humor to keep the audience attentive. However, it was the sort of humor, directed at women, that hasn't been heard in an open speech in the United States for nearly fifty years. It wasn't directly hostile, just offensive to people like us who really believe in the equality of women. He joked about women's weight, age, attractiveness, and role in the household. I winced with every barb. He got laughs, but

I just kept wondering what the primarily female audience was really thinking. Did they just accept it as harmless as women would have done in the United States fifty years ago? Or were they being outwardly polite while seething inside? There was no way to know.

Producing Cotton, Milk, and Pork

With Insights on Race

$\mathcal{L}$eslie went to Washington DC for a series of meetings, so she asked me to attend a meeting of the Swaziland Organic Cotton Task Force, which was working to develop the potential for growing organic cotton in Swaziland. With the increasing global interest in preserving the environment, a nascent market for organic cotton clothes had emerged. A large global retailer specifically had become interested in offering clothes made from organic cotton and had communicated this to one of their clothing subcontractors, Tex-ray, located in Swaziland. Since much of Swaziland's textile and clothing industry had migrated to China in recent years, the government was greatly interested in retaining some clothing manufacturing in Swaziland. Also, organic cotton growing presented an opportunity for a large number of Swazi farmers. Traditional cotton had been grown in Swaziland in the past, but as world cotton prices collapsed, Swazi farmers found they couldn't make a profit so let their land lie fallow or switched to other crops.

Organic cotton presented a big opportunity, but it also presented big challenges. The first was simple economics. The projected cost of producing organic cotton was more than three times the cost for producing traditional cotton. Consequently, the biggest question was, "Will there be a market for organic cotton?" Would consumers be willing to pay the premium to have their clothes made from organic cotton, which, unlike organic food, offers little direct benefit to the individual? And if there was a market, would it be large enough for the large global retailer and others to pursue on a continuing basis? Or was this a fad? Beyond the basic economics were all of the challenges to actually producing organic cotton, without typical fertilizers, pesticides, or herbicides; on certified, uncontaminated land; not close to the spraying of other crops, etc. However, at this early stage, the opportunity outweighed the challenges, and there was great interest in government and private industry to move ahead. Hence the task force.

There were about twenty people in the meeting. The chairman came from the Ministry of Agriculture as did a number of the other participants who represented different departments within the ministry. Several agricultural research stations were represented as was the engineering department responsible for designing irrigation systems and the land survey department. Tex-ray and the Cotton Board were also represented. The Cotton Board was a parastatal (quasi-government) organization, somewhat separate from the ministry of agriculture, and was responsible for regulating and promoting the cotton industry in Swaziland.

The meeting began with a prayer, as most public meetings did in Swaziland. The chairman then made a few opening remarks about the importance of the opportunity and exhorted everyone to work hard to make it successful. Then we reviewed and corrected the minutes from the last meeting. After correction, the minutes were accepted. The primary item on the agenda was the planned pilot planting of organic cotton, which had to occur within a month or the opportunity would be lost for a year. Many things had to happen before the pilot planting could occur, and these activities depended on a lot of different organizations. The person most on top of all of the dependencies and with the greatest motivation seemed to be Dr. Dan, the agricultural expert from Tex-ray. Dr. Dan had made a lot of calls trying to get the many required parties organized. He had also gotten Tex-ray to make a number of commitments necessary for the project to move forward. At this point, he was mostly reiterating the actions and related responsibilities necessary for the pilot. Tex-ray had committed to buying the cotton coming out of the pilot at an attractive price. Tex-ray was also arranging and paying for the land to be certified as organic. Dr. Dan reiterated the need for the Cotton Board to advance the money for the planting materials to be paid back after harvest. The most difficult commitment seemed to be the need for the Agricultural Ministry to pay for irrigation to be installed.

Regarding the irrigation, the chairman called on the representative from the engineering department who had been asked to design and ultimately construct an irrigation system for the pilot land. The engineer said that he had a problem locating the precise plot on his maps so wasn't sure what the access to water would be. Then he went into the advantages and disadvantages of a drip system versus a standard spray system. Several other people joined in the discussion, and we learned a lot about irrigation systems. The consensus seemed to be that drip would be better from a long-term conservation and uniformity of watering perspective, but it would require more precise design engineering, would cost more, and take longer to install. We were reassured that a spray system would not damage or stain the cotton bolls. In the end, it was decided to pursue a spray system because it seemed to offer fewer short-term roadblocks, and we only had a month to get it installed. The chairman then reminded everyone of a larger roadblock. Although they would make every effort to get the Agriculture Ministry to pay for the irrigation, everyone needed to remember that the government was running out of money, so it was difficult to get money for any new projects. In fact, the local phone company had cut off service to many government offices (for nonpayment), and the government employees were making calls on local pay phones.

This wasn't the only challenge. There were also questions as to the tenancy of the land and who would do the farming. Regarding the land tenancy, much of the land in Swaziland was not individually owned. It was owned as Swazi Nation Land and was given to specific people for beneficial purposes by the local chiefs. If the land was used for the intended purpose and generally benefited the community, the occupant of the land could possess it in perpetuity. However, if it was not used beneficially, then it could be taken away, although the process for doing this was not clear. The land designated for the pilot had been given to another group for farming, but this group had stopped farming several years prior. The task force had gotten permission for the pilot, but it wasn't clear whether the land would be available in the future if the pilot was successful. Someone was designated to investigate this situation and to navigate the political processes with all the players to secure the rights to the land going forward. A final issue was who would do the farming for the pilot project. A group of needy women from the local area had been found to do the farming, but the interest of the local politician was primarily that the women make sufficient money from the project, not necessarily that it be a good test as to whether it would be a viable crop. So despite the fact that this was a high-priority project for a lot of people, many large challenges and conflicts remained; and there was only a month to go before planting must occur. The meeting closed with another prayer, maybe because we would need divine help to make the pilot successful.

Cotton wasn't the only new sector I was learning about. In parallel with my other projects, I had been supporting Mkhululi in his work with smallholder dairy farmers. Their problems were inconsistent profitability and inability to expand. At the time, Parmalat (the dominant dairy processor in Swaziland) didn't want milk from the smallholder dairy farmers because they milked their cows by hand, which didn't conform to the sanitary procedures that Parmalat required. However, even if Parmalat would have accepted their milk, the farmers didn't want to sell it because they couldn't make money at the price that Parmalat was paying. These small dairy farmers could and did make money selling their milk or milk products (such as emasi) directly to consumers. In this way, they cut out the middleman. The consumer got a lower price and the farmer got a higher price. However, this informal market usually went only slightly past the neighbors of the individual farmer and no farther. The margins were good, but the demand was not consistent, and there was no opportunity for growth.

TechnoServe was looking for an opportunity to change the market. We knew that the small farmers could not compete on price; they had to have some way of differentiating their product. Mkhululi and I had heard that Dalcrue, one of the larger dairy farms in Swaziland, had just advertised the introduction of their branded products to the market. We thought that this might provide an opportunity, so we went to meet with their CEO. Although Dalcrue was one of the larger dairy farms in Swaziland, it was small compared to many dairy farms just across the border in South Africa, which could be twenty times larger. Dalcrue had been supplying most of its milk to Parmalat for processing and sale. However, at the price that Parmalat was willing to pay for milk, Dalcrue was barely making a profit. To become profitable, Dalcrue felt they had to go to the market themselves with their own brand.

We thought the Dalcrue brand might provide a channel for our small farmers to differentiate themselves in the market. Our only previous idea was based on the fact that the small dairy farmers generally owned Jersey cows versus the Friesen cows held by the large dairy farms. Jersey cows don't produce as much milk, but their milk is richer and better suited for certain cheeses and other dairy products. We hoped that the small dairy farmers could find a manufacturer of cheese or other dairy products who would be willing to pay more for their Jersey milk because their consumers would appreciate the Jersey cheese. We hadn't found one, but we thought Dalcrue might be a possibility. In our discussion, we discovered we were very premature. Dalcrue had only just announced their brand, and they had a lot of work on their hands just to fulfill their immediate plans. They weren't ready to even talk about taking on a new endeavor. We still had a pleasant conversation and agreed to stay in touch.

After hearing that, even Dalcrue had trouble making money in dairy; my opinion on the potential for a dairy industry in Swaziland declined even further. As I had presented to the people in our office, we needed to focus our resources, and I didn't think the dairy industry was one to focus on. However, Leslie and Mkhululi weren't ready to give up on dairy. They felt that even if it wasn't commercially attractive, a dairy industry might provide a source of income for smallholder farmers. I argued that if it wasn't commercially viable that it wouldn't be independently sustainable, a very important concept for TechnoServe. TechnoServe does not believe in being a long-term source of charity or subsidy. Their objective is to establish market systems that can survive on their own and then let them go. We couldn't agree on whether a dairy industry could sustain itself in Swaziland, so we continued to explore possibilities. As we continued to search for ways to help the small dairy farmers, Mkhululi and I were invited to a meeting of large and small farmers at the Dairy Board offices. We had also been invited to share our ideas on the milk industry with the director of the Dairy Board in a private meeting.

Many African countries have "boards" to regulate and

promote the production of various commodities (such as cotton, mentioned earlier). Sometimes these boards actually help. Frequently, they just distort the free market and offer opportunities for corruption and political manipulation. Usually, these boards are heavily lobbied by farmers to institute minimum commodity prices and to limit imports. Purchasers and processors of the farmers' produce usually lobby the boards to let the free market reign, which typically drives down their costs. Schemers on both sides often lobby the boards to institute particular regulations so that they can manipulate the market to their advantage. I hadn't seen this type of behavior in my limited exposure to the Cotton Board, and I was curious as to what I would see when I went to the Dairy Board, the analogous organization for the dairy industry.

As part of the Dairy Board's efforts to grow the industry in Swaziland, the meeting with farmers was intended to get them all (large and small) to form a united front for the anticipated meeting between the dairy farmers and the production/marketing companies. The hope of the Dairy Board was that they could get local dairy farmers to provide a reliable and continuous supply of milk to the formal market. On the other side of the equation, the Dairy Board wanted to get the production/marketing companies to buy the local milk at a price that would allow the dairy farmers to make a profit. It was a huge challenge, but the Dairy Board had resources beyond the normal market mechanisms to make things happen. For example, the local milk production companies had been importing powdered milk from South America at a very low price and reconstituting it to sell as whole milk in Swaziland. The Dairy Board put an import tariff on powdered milk. This hurt the profits of the milk production companies and got their attention. They became more willing to explore options for using local milk, and so the meetings began.

This first meeting in the planned series indicated that the

process would be long and difficult. We only stayed for the first three hours, but the general tone was pretty acrimonious. The dairy industry in Swaziland, a very small country, was very fragmented. There were a few moderately large dairy farms, but even those had only a few hundred cows each, much smaller than the successful dairy farms in South Africa. On the other end of the scale, many small dairy farmers had only a few cows. Some of these small farmers were organized into associations or cooperatives, but none of these organizations spoke to each other. The only things that the collected participants could seem to agree on were that the selling price of raw milk was too low and that the government (including the Dairy Board) was not doing very much for the dairy farmers. As an independent party with no vested interest in the industry and a personal orientation to free trade and comparative advantage, most of the comments sounded to me like self-serving statements from a very parochial point of view. On the other hand, isn't this what happens with every industry in every country with the outcome based more on politics than economics? Just look at the history of sugar, cotton, corn (including ethanol), steel, dairy, and computer memory chips in the United States. We preach free markets to the developing world but manipulate as much as possible with subsidies, import tariffs, etc., for the benefit of narrow interests (with political influence) at home.

At the break in the meeting after the first three hours, we took our opportunity to meet with the director of the Dairy Board. I had not met the director before. I was anticipating a political hack with unreasonable goals and no plans for accomplishing them. I was totally wrong. The director was an intelligent, articulate youngish man with a degree in veterinary medicine and an MBA from Leeds University in England. He listened intently as we presented our view that the commodity milk industry was not viable in Swaziland because of the high cost of production compared to the much larger farms in

South Africa. We went on further to say that we thought the only opportunity for success was to develop a branded specialty dairy industry by integrating forward and promoting the desirable qualities of the Jersey milk produced by the local farmers.

After we had finished our presentation, the director thanked us, and then went on to explain, very thoughtfully, why the Dairy Board was not going to follow our approach. He explained the political issues, mentioned the huge level of unemployment, discussed treaties on trade, discussions with the South African government, actions taken by Namibia to close their border to dairy products, etc. In the end, it all came down to the imperative of developing a broad Swazi dairy industry. Politically, he had no choice, and he intended to aggressively pursue the mandate he had been given. He knew that he had a lot of work to do on all sides of the equation. He knew that he had to convince the local processors/marketers to take the local milk at a reasonable price. He knew that this would be difficult, but he thought that he had enough regulatory and financial clout to get their participation. He also felt that the larger challenge would be to organize the local dairy farmers to provide a reliable, continuous supply of milk that the producers could access. He wanted to get the small farmers to organize into associations or cooperatives with centralized milk collection centers to reduce costs and allow the producers to economically collect their milk. It was an incredibly ambitious, but logical, plan with many political and economic hurdles to overcome. TechnoServe had helped smallholder farmers with a similar approach in Kenya, and it had been very successful. However, Kenya didn't have the huge dairy farms of South Africa sitting just across the border, and the price that Kenyan dairy farmers received for their milk was approximately equal to the Swazi farmers' cost of production. We wished the director well and offered our help in setting up the cooperatives once his concepts had been accepted and the dairy farmers were ready.

At the end of the day, Mkhululi got a call from the director of the Dairy Board. While we were having our private meeting, the larger meeting had restarted and the participants had hijacked the agenda. When we left the meeting, the dairy farmers were being facilitated through a SWOT (strengths, weaknesses, opportunities, and threats) analysis of the dairy industry in Swaziland. While the director was out of the room, the dairy farmers had revolted against continuing the SWOT and had said that their only purpose for the meeting was to agree on a price to demand from the milk processors. They agreed that they should demand E4.5 per liter, roughly double what the processors were paying for milk. All of this was completed by the time the director got back into the meeting room. He definitely had his work cut out for him!

One of the fascinating things about international development and particularly the TechnoServe approach is that you learn the details of topics that you could never have imagined that you would understand. My background in consulting was useful because for every consulting project, I had to quickly learn at least the essentials of the client's business. Most of my consulting was in computer hardware, so I was pretty knowledgeable about computer marketing, manufacturing, product development, and customer service. I understood the details of manufacturing disk drives in China and how to configure personal computers in Ireland to ship to different countries in Europe. I had even branched out into understanding semiconductor manufacturing and software development. But I knew nothing about agriculture. In Africa, I had gotten introduced to the specifics of cotton and dairy production, and I got really familiar with pigs. Coming from an educational background in electrical engineering and business plus my career in the high technology industry, I could never have imagined that I would become so knowledgeable about the pork industry. Mkhululi was the business advisor for all of the feed and livestock industry and had concluded that not only could the pork industry be very viable in Swaziland, it could also provide income to a large number of poor rural farmers. His analysis caught my attention and interest because it suggested so much potential. In addition, I was enthralled with the unique terminology used in the industry. My favorite word was *weaner*. This, as might be suspected, is a little pig that has just been weaned from its mother. What made it funny to me was that these weaners would be fattened up and then sold to a butcher who would turn them into wieners. I know it's silly, but every time I hear the word *weaner*, I still envision a little sausage with a head running around on four tiny legs.

Only slightly more serious, when pigs are born, they are suckers, who soon become weaners. They are then fed to be fattened up and grow into porkers. Most of the male porkers get sold to be slaughtered and turned into pork. Among the females, most of the culls (not chosen to become reproducing sows) also meet this fate. Some of both the male and female porkers get fattened up further to be sold as baconers. However, the best females are raised to be gilts (analogous to a heifer) ultimately to become breeding sows. When they have achieved a sufficient age, the gilts are serviced by either a boar or artificial insemination. Four months later, as sows, they give birth to approximately ten suckers. This cycle continues twice a year for about three years. By this time, the sows have become tired sows (no wonder), and they don't produce as many suckers. So it's off to the abattoir for the tired sows that get replaced by new gilts.

Although the terminology is amusing, the pork industry is a very serious business. Large piggeries can have thousands of animals at one time in all of the above stages. They plan and closely monitor all of the critical steps in the breeding and growing processes and the associated financials. They know how much feed an animal should eat at each stage and how much it should cost. They can tell you how many kilograms in weight a pig gains for each kilogram of feed it eats at each stage of a pig's life. They know that a sow produces 9.8 piglets per litter and has 2.2 litters per year. It was fascinating, and I could work with the numbers.

On the other hand, the pig business stinks, literally not figuratively. I mean anywhere near a pig farm, it really smells bad. And you don't get accustomed to the smell as you do with other odors. At least not during the several hours I spent on a pig farm.

More specifically, I had been helping Mkhululi with his modeling of a pork industry in Swaziland. Mkhululi had envisioned a pork industry with three tiers. At the top would be a "multiplier." The primary objective of the multiplier would be to produce gilts (future sows). These gilts could then be sold to small farmers who would own one to a few sows. These breeding sows would produce piglets that would be sold at the weaner stage to larger growing farms that would fatten up the weaners and sell them to be slaughtered. Mkhululi thought that the business of owning sows and producing weaners could be a simple, profitable business not requiring much capital. For these reasons, it could be operated by relatively poor farmers, even starting with one sow. It sounded like just the kind of business that TechnoServe liked to develop.

However, Mkhululi had been having some trouble with the numbers. As he had conceived and modeled it, the multiplier wasn't profitable. He knew that something must be wrong because there are people in the business, and they do make money. We had checked all of his assumptions on costs, birth rates, etc.; and still things weren't coming out right. He needed experienced help, much more than I could give him. I suggested that he meet with one of the experts he had previously contacted to go over his numbers in detail and figure out the problem. He thought that was a good idea and that I should go along. I agreed. So we set out on a two-and-a-half-hour drive into South

Africa to visit a gigantic pig farm and the manager who had graciously offered to help us.

Mkhululi had been to the pig farm before and thought he remembered how to get there. He didn't ask for directions and didn't need a map. As an interesting sidelight, most Swazis I met didn't use maps. I later observed the same phenomenon in other African countries, but it was more pronounced in Swaziland. It might be that maps have historically not been available, but many Swazis will freely admit that they are not good at reading maps. However, they are very good at directions. When they go to a place, they just memorize how they got there and the landmarks that they passed. I had experienced this many times, so I wasn't worried about Mkhululi. We should have gotten directions. He remembered perfectly how to get to the piggery except for one detail, the highway exit where we needed to turn. So we got off the highway at a number of exits to let Mkhululi look around and see if the terrain looked familiar. Finally, we got off at an exit and were able to stop a truck driver who told us that we needed to take the very next exit. Once we got off at the right exit, Mkhululi knew exactly how to get to the farm and how to maneuver down the farm's many dirt roads to get to the piggery office.

The manager of the piggery was a very pleasant and helpful person. He voluntarily gave us his whole afternoon to go over our projections and explain how they related to the actual production figures from his operations. He had worked on this pig farm for over twenty years, I think since he graduated from college, so he had many figures readily available in his head. For those he didn't, he accessed files in his office and gave us very detailed information. As we went through the model, our heads were spinning with all the numbers. However, we found at least part of our problem. In Mkhululi's model, he had assumed that the multiplier would sell most of its piglets at weaner stage and only keep a few who would grow into the gilts. It was hard to sell weaners at the right price to make money. The money got made in fattening up the pigs for market. Mkhululi needed to restructure his model.

Besides the numbers, our meeting with the piggery manager had some other interesting aspects. As we were listening intently to some other dimensions of pig farm management, we heard a little noise from the bookcase behind the manager. I looked up at the device that had made the noise but couldn't figure out what it was. Shortly, however, the smell of pipe tobacco began to fill the room, but no one was smoking. As I mentioned previously, the stench of the pig farm was pervasive, and it definitely penetrated the manager's office. I deduced that the little noise must have been from an air freshener that was dispensing the fragrance of pipe tobacco. I don't know if eau de pipe tobacco was chosen because it's a manly smell or because it may be the only fragrance that could cover up pig stench. In any case, it worked for a while, but it didn't take long for the pig smell to dominate again.

Another interesting dimension to the conversation emerged when the manager made a comment about farm management and employees. The huge farm had been divided into smaller units to allow each of these units to be more tightly managed, which had been a successful transition. The manager further explained that this simplification allowed the "black chappies" that they employed to control their operations without a lot of supervision.

I'm sure it was meant as a simple statement of fact with no ill intent. However, to my politically sensitive American ears, it set off alarm bells. When I talked to him later, Mkhululi said I visibly straightened in my chair as I heard the words come out. There is still a lot of racism in the United States, so I must admit it hadn't been that long ago since I had heard an intentional racist comment made in informal conversation. However, it had been many years since I had heard this type of inadvertent racism in a work situation, especially from someone in a responsible position, who otherwise seemed like a nice, intelligent individual. It would have been fine if he had talked about hiring the locals with limited education, but there was that implicit assumption of the tie between race and the lack of capability. And he said it right to Mkhululi, who of course is black.

I discussed this with Mkhululi on our drive back to Swaziland. I explained that this type of phrasing had been considered professionally unacceptable and racist for many years in the United States. I wondered what the standard was here. Mkhululi explained that in Swaziland, this type of phrasing was definitely unacceptable. He suspected that in sophisticated society around Johannesburg and other South African cities, it would also be unacceptable. It was probably just in the more isolated rural areas where this manner of speaking still existed.

Race and racism are interesting, if usually unpleasant, topics. It is fascinating to me how people can devise complex schemes to discriminate against their neighbors and fellow citizens. It's also fascinating, and of course sad, to contrast the differences in the way the United States and South Africa practiced discrimination. Mkhululi pointed out that the former king of Swaziland, Sobhuza II, had been very wise in this regard. When Swaziland had gained its independence from Great Britain, Sobhuza had not expelled the whites from Swaziland or even quickly replaced them in their important jobs as had been done in most other African countries. Sobhuza had believed that the different races could live peaceably together and that the Swazis should benefit from the accumulated knowledge of the whites who were in the country. The transition in Swaziland was peaceful and successful, and Mkhululi insisted that Nelson Mandela had used Sobhuza II as his role model for the transition in South Africa. Most Swazis are very proud of their heritage but have a slight tendency to embellish their history.

Several weeks later, Mkhululi and I visited another smaller pig farm and an abattoir. We got more information, and I learned a new word. A cutter is a pig between the size of a porker and a baconer. They get cut from the group if they eat too much food and don't gain enough weight.

We also confirmed our financial analysis that said the best economic return for a pig farmer would come from selling all of his pigs at the baconer stage. However, we learned the market would not accept all of its pork in cuts that large. There was a sizable demand for porker or cutter size cuts of pork in the markets. Consequently, most farmers couldn't realistically sell everything as baconers. Who knew? Mkhululi and I were becoming so informed!

Tasty Meals Business Plan and the Bank

*F*or a number of weeks, I had spent many hours developing the Tasty Meals business plan. Tasty Meals needed financing to restart their operation. We had to go back to their bank and demonstrate how they could be successful with additional financing. Without a really solid business plan, there would be no hope, and Tasty Meals would become just another one of the hundreds of businesses around the world that fail every day. The business plan would show that they could be successful, and it would show how. There would be two crucial pieces, one describing how Tasty Meals would assure a year-round supply of mealies and the other describing how they knew that they could sell enough mealie bread to be reliably profitable. But in addition to these two crucial pieces, there would be a lot of other required sections. When financing a business, the investor has to know how all parts of the business will work. He has to know that all the pieces will be integrated without weak links to endanger the business. I had to convey this information in two forms, text and pro forma financial statements. The text described the market, the consumers, and the competition. It then explained how the business would satisfy customers, overcome competition, and garner enough market share to be successful. The pro forma financial statements showed how everything in the text got converted into financial numbers, which was, of course, the bottom line. Developing each of these required a lot of work.

A good business plan must describe very clearly how the business will operate to show that the entrepreneur has thought very deeply about the business and the many alternatives for running it. It shows that the entrepreneur has selected consistent approaches for all aspects of the business to support the overall strategy. Both the text and the financial statements must all be internally consistent. That leads to one of the challenges in developing the business plan. Everything is linked together, and a small change in one area ripples through with implications for everything else. For example, a decision to do more advertising in the early stages of the business naturally increases expenses on the income statement. However, it also generates the need for additional financing, which changes the cash flow statement. But the additional cash required means that the loan payments and interest charges must be recalculated to again update the income statement and the cash flow statement. The increase in expenses means that the breakeven production volume has to be recalculated as does the loan payments coverage. Fortunately, another TechnoServe colleague had developed a package of ten linked spreadsheets that allowed for a lot of the financial statements to be updated automatically, but the numbers had to be checked, and the related textual comments had to be updated manually and individually.

As I continued to make adjustments and refinements, I waited for our controller to produce up-to-date Tasty Meals financial statements so we would have a starting point for our projections. When they were finished, it was great to have real numbers, but the numbers were very depressing. Tasty Meals had gone through (i.e., lost) $70,000 in the seven months they had been in business. This included a $50,000 bank loan plus a $20,000 line of credit. Now we were going back to the bank to ask for $40,000 more! On the other hand, the business plan looked solid. If the bank wouldn't grant the new loan, they would have to foreclose on the property that Phiwa put up as collateral. Originally, I had been thinking that this would be a difficult decision for the bank, but I was just being too hopeful for my client. When supporting hopeful entrepreneurs, it was very easy to get sentimental and let hopes and dreams for their success get in the way of cold, hard, realistic thinking. I thought Leslie and Mkhululi were letting their emotions cloud their thinking on dairy, and I was doing it myself on Tasty Meals. If we had been dealing with an equity investor, he could have seen a potential upside from a successful business. Realistically, I knew the bank would just see more risk, and I knew that banks hate risk. In my experience, when banks lend money, they want to have at least two ways of getting their money back. First they want to see pro forma financial statements from a successful business plan that shows the company generating more than enough cash to pay back their loan. But this is never enough. Banks also want to see how they will get paid back when things don't go well for the business. Typically this means collateral. The banks want access to the customer's assets that the bank can sell to pay off the loan if things don't go well. I thought we had a great business plan, but Phiwa had no more collateral to pledge against a new loan. I resolved to remain hopeful, but the feeling in the pit of stomach told me what was going to happen. I knew times would be tough for everyone involved but especially for Phiwa.

Finally, Leslie and I accompanied Phiwa to the bank to request the additional loan for Tasty Meals. The meeting went about as well as could be expected. We had given the bankers the Tasty Meals business plan the day before, but they had not had time to read it. So they hadn't had a chance to be impressed by our wonderful prose or elegant pro forma financial statements. Actually, the current balance sheet didn't show in our favor, and I don't think bankers ever get impressed by nice prose. In any case, after Phiwa's overview of the loan request, the lead banker asked the predictable questions. I can actually say they were predictable because I had coached Phiwa on them ahead of time. The banker wanted to know what arrangements had been made to secure the green mealies. She asked why he had lost so much money in such a short period and how it would be different with a new loan. She asked about competition. She especially asked about additional collateral that certainly would be required and Phiwa didn't have. Finally she suggested that Phiwa get a partner who could provide management help as well as additional capital. She said that they would read the business plan, do their own analysis, and then get back to Phiwa.

Phiwa remained upbeat throughout the meeting, and we assured him that he had responded well to the questions. It was just that from the basic situation, it was nearly impossible for the bank to justify a new loan. He said he would look for a partner.

Wrapping up in Swaziland

*D*ecember came quickly, and it was time to wrap up our work in Swaziland, not because we had accomplished all that we had hoped for, but because our planned stay was nearly finished. But before we left, we had one last adventure. Our good friend Carolyn had come for a visit, and we got to do some touring with her. On her last day in Swaziland, I played chauffer for a shopping day, taking Carolyn and Wendy to many different locations that sold various Swazi craft items. Our last stop was Ngwena Glass near the border with South Africa. After sizable purchases by both Wendy and Carolyn, we were ready to leave and noticed that the weather was becoming threatening. Large black clouds were moving in our direction from the west. After driving for a while, the rain started and then began falling hard. I told Carolyn not to be surprised if it began to hail since we had experienced hail several times over the past months. Within thirty seconds, we began to hear the pitter-patter of hail as it bounced off the car.

I don't know precisely why it is, but I think the mountainous terrain of Swaziland combined with its geographical location generates extreme weather patterns. Although the terrible windstorm we experienced when we first arrived was unusual,

Swaziland frequently has very strong winds at certain times during the winter. Also hail was not uncommon. For the nonmeteorologists, hail is generated by turbulent weather that causes raindrops to be swept up into the upper atmosphere where they freeze before falling to the ground. Very turbulent weather can carry small hailstones, which accumulate more water on their downward journey, back into the upper atmosphere to refreeze into larger hailstones. This process can continue until the turbulence can no longer lift the large hailstones, and they fall to the ground.

This is relevant because, as we drove along, we were about to experience very turbulent weather and very large hailstones. The best way to describe the experience is to recreate the dialogue in the car as closely as I can remember it.

"It's hailing, just like you said."

A small amount of time passes.

"Wow, those are hitting really hard."

"Those hailstones are getting bigger."

"Wow. Those are really big. They could be dangerous."

"Oh my god! If one of those hit the windshield, it could break."

"Oh my god! That broke the windshield."

"There's another break in the windshield, and that one dented the hood."

We continued to drive through the bombardment. I felt like an unwelcome American in a foreign country where people were pelting the car with large rocks. Some of the hailstones were the size of softballs but irregular in shape. Fortunately, the car was protecting us, and although the windshield was being cracked into a mass of overlapping spider webs, it held intact.

"Oh my god! The back window just shattered. I'm covered with glass. I'll try to hold my raincoat up to keep the rain from coming into the car."

In many action movies, there is a car chase scene where the pursuing car shoots out the back window of the fleeing car in front. That's how it felt for us, but we were being pursued by a hailstorm, not gangsters with shotguns. It didn't't matter, in both movies and real life, the tempered glass windows literally explode into a shower of tiny pieces that won't cut the passengers, but the glass goes everywhere.

"Is there anywhere we can go for protection?"

"I'll look, but I don't even see any trees we could pull under. I'll just keep driving slowly. You look for some overhead protection."

We drove on at a snail's pace for the few remaining miles to our cottage, and as we drove, the hailstones got smaller, down to golf ball size. As we got closer to home, I was feeling good that we were safe, but I couldn't help remembering that I had taken the $2,000 deductible option for insurance on the rental car.

We entered the Emafini grounds and started up the road to our cottage, but our path was blocked by a downed tree. It was still raining and windy. I wanted to get the car into the carport to at least limit the water damage to the interior. We were close to Mark and Liz's house, so Wendy jumped out of the car and ran up to their door to see what could be done. It was Sunday afternoon, and Mark was home, but he still had on his nice church clothes. He came out in the rain to survey the situation and then quickly disappeared to pursue the solution.

Mark was in his early seventies. He started his career as a policeman and over the years, with Liz, built up their hotel business. He was a very good and practical businessman. In Swaziland, he was considered relatively well-to-do, but he and the rest of his family were very unpretentious and hard-working. He saw our situation and knew what to do. Although there were a number of workmen on the Emafini property, as Mark disappeared over the hill, it was obvious that he was going to take care of the situation himself. Only a few minutes later, Mark re-emerged over the hill perched at the controls of a gigantic front-loader. He looked like a storm trooper from Star Wars piloting one of the huge war machines. From the stories told by his family, he had purchased this massive piece of road building equipment a few years earlier, over their objections. It was used periodically for maintenance at Emafini, but most family members still thought the purchase was unjustified. I didn't know the story and so was shocked to see this elegant gentleman, in dress shirt and suit pants, skillfully maneuvering this imposing machine. With great dexterity on the controls, Mark made short work of the barrier to our progress. He chose the right points for leverage and, with just a few paths back and forth, pivoted the tree off the road. Then I drove the car up the hill and into our carport.

After I got out of the car, I surveyed the damage. There were approximately fifty dents in the sheet metal body of the car. The back window was gone, and there were bits of glass throughout the interior of the car. The windshield had taken sixteen major hits. The exterior mirrors were gone and head-lights were destroyed. Once again, I was thankful that we were safe, but I also knew that I was $2,000 poorer. I couldn't reach the rental car company by phone, but I knew that when I did the conversation would be painful for all of us. I had gone over five months without even a slight scratch, and then this happened two days before I was to leave. There was nothing I could do, so I laughed.

The next day, we were able to assess the storm damage from a broader perspective. The area where we had been driving was the worst hit. As we drove around town, we saw numerous cars with multiple dents and lines of cars at the glass shops where windshields were being replaced. There was a lot of damage. Sadly, the storm had killed five people. We all felt very fortu-nate.

The rental car company delivered us a replacement car. Two days later, we finished packing and headed to the airport. The rental agent at the terminal had become friendly with me during our stay and was very apologetic as she handed me the bill, but she had no choice.

We checked our luggage and waited for our plane. We were facing another long trip, but we were going home to family and friends.

As I sat waiting for the plane, I thought back on our experience, and my intellectual musings and conclusions were mixed with emotions. As I remembered my day at the bank with Tasty Meals, I was feeling really bad, but then I remembered my wonderful experience the very next day, and it lifted my spirits all over again.

One additional facet of TechnoServe's initiative in Swaziland had been a business plan competition called "Believe, Begin, Become" (BBB). The purpose of the competition was to promote entrepreneurship and specifically to promote the start up of small and medium enterprises. In addition to the recognition and prize aspects of the competition, there were also educational and mentoring components. Throughout the competition, the number of contestants got narrowed down as they passed more hurdles and got more training and coaching on developing their business plans. Ultimately, six winners would actually receive cash prizes that could be used to finance the start up of their businesses. Managing all of the BBB activities created a huge load on the office, so everyone pitched in to help. In addition to helping with the many administrative activities, I judged some of the business plans, and Wendy and I both conducted classes as part of the training.

Shortly after Wendy and I returned from our trip to the Junior Achievement meeting and the TechnoServe office in Nairobi, all of TechnoServe Swaziland gathered for the graduation ceremony of the top sixty candidates from the competition. This was held at the most unusual graduation venue we've ever attended: a disco club called the House on Fire. "Building" is a loose term for this series of tin roofs and caverns, nooks, crannies, sculptures, and balconies. Various parts were made of wood, rocks, glass, concrete, mosaic, or a combination with fire pits in each "room." But somehow, House on Fire proved to be a fitting location to celebrate sixty budding entrepreneurs' completion of five intense weeks of workshops. All of the sixty semi-finalists had met the most rigorous business challenge: creating a bankable business plan that could be funded either by TechnoServe's prize money or by a local lender. Unfortunately, the graduation of the semi-finalists was quickly followed by the announcement of the twenty finalists, so many people were left disappointed. Although only twenty competitors could go on, all of the men and women had demonstrated admirable perseverance.

Despite our limited involvement in BBB, it led to wonderful experiences for both Wendy and me. For Wendy, the experience occurred after she taught the marketing class. A young man came up to her to ask for any special insight she had on starting a business. She replied that most U.S. entrepreneurs fail at least once in starting a business so to be prepared to be challenged, make mistakes, and perhaps fail. However, ultimately perseverance and belief in yourself would help as much as any classroom learning. He came up to her at the graduation and thanked her for that advice. Wendy hoped that she'd made a difference in at least that one young man's future.

My uplifting experience came at the Swazi Sun Hotel the day after the bank visit with Tusty Meals when a young man, Thembisa, came up to me and introduced himself. I didn't recognize him at first, but he knew I was from TechnoServe and said that we had met before at some of the Believe, Begin, Become activities. He had submitted a business plan for a mobile hair salon, basically going to customers' homes during typically nonbusiness hours to cut, color, etc., their hair. Thembisa had been a semifinalist, but his plan had not been selected to be one of the finalists. He was glad that TechnoServe was doing a follow-up event for the semifinalists who didn't make it into the finals. Moreover, he wanted to thank me and tell me how wonderful the Believe, Begin, Become program had been for him. Thembisa said that he had been thinking about starting his own business for quite a while. He had confidence in some aspects of his capability to start and run a business but not in others. He said that the TechnoServe program had given him knowledge in areas that he was lacking, and now he had the confidence to go ahead with his business plan. He was very grateful for TechnoServe and thanked God for sending us to Swaziland. I spent some more time with him discussing his concept and urging him to press forward because I knew he could succeed. At the end of our discussion, Thembisa thanked me again for TechnoServe. It was very inspiring, and I felt I had been rewarded more than I deserved.

Looking at the bigger picture, my biggest lesson learned in Swaziland was how much must go right for economic development to happen. Although most free-market economies with the right legal and macroeconomic environment do experience economic growth, it doesn't have to happen, and it especially doesn't have to happen fast. Many years ago during the depression, John Maynard Keynes showed that economies can stabilize in suboptimum conditions. When this happens, there has to be an outside intervention to change things and offer an opportunity for improvement and growth. That's what economic development work is all about, intervening to promote economic growth. However, there's never just one intervention that's necessary, and multiple factors must exist for an intervention to lead to sustainable progress. That's why it's so challenging and why it requires perseverance.

Of course, Wendy was extremely proud of her and Atiba's

successfully launching the pilot classes of JA Swaziland. On the other hand, she felt that her biggest lessons learned were threefold. Launching a youth entrepreneurship program, even supported by the structure of global organizations like Junior Achievement and TechnoServe, is incredibly difficult in a developing country where taking initiative and risks are not part of the culture. She also had reinforced for her the fact that no project is as straightforward as it might seem, particularly when dealing with partners (such as UNISWA and JA). Finally, it was important to not just accomplish something personally but to build the capacity of the people with whom she worked because that would hopefully last long after her personal involvement. Wendy most greatly enjoyed her mentoring: expanding Atiba's already strong skills and building the capacity of LULOTE staff who were unfamiliar with international organizations, entrepreneurship, and launching new programs. I had hoped that during my time in Swaziland, I would have enabled one or two companies to start on their path to sustainable success. Clearly I was naive and my objectives were totally unreasonable. I believe I made good contributions to the paths of several companies and helped to develop a number of colleagues, but the real results would depend on the work of those colleagues after I left. It wasn't what I'd hoped to accomplish, but with a more reasonable perspective, I felt good about what I'd been able to do. I understood economic development better now, especially from the perspective of being on the ground as well as the high-level overview. I'd learned that the economies of developing countries can't be transformed overnight, but we can accelerate their growth. And if we can increase the annual growth rate of developing economies by only a few percentage points, it will mean that millions of people spend many fewer years in extreme poverty. That's a realistic goal.

The Interregnum

$\mathcal{T}$he trip home wasn't permanent. Wendy and I were feeling that our time in Africa hadn't been long enough, and we hadn't contributed enough. Although we had worked hard, the length of our stay felt more like an extended vacation. We had arranged it this way on purpose because we didn't know how well we would survive living in Africa. Well, we had survived just fine. It had been an exciting adventure. We'd had many new and mind-expanding experiences. More importantly, we felt good about the work we had done. It hadn't been a hardship, and we felt as if we were contributing, so we wanted to do more. We weren't ready to commit our lives to working in Africa, but we were ready to invest an additional year.

I talked again with Simon, TechnoServe's vice president for Africa, and told him that we would be interested in staying on in Africa, but wanted to work in a different country if there were opportunities. He quickly responded that he had opportunities for both of us in Kenya. TechnoServe's country director in Kenya was about to leave and go back to the United States. The country director had two deputies. One of the deputies was being promoted to become the new country director for Kenya. The other deputy was being promoted to become the country director for Uganda, where TechnoServe was starting up a new program. The senior management ranks in these two important countries would be thin, and Simon thought we could help. My consulting experience in operations improvement could be applied to enable the new country directors to establish or improve strong administrations. Wendy was excited because she would not only again leverage her youth program experiences, but also apply her interests in women, entrepreneurship, and education as well as her marketing communications and fund-raising skills.

He answered so quickly that I was concerned. I didn't want to be taken lightly just because we had been volunteers, and more importantly, I wanted to make sure that our roles would be substantial. So I asked for a salary (or salaries). I didn't specify an amount, and I didn't care specifically how much it was. I just wanted it to represent a commitment from TechnoServe that they would value our efforts. Simon didn't hesitate. He said yes, in general, and that we would work out the specifics. In the end, it turned out that it would be easier, with my background and the role that I would fill, for me to get a business visa than for Wendy. So I got a salary, and Wendy remained a volcon with her per diem.

So in January we would be headed to Kenya.

I was in the United States for about a month, Wendy a little longer, but it was a whirlwind tour. We arrived at our home just in time to prepare for the holidays. Our house sitters had kindly gone on vacation for two weeks and left the house to us. We immediately cut a fresh Christmas tree and decorated the house for Christmas and Hanukkah in anticipation of the arrival of our kids, Adrian and Diana, along with Adrian's dog, Scooter.

The kids were around for eight days and the decorations up for ten. During that time, we attended multiple Christmas, Boxing Day, and New Year's parties, and then we left for the east coast. First we visited with my family in Washington DC, including my mother, two of my sisters, their families, and some cousins. Then we flew up to Boston to see Adrian, Wendy's aunt, uncle, cousins, and some friends from college days.

I flew back to California to prepare for my flight to Nairobi. Wendy stayed on a little longer. When I took off for Nairobi, the time in the United States was already a blur.

Kenya

First Impressions of Nairobi
And TechnoServe in Kenya

Flying into Kenya was very different from our arrival in Swaziland. Nairobi's Jomo Kenyatta Airport is a large international, if run-down, facility in a capital city of four million people. Like many international airports, it has an endless concourse filled with similar-looking shops selling similar-looking "duty-free" goods. There were long lines at immigration with a longer one at the visa desk. And after I picked up my luggage and exited the customs area, throngs of prearranged drivers with signs were trying to make themselves seen by their intended riders. These were competing for space with the horde of entrepreneurs who were opportunistically soliciting for passengers. This, of course, was occurring right below the sign that said, "Soliciting for Passengers Prohibited."

Despite experiencing this scene many times in my life, I am always slightly panicked that I will miss my driver or that he won't be there, and then what will I do? In Nairobi, I didn't know where I was going; I didn't have a cell phone to call someone, but that didn't matter since I didn't know who to call anyway. The driver just had to be there. On rare occasions in the past, the driver wasn't there, which could be very inconvenient or somewhat scary depending on the situation. (We were pretty nervous in 1994 when we flew into Hangzhou, China, and our guide wasn't at the airport. The fact that the woman in front of us at immigration had an altercation with the authorities and was arrested also didn't help our sense of comfort.) Arriving in a foreign country without easy access to communication and not knowing who to trust for help always worries me, but things usually work out the way they're supposed to; and when they haven't, I've still survived. Yet, that brief moment of worry always grabs me as I look for my name amongst the dozens of signs being held up. This time, I passed my driver three times before I saw my name. Seeing your own name in a strange place always provides a great sense of comfort.

Although there was more hassle in the arrival, the flight from the United States to Nairobi seemed much easier than to Swaziland. It was considerably shorter. The flight from Nairobi to Johannesburg would have been another four hours, and the flight onward to Swaziland would have been an additional hour plus the layover. However, the difference seemed to be even greater. Of course there was one less stop, and because of the timing of flights, the layovers were shorter. All of this resulted in one overnight during the journey rather than two. I felt much less exhausted. And it didn't hurt that I had gotten upgraded on two legs of the flight and had an exit row seat with lots of legroom on the third to accommodate my 6'3" frame.

The flight arrived in Kenya at 9:00 p.m., and so the driver took me straight to my initial apartment. I thought the late arrival might be inconvenient, but it turned out very well. Since the airport is southeast of the city center and we would be working and staying in the northwest, the trip between the two had to go directly through the city center. During rush hour, this can be a two-hour ordeal. For us, it was an easy forty-minute ride.

My apartment had been occupied by a TechnoServe volunteer consultant (volcon) who was leaving the next day. It turned out that he came home from a long night of celebrating at 4:30 a.m., took a shower, and left at 5:00 a.m. so I didn't get to have an extensive conversation with him. I'm not even sure what he looked like because I barely woke up when he came in.

The next morning, I went outside to survey my surroundings. The apartment complex appeared nice but modest. It could easily have been in a middle-class neighborhood in Los Angeles, except of course for the high wall topped by barbed wire and an electric fence with a large locked and guarded metal gate. It wasn't really like a war zone. During the daytime, it was perfectly fine to pass through the gate and walk around in the neighborhood outside the wall, but at night, it was strongly discouraged. There was a lot of crime in Nairobi, and some of it was violent. Even though we were in a "nice" neighborhood, there was no point in taking chances. Philosophically, I didn't like the implied elitism and isolation, but personal safety trumped philosophy. Practically, it was nice to know I was safe and could concentrate on other things.

Later in the day, I had a beer with Fred, the new TechnoServe country director to whom I would report. He was very warm and really wanted to welcome me. Fred was a big, outgoing man with an effusive personality that immediately engaged me. I really liked our first interaction and felt very comfortable that I would enjoy working with Fred. The next day, I had lunch with Fred, his family and Erastus, who was the newly appointed country director for TechnoServe's future office in Uganda. Erastus was also a very warm and engaging person. He was not as big as Fred or as effusive, and he was more intense. They were both obviously very intelligent and committed to what they were doing, so it was easy to see why they were selected to be country directors. I was looking forward to working with both of them.

During my first few days in Nairobi, I began to develop impressions and an overall sense of the city. My primary frame of reference was Mbabane, Swaziland. Although Nairobi was a very large city and Mbabane a very small one, they had more in common than either did with any U.S. city. Primarily, they were both in developing countries in Africa with all of the implications. But they also had tremendous differences, which were often the same as differences between large and small cities throughout the world. Mbabane was a small pleasant city that felt very comfortable and safe like many small U.S. cities. Lots of people knew each other, and many were related or close friends. At the one supermarket in Mbabane, it was typical to meet someone you knew. Houses and apartment complexes in Mbabane had some security features, but they didn't have eight-foot-high walls topped with electrified barbed wire and twenty-four-hour guards. On the other hand, Mbabane had only a few really nice restaurants, no movie theaters, and you could walk through every street in the central city in less than an hour.

Nairobi was totally different. Nairobi was analogous to New York City. There were many nice restaurants, multiple shopping centers, movie theaters, and nightclubs; and Nairobi had an edge. Like New York, it heightened one's senses. It made my adrenaline flow. Both for self-preservation and for enjoyment, I was more alert. There was more to take in and more to worry about. There were more cars and more people, which moved faster, except in rush hour when traffic came to a standstill for miles. Although people didn't walk as aggressively as in New York, there was a very different feel from Mbabane. Hawkers were also much more pervasive, not too aggressive, but selling everything. I was familiar with hawkers walking through rush-hour traffic selling flowers and crafts, but I was surprised to see them in Nairobi selling puppies, television antennas, coat racks, pillows, and pruning shears.

Traffic and driving were also very different from Mbabane. Nairobi driving habits were not as bad as Kathmandu or Bangalore, but they were worse than any place in the United

States. The matatus (mah-tah-toos) were especially aggressive. Matatus are the small independent vans that substitute for buses and in other countries are called combis or micros. The drivers of these vans seemed to be frustrated race car drivers who felt that a moment's delay would seriously decrease their income. They were really independent cowboys, and everyone complained about their driving style. While driving in Swaziland wasn't too unpleasant (after learning to drive on the left), I decided to avoid driving in Nairobi. I knew I could manage Nairobi driving, but I didn't want to. The combination of the very heavy traffic and aggressive driving would have made it quite stressful and the office and shopping were only short rides or walks from our apartment.

Another factor that influenced my decision was that riding in a taxi with a local driver seemed more secure than driving our own car. Part of Nairobi's edginess was the backdrop of crime. Most expats didn't personally experience this on a regular basis, but crime was always in the background. Carjackings happened. Shortly after I arrived, two women were shot dead by carjackers because they didn't vacate their United Nations SUV quickly enough. I felt safer being in the backseat of a beat-up taxi with a local driver than being a big white guy driving a nice, new rental SUV.

The next week, the news reported another carjacking just outside Nairobi in which the occupants were murdered because apparently they resisted. I also heard that two other UN vehicles had been carjacked recently, but they didn't make the news because no one was killed. It made me nervous about our decision to come to Nairobi, and I did consider whether I should tell Wendy not to get on the plane. However, after carefully processing my concerns, I was mostly able to put them into the background. Except, they definitely reinforced my plan not to drive in Kenya.

Helping me to process the violence were Kenyan friends

who told me that these fatal carjackings were very unusual, and they suspected Somali refugees. Kenya had definitely been experiencing a recent upsurge in violence, which many people attributed to the fighting in Somalia. Many Somali refugees were fleeing to Kenya, and sometimes they brought along their military weapons. Because I had registered on the U.S. embassy website and included Wendy's information, we both received e-mails with the embassy's travel warning referring to the violence. I had read earlier embassy warnings and this new one wasn't much different, so I was disturbed, but not too much. Since Wendy hadn't seen these warnings before, she was seriously taken aback and initially very nervous. However, I was able to reassure her. I thought with a few precautions, it would be easy to minimize, but not totally eliminate, our exposure to violence. Everyone knew to take taxis wherever they went, especially at night. The area where we were living and working was quite safe to walk around during the day but, once again, not at night. Based on empirical evidence, I had already developed what I believed to be important safety rules: Rule # 1: Don't drive around anywhere in a large new SUV. Rule # 2: Don't drive alone in isolated areas in any kind of car. Rule # 3: If held up or carjacked, don't resist or scream; do whatever the criminals request.

While getting accustomed to my new living conditions in Kenya, I was also developing an understanding of the Kenya TechnoServe operations. Before arriving, I had begun to form a conflicted view of the state of TechnoServe's Kenya office from the bits and pieces of information that I had received and my earlier visit. In one sense, Kenya was a star because it had secured large amounts of funding in the past few years and had tripled in size. It also had very successful projects producing clearly demonstrable benefits for many smallholder farmers. On the other hand, I was getting the impression that the rapid growth was not necessarily under control.

After the first week, I had seen things that supported both points of view, but I didn't have enough information to form a complete and detailed picture. However, I did think that there was an opportunity to improve the overall management of the Kenya office and to establish good management practices in Uganda. And that's basically what I was there to do. Because of the huge growth and the new country directors, TechnoServe's regional VP thought that the Kenya (and Uganda) office could use some support from someone like me with years of business management experience, especially in consulting, providing advice to senior executives in high-growth companies. It seemed like a perfect fit and an opportunity for me to make a significant contribution. My role was going to be very different from the direct client work I had done in Swaziland, but I was looking forward to it. I had put together my objectives, based on my job description from the regional VP, but I needed to sit down with Fred and Erastus to make sure that my ideas aligned with theirs.

After two weeks of work, I had a better understanding of TechnoServe's operations in Kenya. I'd even started to contribute. The TechnoServe programs in Kenya were mostly doing the right things and helping people the way they were supposed to but without a consistent approach for assuring they were under control. Success relied heavily on the experience and skills of each individual program manager. Like a lot of rapidly growing companies that I'd worked with in Silicon Valley, TechnoServe had grown beyond the informal management systems and processes that worked when the staff was smaller and the projects less complex. Fred, as the new country director, readily admitted the need for more management rigor and had already taken steps to improve the situation. He knew that getting things more thoroughly under control would only enhance his ability to manage and expand the Kenya program. It was good to know he supported this direction and welcomed my help because not all personalities would have. For example, as Fred and I were reviewing the annual budget with our controller, I asked a number of specific questions, which brought up a number of issues regarding our financial situation and management practices. Fred insisted on the spot that we have an offsite session with all of our professional staff to talk about operational management including a big component on financial management, which I would develop and present.

We held the offsite meeting within a week. Fred reviewed our overall budget for Kenya and the funding pattern of our programs. He highlighted the ones that would run out during the year and the need to replenish donor funding to allow the affected teams to continue their work. I gave a presentation on program management with a heavy financial component and explained that Fred and I would be initiating more formal program management procedures with detailed monthly reviews. No one complained because everyone seemed to believe that more of this discipline and structure were needed. Donors, particularly those with a background in the private sector, were becoming increasingly attracted to the TechnoServe approach for development that emphasizes private sector business. However, these donors also demanded very rigorous management of projects and monitoring of results. As these donors contributed more and demanded more, we needed to demonstrate that we could reliably and consistently deliver the results they wanted.

As I learned more about the details of our projects in Kenya, I learned that they were typical of the type of work that TechnoServe was doing in many developing countries. TechnoServe's tagline is "Business Solutions to Poverty," and it is essentially a training and consulting organization. Since 80 percent of the world's poor are smallholder farmers, TechnoServe primarily worked to improve agricultural value chains consisting of smallholder farmers, their suppliers and the buyers of their produce to raise incomes for all of them. This was accomplished by better connecting the various stages of the value chain and improving performance within each stage to produce a self-sustaining market system. In many ways, TechnoServe's work was analogous to the consulting I had done for many high-technology companies, except we were talking about bananas, milk, cashews, pigs, and coffee instead of computers, semiconductors, and software.

For example, most smallholder farmers are not well connected to markets where their crops can ultimately be sold to consumers. Poor infrastructure, lack of transportation, and wide dispersion often prevent smallholder farmers from selling produce in any market. If a smallholder farmer can sell his produce, beyond what he needs for subsistence, the process typically involves inefficient middlemen (often multiple layers) between the farmer and the consumer. Each of these middlemen wants to make a profit, and so the farmer ends up with a very low price for his produce. Individually, smallholder farmers do not have the resources to do anything about this situation. From the other end of the value chain, it is much too difficult for supermarkets to interact directly with individual small farmers whose output is tiny, often unreliable, and possibly of low quality. In electrical engineering systems, this is known as an impedance mismatch. The solution to the problem in both electronics and economics is to design and implement an interface that doesn't result in large losses, like those created by the middlemen.

TechnoServe has a comprehensive approach for dealing with this very common situation. First, smallholder farmers are organized into producer groups. These groups have different names and different legal structures, but all have a number of attributes in common. They all allow small farmers to mass their produce and have more direct purchasing arrangements with large buyers, such as food processors or supermarkets. This allows the farmer to have a consistent market and receive a better price for his produce since numerous middlemen margins are eliminated. The farmer group also facilitates interaction with providers of goods and services that will enhance the individual farmer's productivity. In a simple example, TechnoServe encourages these groups to procure fertilizer and high-yielding seeds in bulk to make them more affordable to each farmer. Also, these groups can contract in quantity for services such as veterinary visits and artificial insemination for dairy cows. Beyond organizing farmers and agricultural value chains, TechnoServe frequently provides training in basic business concepts, agronomy, and the management of cooperatives.

While simple in concept, the changes promoted by TechnoServe are always challenging to implement. People all over the world, in every environment and at every intelligence and economic level resist change. However, if these types of changes are implemented, they can often double a farmer's income. This can mean moving a farmer from the category of seriously poor (earning $1 per day or less) to working poor (earning $2 per day or more). It can mean that a farmer can pay his children's school fees, give them decent clothing, and provide for health care. In sum, it can make a huge difference.

Moreover, as a farmer begins to generate a surplus of crops beyond the minimum for subsistence, he can begin thinking about investing that surplus in better tools, equipment, or additional crops that can further improve his economic situation. And the best part of this whole story is that once the markets and the fully functioning value chain are established, they are self-sustaining. They operate on standard free-market principles and can maintain themselves without TechnoServe's involvement. They continue to be subject to the same threats that challenge any business in a free economy, but they don't need charity, and that's what really appeals to me. The economy of the region receives a permanent upgrade, so it can continue to develop from a higher level.

My first field visit in Kenya was to a project that clearly demonstrated the TechnoServe approach in working with banana farmers. TechnoServe and Africa Harvest had been funded by the Rockefeller Foundation to promote banana growing by small farmers north of Nairobi. Africa Harvest is known for its development and promotion of improved banana plants, so it was chosen to help the farmers access, plant, and nurture these plants. TechnoServe's expertise is in business and value chains, so our focus was on organizing the farmers, training them, and connecting them to reliable markets for their produce.

Although many people believe that successful capitalism just happens, without a push, it can take a very long time. In developing countries, markets are often not efficient or non-existent, so it's very easy for value chains to stabilize in sub-optimum conditions and not improve. For example, before the Africa Harvest/TechnoServe intervention in Kenya's banana industry, the value chain operated as follows:

Poor farmers grew bananas primarily as one of their subsistence crops. Sometimes they would produce more than they could consume so would attempt to sell the excess. With no local market for the bananas and no means of transporting them to a major city, smallholders had to rely on random purchases from ad hoc traders. These traders would periodically visit banana farms in a particular area and ask farmers if they had any bananas to sell. If the farmers had bananas to sell, they were at the trader's mercy in terms of the selling price. If the trader did not buy, then the bananas would not be sold and would ultimately rot. When the farmer had bananas for sale, the trader would eyeball them for quality and weight and would offer the farmer a price. Usually, the farmer accepted.

Although it sounds as if the traders had the upper hand

on the farmers, the system was bad for everyone. The traders could find themselves driving through a rural area with very bad roads, expending their time and fuel money, and finding no bananas for sale. They could also find that the available bananas were only of poor quality and not readily saleable in the urban markets at a good price. All transactions were opportunistic. Supply, price, demand, and frequency of transactions were all random. And the most important fact to note about this situation was that none of the small participants involved could change it! Economists call this a market failure. No one had the resources to rationalize and improve the value chain. Without outside intervention, this value chain could have continued in its inefficient state indefinitely. Free markets are great, but sometimes they fail.

TechnoServe's first step in changing this situation was overcoming a psychological hurdle. In this region, most everyone grew bananas because they were easy to grow and a good source of nutrition for their families. Since everyone grew bananas, many farmers could not understand how bananas could be grown as a reliable and worthwhile cash crop. They didn't think about the four million inhabitants of Nairobi only fifty miles away who had no farmland. And if they had thought about those potential buyers, it would have seemed a dream that they could connect with them. As individual farmers became convinced of the opportunity, they were encouraged to purchase the new varieties of banana plants, to plant them carefully, in sufficient quantity, and to nurture them with appropriate water, fertilizer, and pruning. By following good direction, the farmers were able to produce excellent quality bananas in consistent volumes. However, better bananas in larger quantities were not sufficient. Many past economic development initiatives had taught farmers how to produce more and better crops but had not connected them to markets to sell their newfound abundance. Without connection to a market, a farmer just ends up throwing away more produce. This project was different. It attacked the overall value chain problem from both ends.

While farmers were being taught to grow more and better bananas, TechnoServe was also developing the demand side of the value chain. Banana wholesalers from Nairobi were recruited to visit the banana farming area with the promise of consistent availability of large volumes of high-quality bananas. This was attractive to the wholesalers because it allowed them to reduce their costs for finding high-quality bananas. The consistent availability also made the wholesalers into reliable suppliers to their retail customers. As the two ends of the value chain came together, the farmers and the wholesalers agreed on specific market days to meet and conduct their transactions. They also agreed to price bananas by weight and grade (quality level). Certain individuals within the farming community were trained to become official banana graders. After the new system began operating successfully, a physical market building and surrounding fenced yard were constructed for the collection, overnight storage, weighing and grading of the bananas on market days. The whole system, although seemingly incredibly simple, had become a tremendous success.

The wonderful thing was that these were real markets, just like those in the economics textbooks. Supply and demand were matched up reliably on a consistent basis, and this is the most important aspect for farmers who are trying to climb out of poverty. Although everyone involved anticipated that the most important result coming from this project would be that farmers were getting better prices for the bananas, it hadn't been the case. The most important result for farmers had been the certainty and regularity of income. Farmers now knew that if they produced good bananas, they could sell them. That allowed families to plan their finances rather than being constantly uncertain as to whether they could afford to purchase clothing or pay school fees for the children. Many of the farmers had doubled their income. Needless to say, I was very excited with the project and what it had been able to accomplish.

As part of the banana trip, we got to see the actual market taking place with bananas being graded and weighed. We also visited several banana farms to see their growing techniques including, in some cases, new irrigation systems. The irrigation systems had been purchased with the farmers' increased incomes enabling them to produce more bananas in the dry season when selling prices are the highest.

As an aside, as we drove around the area, I noticed a large compound with a very nice house at the center. I inquired as to who owned this impressive homestead and was told that it was the local MP (member of parliament). I asked, somewhat tongue-in-cheek, if this person had been wealthy before becoming an MP. Everyone in the car laughed loudly and said of course not.

A few days after the banana trip, Wendy arrived in Kenya and learned what her work for the next year would entail. While about 80 percent of TechnoServe Kenya's project work related to agricultural value chains, such as the banana project, the remaining 20 percent was focused on more general entrepreneurship and consisted of three specific initiatives: Young Women in Enterprise, a national Believe, Begin, Become (BBB) business plan competition, and a small business growth program called "Upscaling." Wendy would spend her time in Nairobi working on all three. The projects were a good fit with her interests and leveraged her experience in business plus the lessons learned in Swaziland

The banana trip had meant a two-hour drive each way on relatively bad roads. The week after Wendy arrived, she and I went with the TechnoServe Upscaling team for a three-hour drive each way over worse roads. Wendy was starting to help this team in supporting very small businesses to identify and overcome the barriers that prevented them from growing and creating more jobs. Our first visit was to a small honey process-ing company. It was owned by Mr. and Mrs. Ndambuki but had really been started by the wife. The husband was a pharmacist, and the couple had owned and operated a pharmacy in a small town for many years. They were not rich, but seemed to have a good and stable income, which put them in a better position than most. The honey business was a recent start-up. The honey business had begun serendipitously when an old acquaintance of the wife had come to town in desperate financial condition. Before moving to town, the wife had come from a not too distant rural area. This rural area was quite poor, and the local farmers were always at the mercy of the weather, which that year had not been good for the crops. Many of the farmers were strug-gling to feed their families. Fortunately, some of the farmers kept bees, which produced saleable honey. Although this honey had usually been consumed by the families, her friend had come to town to sell what he could to buy staples. The wife bought the honey, primarily out of charity, and the desire to preserve her friend's dignity. She then had to figure out what she would do with it. Since it was too much to personally consume, she decided to process it and sell it in the pharmacy. It worked and she decided to help more of the struggling farmers by purchas-ing more honey. She processed and sold their honey, and her husband even developed a cough syrup and other pharmaceuti-cal products that incorporated honey.

Mr. and Mrs. Ndambuki now had an additional small business with only one full-time employee, but both were enthu-siastic about it because it had been able to help a number of poor farmers. The business had been able to generate enough profits to provide the small amount of cash required for simple equipment and working capital. While it hadn't contributed to the couple's disposable income, it hadn't been a cash drain. They wanted to expand, and that's how TechnoServe was helping them. The TechnoServe business advisors had helped them to formally register their company and to develop accurate financial statements. Both of these were always prerequisites for obtaining any kind of financing, which the company expected to need soon for growth. The honey business also needed a strategy if they really wanted to grow. Although they had created a brand and packaging for their honey, like many small businesses we saw, their products were mostly undifferentiated.

Many of TechnoServe's clients sell mostly undifferentiated raw agricultural produce, which is fine if there is a sufficient market and you're willing to accept the prices that the market offers. However, trying to sell processed, packaged goods is more challenging. To sell these goods, ultimately a consumer will have to choose your product from a retail shelf, where it usually sits competing for attention with other similar products. How do you get the consumer to choose your product or even get the retailer to put your product on his shelf? It is very difficult to break into supermarkets with this type of product when they already have multiple competing brands on the shelf. Selling honey wasn't as bad as trying to set up a bottled water company, but it was still a big challenge.

We advised the honey company not to aggressively pursue supermarkets in Nairobi unless they could really differentiate their honey. Alternatively, we suggested a more regional marketing strategy and perhaps pursuing second-tier stores and informal markets in Nairobi where the potential volumes might be lower and the logistics more cumbersome, but the competition would be less fierce. We also suggested emphasizing the honey-containing, proprietary products that they had developed. We felt these could be differentiated and would face less direct competition. The proprietors thanked us for our advice and, as we left, gave us a bag of mangoes from one of their trees. We also got a sample of the honey-based cough syrup.

As we discussed this business in the car, we concluded that there are a lot of similar small businesses with undifferentiated products. They can typically succeed in a small market with a lot of hard work and personal touch from the owners. Good customer service in a small area combined with personal relationships and supported by hard work allows them to provide enough profits for a decent income. However as those who work in marketing and sales know, to expand beyond this size, these businesses cannot rely solely on the charisma and energy of the owners. At this point they need to have some other distinguishing characteristic and/or unique position in their market if they are to grow. This to me is always the largest challenge to business growth (in any country in the world). I hoped the honey business would succeed and grow, but unless they developed their proprietary products, I saw them quickly hitting a ceiling.

Our visit the next day was to a slightly larger firm with better short-term prospects. The company produced and bottled yogurt for sale to retailers. The company had been started by a young accountant who had waited for it to grow before leaving his accounting job to work full time making and selling yogurt. The company provided twelve jobs. It also benefited small, local farmers by purchasing eight hundred liters per day of their milk output. This milk was pasteurized in a large cauldron in a small shed outside a house that had been the accountant's home. He had originally set up the business in his home, but when the business grew too large, he and his family moved nearby and let the business take over the whole house.

The yogurt production process was pretty simple and very manual. After the milk had been boiled, it was poured into large containers and the yogurt culture was added, which turned the milk into yogurt. Some of the yogurt had strawberry or vanilla flavoring added before bottling for sale. The bottling process was not what you would see in a large beverage company. Two liter pitchers were filled from the large yogurt containers. The contents of the pitchers were then carefully poured into 300 ml and 500 ml plastic bottles, which would be sold at retail. The bottles received heat seals, which were carefully placed by hand and then affixed with the heat from a common laundry iron. The next step was manually attaching the labels and adding the plastic screw cap. The completed bottles were then grouped into dozens and covered with heat-shrinkable plastic. The plastic was shrunk to fit with an industrial strength heat gun. The employee performing this operation said that the business originally used inexpensive handheld hair dryers, but they wore out too quickly.

The owner said that he had more demand for his yogurt than he could supply, so planned to double his capacity. TechnoServe was helping him to get the necessary financing. I asked about product differentiation. He said that people just liked his yogurt. He thought it might be a little thicker than the large commercial brands. One of his larger competitors was beginning to worry about the competition from our entrepreneur's increasing sales and thought that his success was due to his salespeople. The competitor hired away all the salespeople at much higher salaries, but it only caused a short-term problem for our entrepreneur, and he kept on growing. He was selling locally as well as to many small shops in Nairobi. It sounded as if the short-term prospects were very good for him. Of course, he couldn't afford to compete head on with the large dairy products company, but he could potentially grow to a company with fifty employees while purchasing milk from hundreds of small farmers. This was already a success story, and it was growing. It was another heartwarming experience where an entrepreneur's pursuit of profit was creating opportunity and economic growth, and it helped to reassure us that this was a proven path to helping the poor.

A few weeks later, Fred showed us another success story based on another of TechnoServe's proven approaches to helping the poor. Fred had been really busy and felt the need to take a weekend break out of town with his family at the Outspan hotel in Nyeri. Fortunately, he invited us to go along and made special plans for us. First of all, he took a circuitous route to Nyeri to show us the variety of Kenya's terrain north of Nairobi. In this area, the Rift Valley meets the watershed of Mount Kenya and evolves into the plains of northern Kenya. As we drove, the landscape varied dramatically depending on the direction of the view.

Fred also wanted to show us the Nyala dairy, a very successful TechnoServe project that he had initiated many years ago. The "dairy" was actually a collection point for the milk from over five thousand smallholder farmers, each of who had typically less than four cows. The farmers delivered their milk by whatever means they could, such as by bicycle or donkey, to Nyala, where it was weighed and tested for quality before being put into the large cooling tank. Once a day, a large tank truck from a commercial milk producer would pick up the milk from the tank. In this way the farmers were assured of a reliable buyer for their output. Based on their record of milk deliveries, farmers could also access credit to purchase supplies such as feed and veterinary medicines. Dairy programs, such as Nyala, had become a model for increasing farmers' incomes. Dairy farming is particularly attractive in this respect because, in contrast to seasonal crops, it produces output every day.

It was during the trip with Fred and family, while observing many small towns and varying terrain, that I finalized my concept of the Walleigh Bare Dirt Index of Development, for which I expect to be immortalized in the economic development community. My proposition is that the amount of exposed bare dirt in a community is inversely proportional to its level of economic development. Poor communities have a lot of exposed bare dirt, e.g., parking areas in front of stores, side streets, and even main roads. At the other extreme, the most developed communities, e.g., cities in the United States, have no exposed bare dirt. Every square foot of ground is covered by concrete, asphalt, or deliberately planted grass or shrubbery. There is no bare dirt to be muddy when it rains or dusty when it's dry. Because poor communities have no money to spend on paving roads and parking lots or planting landscaping, as foot or vehicle traffic increases, the natural vegetation is worn down and bare dirt is produced. As a community improves its economic condition, limited funds begin to go into paving and landscaping, but a lot of bare dirt persists. The amount of bare dirt ends up being proportional to the level of poverty and inversely proportional to the level of development. QED. I'm just waiting for the recognition.

Although Wendy worked on all three Kenya entrepreneurship programs, she spent the majority of her time on Young Women in Enterprise (YWE) sponsored by Nike. This innovative program encouraged young women to become entrepreneurs. It provided training in both urban and rural settings around Nairobi, and participants included both high school students and school leavers (meaning dropouts) some of whom were already mothers. Since the Kenyan economy didn't generate enough jobs to employ all of the people leaving school each year (either through graduation or dropping out), self-employment was seen as a very viable alternative for achieving an income. The YWE program taught young women interpersonal and life skills as well as about business and concluded with each of them developing a short plan for a business that they would actually like to start. These plans were judged, and some of the most promising were awarded small cash prizes, which could be used to help start the business. The girls in all of the sites had completed their assignments and so TechnoServe teams had been going around to the sites to judge the business plan submissions and award prizes to the best.

As part of her YWE role, Wendy had participated in several of these events around Nairobi, but we had both been asked to participate in an all-day session of judging and awards at our most distant rural site. It was about two hours away over mostly poor roads, some under repair with long diversions over stretches of dirt and gravel. Since it was far away, we had been told to be ready to leave the office by 7:00 a.m., so Wendy and I arrived at 6:45. This being Africa, someone didn't get the word about the 7:00 a.m. departure, so we waited for her and left at 8:30. We already knew it was going to be a late day, but this would obviously make it later.

After the uncomfortable, but not terrible drive, we arrived at the rural school where we were to have the judging and the awards. The school buildings had local stone walls and mostly dirt floors. The small assembly hall had a concrete floor. All of the windows were just openings in the walls that could be closed with steel shutters. There were no lights in the classrooms. The outhouses were behind the school buildings. The exterior features of the outhouses were unremarkable and the interiors were Spartan, a concrete floor with a rectangular opening.

The TechnoServe team set up our operation as quickly as possible, but we were obviously way behind schedule. There were forty-two girls that we would interview. We had planned to have four panels of judges, but we only had enough of us for three. That meant each panel would have to interview additional girls and that would put us even further behind. We plowed ahead.

The process was that each girl would come into one of the judging rooms, briefly describe her business, and then the panel would ask questions. Evaluating the young woman's answers and her written plan, the judges would award points based on standard criteria. I had no idea what to expect. Our first contestant had me very worried. She came in, said a few quiet greetings, and sat down. The head judge greeted her and tried to make her feel comfortable, explaining that she could answer in

Swahili or English, whichever was easier. Then someone asked her to briefly describe her planned business. She just sat there. After a long pause, the judge tried to coax her a bit, offering a question with a simpler answer. The girl finally uttered a few words. It continued in this way for the next twenty minutes. I'm sure it was painful for her. It was definitely painful for the judges. We hoped that all the interviews wouldn't be that difficult.

The next girl came in, vivacious and confident. She explained her business and why it was going to succeed. She told us how, if she couldn't raise all the money she needed, she would start the business in a different way with just a small amount and bootstrap it to a larger size. She had already started an informal business doing essentially the same thing. The contrast between the two girls was amazing. Throughout the rest of our interviewees, the diversity was wide. One or two others were very confident and knowledgeable, but there were girls who couldn't answer the simplest question about a business plan that they had ostensibly written. We suspected a number had been written by their counselors or older siblings.

At the end of the judging, which finished over two hours late, the panels got together and selected the overall winners. We wolfed down some very late lunch and then presented the awards. Parents and relatives of all of the girls had come out to the awards ceremony as had local government officials and politicians. In addition to the prizes for the best plans, each girl got a graduation certificate. Both the parents and the girls were excited. Many of the attendees couldn't fit in the small assembly hall, but the open doors and windows allowed us to easily observe from outside. As the awards were given, the audience clapped joyfully, especially the parents of the girls who won prizes. At the end of the awards, one of the students gave a brief, impromptu speech thanking everyone for the training and the associated opportunity. Then, one of the fathers stood up and asked to speak. He was an older man; he looked as though he could have been a grandfather, but his daughter had won one of the awards. He mentioned that he had started his own business many years ago and that it had allowed him to provide for his children and send them to school. He was thankful for his own success, and he wanted to thank everyone for the opportunity that was being given to his daughter and all of the other young women. Although he spoke in Swahili, and I didn't get the translation until later, you could tell that it was a very moving speech by the standing ovation at the end. After his speech, the ceremony was closed with a prayer, and we were ready to pack up and drive the two hours back to Nairobi. It had been a long but rewarding day.

Over the following two weeks, the scene was repeated in a number of communities around Nairobi including several major slums where most of the girls were school dropouts and many of the teenagers had their own children. After participating in many of these sessions, Wendy had an interesting observation. While the quality of plans and the determination of the girls varied in each location, all of the best plans and the highest levels of determination came from school dropouts in very poor areas. I guess it was these girls who understood the economic facts of life and knew that this was a great opportunity for them to change their own situation.

I hoped that once the excitement died down that many of these young women would be able to build on what they had learned and actually start a business. These businesses wouldn't be the next Google or Apple, but they could provide a few dollars a day to help feed a family. We had already seen anecdotal examples of success with new businesses, and clearly all of the young women had gained confidence in their abilities that would serve them well as employees or entrepreneurs.

The U.S. Embassy and Other Concerns

In life, if one wants to worry, there are always things to worry
about. In familiar situations, we learn over time which risks
create real and present danger and which ones can be safely
ignored. In new and unfamiliar situations, we don't have these
rules of thumb, and everything seems scarier. It wasn't clear
to us as to whether the apparent upsurge in violence in Kenya
was really something that we should worry about, but apparently, the U.S. embassy wanted to do something to respond to
concerns raised by the extensive publicity surrounding it. They
called a "town meeting" and invited all of the U.S. citizens
living locally to come to the embassy. I didn't think that I was
going to get any new or useful information, so I decided not to
attend, but their initial invitation and the follow-up message
were additional reminders of the somewhat threatening environment.

I had basically forgotten about the meeting until the embassy's follow-up e-mail arrived. At the meeting, a U.S. citizen
had brought up an issue about the location of the embassy's
parking for U.S. citizens going to the embassy for various
services. Evidently, the parking lot was a significant distance
from the embassy and not particularly secure. The citizen was

concerned, and probably asked if anything could be done about this situation. Well, the e-mail response from the embassy indicated that because of safety and *liability concerns* (my italics), there would no longer be parking available for U.S. citizens going to the embassy for services. They really took care of that problem!

While I had basically gotten over worrying about increased violence from Somali migrants, at this time Kenya presented other opportunities for worrying such as Rift Valley fever, which had broken out in the north. Rift Valley fever is a hemorrhagic fever disease, sort of like a mild form of Ebola (the horrific disease which kills 90 percent of its victims within a few days). Fortunately, Rift Valley fever mostly attacks animals like cows, goats, sheep, and pigs. However, the disease can pass to humans, and more than a hundred people had died. Not everyone who contracts the disease endures a serious case. However, those that do bleed from all body orifices and die within a few days. During the outbreak, the consumption of most meat plummeted and the demand for chicken and fish skyrocketed. Most cases of human infection actually come from contact with live animals, but people were still worried that they could get it from contaminated meat. If you bought meat from a reputable butcher, there was nothing to worry about. My general approach to life is to be optimistic and avoid unnecessary worrying. I didn't change my eating habits, and I didn't even get a bloody nose.

On the other hand, we did worry about malaria, and I was reminded why when I went to the office to ask a colleague, Carl, about the project he was working on. He seemed a little out of it, and when I asked about it, he said he wasn't feeling well. I asked what was wrong, and he said he had gotten malaria, but he'd caught it quickly and was on good medication. He wasn't concerned.

Nairobi, because of its altitude, is a relatively low-risk area for malaria, and so most people don't take preventative medication. However, Carl had been to Tanzania and hadn't bothered to take precautions. Every tourist is seriously warned to take prophylactic medication, but most people who live in Africa don't. The medications do have side effects, both short- and long-term, and many people don't want to take them for years on end. Maybe it's a good gamble if you live in Africa, but for us, there was no question. Wendy and I religiously took the meds. And besides, those other people were missing out on some great dreams. Yes, that's one of the side effects.

When you're a tourist in a malarial area, there are two primary types of preventative medication to choose from, malarone and mefloquine. For short vacations, malarone is generally considered the drug of choice. It is probably somewhat more effective, and it has the fewest side effects. However, it has to be taken every day, and when we went to Africa, it was very expensive if you took it for a long period of time. Mefloquine, on the other hand, was also effective, needed to be taken only once per week, and was much less expensive. However, the potential side effects of mefloquine can be quite interesting. One is hallucinations.

Wendy and I didn't have any daytime hallucinations, but the Tuesday night dreams were exciting. Monday was the day we took our pills for the week, but for some reason, the resulting dreams were most intense on Tuesday nights. Wendy periodically had scary nightmares and talked loudly in her sleep, but my dreams were just weird. I had the usual late to class, didn't study for the exam, walking around naked dreams, but I also had some unique ones as well. One that I remember concerned not having a date for the senior prom. I was very upset that I hadn't asked anyone to the prom and was remembering all the girls I had dated in high school (not a long list) and wondering if I should ask each of them. As I was going through this process, I remembered that I was married and couldn't understand why I was worried about a date. But I still thought I should get a date. My mind tried to reconcile these thoughts, and then I woke up. It was really like going to a weekly festival of strange, short movies.

Although I was looking forward to getting off the medication and experiencing plain old boring sleep, we weren't going to risk that in Africa. When I was talking to another colleague, David, about Carl's malaria, he said, "Oh yeah, I had malaria and almost died." Several years earlier, he had felt feverish and achy, but he was traveling away from home and thought it was just a virus. He hesitated in going to the doctor. By the time he went, just the next day, the malaria had gone to his brain. The doctor immediately told him that he might not survive and put him into intensive care. David was totally conscious and called his wife and told her that he might be dying. He called his brother to discuss his own funeral and burial arrangements and also asked his brother for help in taking care of his wife after he was gone. Fortunately, the doctors pumped David full of medication for several days and he lived. He chuckled as he talked about it, but it was really a close call. Wendy and I paid close attention to the calendar and took our meds every Monday like clockwork.

Carl quickly recovered from the malaria, but he was still feeling bad. He found out he also had an amoebic infestation. Those critters take a week of nasty medicine to get rid of. No, we weren't in Kansas.

Continuing the unpleasant creatures theme, I had learned what to expect regarding animal encounters in our apartment. I had been surprised several times by geckos scampering up the wall to hide behind curtains or other cover. Fortunately, they seemed quite afraid of me and disappeared before Wendy saw them. In the unusual bug category, Wendy had called on me several times to kill some very large invaders (species unknown). They were about an inch wide, two inches long and appeared to be a cross between a beetle and a cockroach. They moved very fast, but ultimately made a large snapping sound as I crushed them under my size 14 work shoes. Overall, however, Nairobi's high altitude and dry climate contributed to minimizing insect (especially mosquito) encounters, for which Wendy was especially grateful since she tends to be a mosquito magnet. Whenever they're around, mosquitoes bite her and not me; I think because she is much tenderer.

While some of nature's threats, such as malaria, are predictable and can be defended against, for others we can be totally surprised and essentially helpless. One day, I was sitting at my desk, and I felt a strange movement coming up from the floor. It wasn't quite a shaking; it was more of a rocking. It was a feeling I had felt many times before in California, but I was in Nairobi, Kenya. Could this be an earthquake, here in Africa? Yes it was, and only the first of a number to come. Who knew they had earthquakes in Kenya? Looking at the geology, I guess it's not surprising. Nairobi is located near the Great Rift Valley and between the extinct volcanoes of Mount Kilimanjaro and Mount Kenya. All of these would be obvious clues to the most amateur geologist, but it hadn't occurred to me.

Wendy sat near to me in the office and reacted quicker when she felt the tremor. She instantly positioned herself in the doorway as we are trained in California (because doorways are more strongly reinforced and can protect you from falling debris in a moderate earthquake in the United States (for advice on what to do in a very serious earthquake, especially outside of the United States, search online for "The Triangle of Life"). Although she reacted quickly and followed the guidelines we had been taught, this would have been a problem in a serious earthquake. The doorway in which she positioned herself was capped by a large glass panel, which would have shattered into many sharp pieces and seriously sliced anyone standing below. Fortunately, the first quake only measured 4.4 on the Richter scale, so was only a little wake-up call.

The next quake hit on Sunday night, and it registered 5.4 on the Richter scale, which meant that it was about ten times as powerful. It hit while I was sitting on the toilet in our apartment. Talk about the ultimate in terms of helplessness. The only solution was to let it happen and hope. Compounding the impact was the fact that I was feeling a little tipsy from the few glasses of wine I'd had with dinner. Boy, was there ever a wrong night to overimbibe.

On Tuesday, a 6.1 quake hit near the end of the work day, and the panic started. It was the strongest quake yet, and the fourth in five days. People streamed out of office buildings and were reluctant to go back the next day. At first, running out of buildings seemed to be a foolish reaction, since that was not what we were taught in California, but later we learned that 90 percent of Nairobi buildings were not designed by professional architects or engineers. Maybe running out of those buildings wasn't a bad idea. I reminded myself that the rules are different in Africa.

As the tremors continued, so did the panic. There had been no destruction of buildings, but this had been the longest string of earthquakes ever felt in Nairobi. Fortunately, the city was 155 kilometers from the earthquake's epicenter in Tanzania, so the impact was lessened. Rumors circulated about a big tremor that was coming and some people slept outside their homes. As rumors of an impending large quake accelerated, including the quake's date and time, experts continued to deny that earthquake prediction was possible and the U.S. embassy was forced to issue an official press release saying that it had not predicted a large earthquake on Thursday at 2:00 p.m. Over time, the earthquakes subsided, as did the panic, and things went back to normal.

Getting beyond the concerns with disease, pestilence, earthquakes, and Somali invaders, traditional crime was still an issue. Within a month or two of my arrival in Nairobi, I had pretty much forgotten about the two fatal carjackings. My friends were probably right; these had been an aberration. However, the city still had a long-standing reputation for nonfatal crime and was nicknamed Nairobbery. There were even anecdotes about the old days when criminals would steal your car at gunpoint but then put you in the trunk and politely drop you off near your home before taking off with your car and your money. Anyone who recounted these stories always followed them up with a warning that modern criminals did not adhere to these old ways and were to be seriously feared. Just in case we were getting complacent, we received several messages that definitely put us on our guard.

The first message was from Peter, one of our coworkers, which he sent to everyone in the office. It said essentially, "Please send any e-mail messages to me in care of my personal e-mail account since my computer has been stolen, and I can't access my work e-mail." On his way home one night, Peter was accosted as he was about to drive into his yard. As with most homes outside the slums, his property was surrounded by a high fence with a locked gate. Although this generally provides protection, it can also provide an opportunity for thieves. People are vulnerable as they arrive home and exit their cars to unlock their gate, allowing thieves to easily attack, which is what happened to Peter. In some senses, Peter was lucky in that the thieves only took his cash, cell phone, and computer. They often take the car. And of course, the situation can be life-threatening as well. From our perspective, it appeared as if Peter mostly took it in stride and just set about fixing the problems. However, it had to be a harrowing experience. Several days later, he got good news; the thieves had been caught, and he was called to the police station to identify them. Although he got through it without serious physical harm, it must have left a mental scar. Several people at TechnoServe had experienced similar trauma. Erastus told me of an incident, several years earlier when he was confronted by a thief with a gun, and he was certain that he was going to die. In another incident, just months earlier, an expat couple who were our good friends had been forced to lie facedown in the dirt as armed thieves went through their pockets and purse.

The second message, which was e-mailed from the U.S. embassy, just reinforced the ideas.

Warden Message: Carjacking of USAID Employee

This Warden Message is being issued to alert American citizens to the ongoing danger of carjackings in Nairobi. On May 3, an American citizen was carjacked on Ridgeways Road, off of Kiambu Road, by three male teenagers, two of whom were armed with pistols. The victim was not injured in the incident.

Extreme caution is advised once you turn off of Kiambu Road, going towards the Windsor Hotel, as there are many blind turns and the ability to maneuver around potential threats is limited. Be aware of your surroundings when driving this or other similar routes, and be especially conscious of any person(s) acting in a suspicious manner, who might be acting as a lookout for potential hijackers ahead. Do not expect pedestrians or passers-by to lend assistance as witnesses are usually unwilling to get personally involved in this type of situation.

If criminals demand to go to your house, dissuade them by telling them you live in a large housing compound guarded by security guards and police.

It is advised that you carry credit cards or ATM cards only when you have a specific need for them. Be willing to give up your valuables immediately; they are not worth your life. It is imperative that you remain calm and let the carjackers know you will comply with their demands and give them all of your valuables. Keep talking to them, listen to their instructions, and comply immediately and fully.

As temporary residents, taking lots of precautions such as only taking taxis and not driving a fancy car along with being able to limit where we lived, worked, and shopped, I thought our chances were good that we wouldn't have this type of experience. But there were no assurances. I felt bad for the local residents who must know in the back of their mind that eventually their luck will run out, and they will be robbed or worse. However, the locals seemed to adapt. They were very attentive to potential danger, while at the same time seemed to take it in stride, as illustrated by an e-mail we got from Henry, another TechnoServe colleague:

On Wednesday, on my way to [a local town] on one of the dirt roads, a saloon vehicle overtook me at very high speed and made me suspicious. I slowed down to observe their movements, and after moving for less than 2 kms the vehicle slowed down and parked near some thickets. The guys did not look good to me, so I turned at high speed and drove like mad to the highway. There, I found another suspicious car, so I drove to the direction of Nairobi and used a different route from the main Nyeri Highway.

I cannot for sure say that these guys were carjackers, but my intuition told me so, and I acted. Better to be safe than sorry.

Let's be very alert particularly with [our TechnoServe Toyota Land Cruiser] Prados on off-road destinations, especially during this electioneering period when their demand has gone to an all-time high.

CHEERS,

Henry

Wendy's increased discomfort with personal safety was obvious as she resisted walking even a block or two in our neighborhood at night to the nearby mall and supermarket. On the other hand, I had pretty much rationalized that we were pretty safe and had put the messages from our colleagues and the U.S. embassy out of my mind. So I talked her into walking to the Phoenician Restaurant near our apartment.

Nairobi had many good, very diverse restaurants, a number of which were located very near to our apartment. What a difference from Swaziland. We had been to several wonderful Indian places, a Japanese sushi bar, an Italian restaurant, a multicultural café that served enchiladas and a Tex-Mex outlet at the food court, as well as the Phoenician, which is Lebanese.

For safety's sake, the general rule in Nairobi is to never walk anywhere at night—always take a taxi. We generally followed the rule. We also lived in a nice area where it was very safe to walk around during the day as the streets were busy with people. Even at night, the area was generally well-lit and occasionally people could be seen walking.

Since the Phoenician was less than four hundred meters from our apartment gate, it seemed ridiculous to take a taxi. We had previously walked at night to the Japanese restaurant that was only one hundred meters from our gate, but it was almost visible from our apartment, and we were always within yelling/running distance from the security guard at one location or the other. Of course, if attacked, you should neither run nor yell, but it still felt very safe. The Phoenician was just enough farther away, around a curve on a tree-lined street that Wendy was very uncomfortable, but I decided we should walk anyway.

We prepared to walk by emptying our pockets of everything except enough cash to pay for dinner and one cell phone between us. Then we set out. During the day, the walk would have been delightful. The street at this point is well constructed with new, paved sidewalks, bordered by trees and other attractive vegetation. It was even brightly lit. The weather was pleasant. It was a beautiful night for a stroll, but it was still Nairobi. As we turned from the street with our apartment to the street with the restaurant, it was nearly deserted. We saw one woman walking toward us. She was walking very purposely and passed us by with no one uttering a sound. Then we heard a man, coming up from behind us. He was walking more quickly than we were. We didn't change our pace, but Wendy squeezed my hand tightly as the man approached. As he passed us and walked on, the only sound we heard was the crinkling of his plastic grocery bag from the local supermarket. Though she continued to look over her shoulder and twitched at the slightest sound, Wendy and I arrived at the restaurant compound safely. We felt very relieved as the security guards let us pass through the steel gate into the restaurant compound.

I had prawns for a main course, and Wendy had some type of Middle Eastern chicken, but we started with several varieties of hummus and pita bread. The décor was simple but charming, and we felt very cozy sitting outside by a fire. However, the most unusual part of the evening was the music. On Friday nights, the restaurant had live music performed by a local duo, one on guitar and the other on keyboard. At first, they were playing instrumentals, some of which were recognizable American tunes. Then it got more interesting. This African duo, in the Lebanese restaurant, started singing, and the first few songs they sang were Kenny Rogers's hits. They went into more country tunes and other popular U.S. hits. Then it really got international. The African duo, in the Lebanese restaurant, in Nairobi, Kenya, began singing a familiar Mexican song, in

Spanish, with a Swahili accent. It was delightfully bizarre and definitely a time and place for all nationalities. We had a great evening.

After dinner, Wendy was a little nervous about walking back. I wasn't, perhaps because of the wine I'd had with dinner. In any case, the walk back was uneventful. There was no one else out walking at that time of night. As we walked back to the guardhouse in front of our apartment and through the large security gate, we wondered what the guards must be thinking about the crazy Wazungu (Swahili word for white people, sometimes used to mean crazy white people, so crazy Wazungu could be considered redundant) who went out walking in Nairobi at night. Eventually Wendy forgave me for coercing her, but we did not walk to the Phoenician at night again.

For a while, I was feeling quite comfortable with the issue of personal safety, but then the concerns came back. I heard rumors going around the office about a robbery and a shootout at a bank only a half-mile from our office. The robbers were supposedly linked to some other criminal activity that had taken place only shortly before in another part of Nairobi. The details were unclear and confusing. The next morning's paper clarified some details but raised more questions than it answered.

Excerpts from an article in the *Kenya Times*, May 18:

Bloodbath in the city
4 cops, 6 thugs killed in shoot-out
By MAXWELL MASAVA

GUNMEN took over control of parts of Nairobi yesterday killing four police officers in what was feared could have been a well-orchestrated killing mission. Three other officers were injured and rushed to hospital in critical condition.

A stab in the country's security shield, the death

drama saw gun-wielding criminals eliminate a CID officer, an administrative policeman and a uniformed policeman in three separate incidents within a span of two hours.

But the officers immediately hit back with ferocity that saw six gangsters killed and a cache of firearms recovered, in the orgy that reminisced scenes of Wild West movies . . .

At Greenfields estate off Jogogo road, a lone police officer who was on undercover mission to investigate the movement of a stolen car ran into a gang of three men who sprayed him with bullets before escaping with his pistol . . .

But as the killing was being carried out in Greenfields, more drama was unfolding in Nairobi's River Road area where a police mission to smash a criminal gang turned tragic with one of the officers being shot dead on the scene . . .

In a quick retaliation, the other group of officers gunned down all the three gangsters and recovered one AK 47 rifle, four pistols and several rounds of ammunition. The officer died while he was being rushed to hospital for treatment . . .

At Westlands, another group of gunmen were plotting a robbery at Barclays Bank next to Landmark Hotel where [an] unknown amount of money was stolen. An administration policeman who was part of the cash-on-transit escorting team was shot and killed. His two colleagues sustained serious bullet wounds after an exchange with the robbers.

Sources say another officer died while being rushed to hospital by his colleagues. A passerby caught in the middle of the shoot-out was also killed. A body of a gangster believed to have been shot during the bank raid was found dumped along Peponi road in Westlands a few hours later. Two more suspects were killed near City Park after they were trailed by police for more than two hours.

Police Spokesman Erick Kiraithe said police were aware of those planning to commit criminal activities across the country and warned that "criminals' days were numbered and that they should expect a full force of the law." He would not, however, rule out any possible link between yesterday's killings to the current circulation of leaflets inciting members of the public against the government.

The killings in Nairobi came as police in Central province confirmed that they had arrested a suspect in connection with the circulation of leaflets in the province.

According to reports, the suspect was said to have confessed to having received money from unnamed people in Nairobi to circulate the leaflets which called on members of the public to arise and fight the current government.

The arrest comes in the wake of police investigations on the circulation of leaflets calling on people believed to be adherents of the outlawed Mungiki sect to arise and protect themselves from alleged government harassment and intimidation.

This was our up close and personal (The Barclay's bank that was robbed was a quarter mile from our apartment, and we had used their ATM several times.) introduction to the clandestine and dreaded Mungiki. We had previously heard about killings in Central Kenya (including several beheadings) but hadn't paid close attention. With events happening in our neighborhood, we became very attentive. We wanted to know who these Mungiki were and why they were doing these terrible things. To satisfy our curiosity, we began asking questions, but the answers we got weren't always straightforward.

As with most aspects of the Mungiki story, their origins are shrouded in mystery. From most accounts we heard, the Mungiki began in the 1980s as either a self-defense force or political action group (depending on your sympathies) promoting the rights and protection of the Kikuyu, Kenya's largest tribe. Supposedly, they modeled themselves on the Mau Maus who led the rebellion against British colonialism in the 1950s. After some years of political action (perhaps peaceful or perhaps violent), the Mungiki morphed from their original form into more of a religious cult whose members wore dreadlocks and promoted traditional rituals such as female circumcision. During this period, the Mungiki seemed responsible for more fear than criminal action. However, in their next incarnation, the Mungiki abandoned any pretense of adhering to principle and became a dangerous, mafia-type gang. Migrating from central Kenya to Nairobi, the Mungiki established criminal enterprises, the most well-known of which were the protection racket and extortion of the matatu (public minibus) trade.

The Mungiki seemed to still have ties to politics and employed ethnic-based violence to influence elections. They seemed to be available to serve whatever politician would hire them. Rumors also swirled that the Mungiki had ties to the highest levels of government and bribed the police to minimize interference in Mungiki affairs. As with the original protection schemes of the Italian mafia, some people initially welcomed the intervention of the Mungiki. At least with one dominant gang, some people felt they weren't in danger from multitudes of independent petty criminals or wars among lesser gangs. They knew who the boss was and felt safe as long as the appropriate tribute was paid.

The matatu drivers felt differently. They received no benefit from being forced to make daily extortion payments to Mungiki members. In most cases, they felt powerless to resist, but during our time in Nairobi, the matatu drivers staged a strike hoping to get the government to take action against the extortionists. The matatu drivers' strike crippled Nairobi transportation for a day and kicked off one of the numerous battles in the Mungiki wars of 2007. Several outspoken matatu drivers and local Mungiki leaders were killed in a series of back and forth reprisals. Some were killed in particularly horrific ways, such as being trapped inside as their houses were burned around them.

A few weeks later, two police officers were shot and killed in the Mathare slum in Nairobi. The next night, the police stormed Mathare looking for the culprits (presumably Mungiki) who had killed the officers, as well as Mungiki members who had been implicated in a string of beheadings. The police killed twenty-two and arrested over one hundred during extended gun battles. In the meantime, the beheadings continued and so did the police crackdown. After the incident in Mathare, it was rare to hear of anyone being arrested, but the killings on both sides continued. By the end of June, the combined death toll was over fifty. Speculation continued about the Mungiki's aim to destabilize the country before the upcoming presidential elections.

For weeks, there seemed to be battles going back and forth between police and the Mungiki. The Mungiki would kill some low-level politicians or police officers, anyone representing the government, often in horrific ways. Then the police would stage a large raid on supposed Mungiki compounds and rarely took prisoners. Politicians would make pronouncements and citizens expressed increasing outrage. For a while, the police seemed to be initiating most of the battles, and then it all seemed to stop. It just wasn't in the news anymore. There was a lot of speculation on what had happened, but apparently, nobody really knew or was willing to say. The predominant story was that the president had become enraged with the lawless killings and had forcefully ordered his security forces to fix the problem. The speculation was that at this point, any political allies of the Mungiki could no longer protect them and the police got free rein to go after them using whatever force and tactics they felt necessary. It wasn't until many months later that any information surfaced, but when it did, the speculation was essentially confirmed.

Nov 8th, NAIROBI
From *The Economist* print edition
Who is to blame for a spate of execution-style killings?

SINCE the summer, 454 bodies have been dumped in mortuaries, mainly in or around Nairobi, the capital, most of them shot in the back of the head. They had all been killed by "state security agents"—at least, that was the extraordinary claim made this week in a report by Kenya's official human-rights commission. The police, it added, had shown little interest in investigating the deaths and had obstructed the commission's work.

The report seems to confirm rumours that the interior ministry organised an undercover squad to hunt down and kill members of the Mungiki sect, a Kikuyu gang that has terrorised central Kenya on and off for years, not least by decapitating its victims. Mungiki foot-soldiers have also been used by politicians to rough up opposition supporters, but a killing spree earlier this year was a step too far. In June the government ordered a crackdown. Many Mungiki leaders have since disappeared.

The head of the police, Hussein Ali, denies any wrongdoing. Where, he asks, is the evidence? The report, he says, showed the "level to which the human-rights commission had degenerated"; the dead were killed in car crashes or in gang violence.

Kenyan police, he insists, do not engage in crime. But some think one reason war was declared on the Mungiki was because they were muscling in on police earnings from bus touts and others in poorer bits of Nairobi. A grave allegation in the report is that some of those killed paid hefty bribes to the police to be let out of prison after a round-up of suspected Mungiki, only to vanish later.

There are calls for an independent inquiry. Many feel sorry for the police, who have lost 15 officers to the Mungiki this year alone. But Mr. Ali's denials fail to answer the main charges: why the lack of a proper investigation, why the execution-style of the killing, and why so many dead?

Another question is what part, if any, the killings will play in next month's general and presidential elections. A crackdown on the Mungiki, whose origins lie in Kikuyu folklore, may placate some of those who complain that the Kikuyus, Kenya's largest ethnic group, have been hogging economic and political power. But the sheer scale of the killings makes everyone feel queasy.

I felt queasy too, but conflicted. How should a developing country, with limited resources, deal with a pervasive criminal element? Whether it's Kenya or a Latin American country fighting drug cartels, what should they do? It seems obvious that they can't afford to take the U.S. approach of gathering detailed evidence on each individual criminal to prove his guilt in a court of law, beyond reasonable doubt, allowing challenges to the admissibility of evidence and subsequent appeals of any guilty verdicts. I think the U.S. justice system is wonderful for us, and I'm glad that it protects the rights of the accused. But it is very expensive, time consuming, and would be entirely ineffective for developing countries. They just don't have the resources to take this approach and protect the rights of probable criminals. On the other end of the spectrum, legitimate governments cannot just adopt the tactics of the criminals and engage in all-out war on questionable members of its society. Where is the right balance? Kenya seemed to have stepped over the line with all of the killings, but order had been reestablished in many communities and citizens no longer felt threatened. I don't know where the line should be drawn, but I'm sure it will remain thin and gray. This dilemma provided just one more lesson in our ongoing education into the challenges of developing countries.

The Mungiki drama just added to all of the other safety issues that one could worry about, but like the rest, it never touched us personally. We were not directly involved and highly unlikely to be directly impacted—nor are the vast majority of visitors to Kenya or Africa. When we returned to the US, I read in the newspaper about gang murders in Oakland, California, just across the bay from Silicon Valley. Then a TechnoServe colleague was mugged in Washington DC. Several weeks later a good friend told me about her daughter having her purse forcibly stolen in San Francisco. Bad things and risks are everywhere. Whether in the US or Africa, people just need to understand the situation and potential risk, take protective action where required, and then get comfortable with taking some chances for the trade-off of a wonderful experience.

TIA, but Some Things Work Quite Well;

And Africans Can Be Very Resourceful

*F*or those who haven't seen the movie *Blood Diamonds*, TIA stands for "This Is Africa." In the movie, the male hero, Leonardo di Caprio, who has grown up in Africa, uses TIA to inform the naive female journalist that things don't work the same way in Africa as they do in the developed world. It's sort of like Dorothy turning to Toto and saying, "Did you think you were still in Kansas?" In our journey, we encountered many versions of the same saying including, "Welcome to Africa," "Welcome to Swaziland," "Welcome to Uganda," and the French version "C'est l'Afrique." All of these were used at various times to explain why some process, equipment, or piece of infrastructure didn't work as might be expected in the developed world. These phrases were often spoken with a shrug of the shoulders, a tone of resignation, and the unstated but implied question of, "Did you really expect it to be any different?" They were also spoken only to newcomers or visitors who have come to Africa with their unrealistic Western expectations of how things should work. The locals are never surprised. They know what to expect.

I never got comfortable with TIA and never developed a standard approach to dealing with it. I couldn't consistently resolve my inner conflict, and maybe that was okay. Maybe a situational approach was appropriate, but it always made me uncomfortable. At times, I would become internally infuriated at things that didn't work properly such as unashamedly poor customer services, bad infrastructure, shoddy products, etc. I knew that the whole acceptance of TIA in society had to change if the economy were to advance. On the other hand, I knew that the people I was dealing with directly had little or no power to makes things different, and that when I complained, I sounded like an elitist outsider who had no real understanding of reality. In work situations where I had some influence, I tried to coach and cajole people to fight the system of complacency and to make positive change. However, outside of work, I often just figuratively threw up my hands, tried not to get too upset, and as much as possible, went along with the flow.

Despite the prevalence of TIA, we were surprised numerous times when things in Africa worked quite well. At other times we were amazed at the resourcefulness of Africans in overcoming barriers and challenges. For example:

When Wendy first arrived in Kenya, I was shocked to see her being pushed out of the baggage area in a wheelchair. When she got to me, she explained that after I left the United States, she had hurt her ankle. She had gone to the doctor at Stanford University Health Center, and they had done an x-ray. The report came back that there was no sign of a break, so she must have sprained her ankle. Wendy explained that it continued to be quite painful, even with just walking. During one airport layover, she had to rush between terminals with a heavy carry-on, and she had really strained herself. Her ankle throbbed throughout the flight, so when she arrived in Nairobi, she requested a wheelchair.

Over the following weeks, she was able to walk, but her ankle still hurt, and she couldn't do any strenuous activity. After more than a month, she finally saw a local doctor and explained what had happened. He ordered a CAT scan of her ankle, and the results came back that afternoon. She had a non-displaced fracture of the fibula. The fracture was healing so there was nothing special to be done, but at least she knew the real story and didn't have to feel that she was just being a wimp. As an aside, the bill for the doctor visit and the CAT scan came to about $120 in total. I'm sure the charges for similar services in the United States would be more than ten times that amount.

Wendy got a copy of her diagnosis and sent it back to the doctors at Stanford. They sent back a very defensive letter explaining how nondisplaced fractures are very hard to detect initially but can be more easily seen after calcium is built up during healing, etc. I'm sure all of that is true, but it was quite amusing that her ankle problem was correctly diagnosed in Africa after having been missed at one of the premier medical institutions in the United States.

Having lived all their lives with TIA, Africans become very creative and resourceful when confronting challenging situations. What in the West is called "thinking outside the box" is second nature to many Africans. For example, as we rode around Nairobi we noticed an innovative Kenyan deterrent to the type of auto parts theft we had seen in Maputo. On many cars, the registration number was sandblasted into the windows, mirrors, etc. It was a very ingenious solution and a value-added business! The world needs more of this type of creative thought.

However, my most memorable encounter with creative African thinking came one evening on a trip to the Nairobi airport with Bruce, the TechnoServe CEO, to catch an important international flight. South of Nairobi, the road to the airport is a four-lane divided highway and after rush hour traffic has subsided, the ride usually goes quickly. On this night, we hit severe traffic. The cause was unknown, but we suspected an accident. Traffic had not stopped completely, so we assumed that perhaps the police were directing one lane of traffic through the backup. As our car moved farther along, we noticed that other cars were passing us on the edge of the median, so thinking this might be the lane that was getting through, Tom, our driver, followed the other cars making a new lane of traffic. We later realized no traffic was getting through. The movement of cars was caused by the creative Kenyan drivers making two long lines of cars into five shorter lines with three lanes in the paved roadway and one each on the shoulder and the median.

At some point, drivers realized that no traffic was actually getting through, but a lot of people must have been really motivated to get to the airport. We were too, but we didn't coach Tom; we just let him take initiative and be creative. Tom noticed that some other cars ahead of us were crossing the median to drive on the other edge, so he followed. The median was wide with two flat edges. In the middle was a deep gully for drainage. There was also a barrier of stone posts to prevent cars from crossing. Tom navigated the gully through a break in the barrier, and we found ourselves on the other side of the highway. We followed other cars along the flat part of the median on the other side, facing traffic! We were making progress toward our destination and the oncoming traffic didn't seem too bothered by us, but the progress was very slow along the soft dirt. At some point, the cars ahead of us decided that there wasn't too much oncoming traffic and that the oncoming cars could share the pavement with us. They pulled out into the oncoming traffic lane, and we followed! I was very happy that Tom only pulled out behind another car so that we wouldn't be the ones to absorb the full impact of a head-on collision. As we proceeded down the highway, the oncoming traffic swerved to avoid the headlights speeding toward them. After a few miles, we passed the accident, which involved a huge truck totally blocking the road. There were a number of policemen standing around, but no one seemed to be making any effort to get traffic moving. Past the accident, we got back onto the proper side of the highway. We breathed easier and got to the airport well ahead of the departure time for our planes. Other people were stuck for much longer, but the jam had trapped so many people that all major international departures were delayed for at least an hour to prevent stranding so many passengers. These types of incidents always provided me with amusement as creative and sometimes subversive individuals overcame the oppression of the system. Despite my frustration with sometimes overwhelming TIA, I retained hope because of the incredible spirit and resourcefulness of some of the individuals we encountered.

Uganda

$\mathcal{P}$art of my responsibility, beyond my work in Kenya, was to support Erastus, TechnoServe's new country director for Uganda as he reestablished our presence, starting with an office in Kampala. So Wendy and I flew to Uganda. The flight from Nairobi to Entebbe (yes, the infamous Entebbe from the 1976 hijacking incident) airport is only about forty-five minutes. However, since it was an international flight, we arrived at the Nairobi airport two hours before the departure time. After touching down at Entebbe, it took us about an hour to go through immigration. Then there was the forty-five minute drive from Entebbe to Kampala; and I left out the drive getting to the airport in Nairobi. So overall it was a half-day trip for a forty-five-minute flight.

As soon as we landed in Uganda, Wendy said that memories of Entebbe and the Idi Amin fiasco associated with the 1976 hijacking began to haunt her. She had seen the movies *Entebbe* and *Last King of Scotland* and their scenes were spinning through her head. Thankfully, Uganda and the city of Kampala have come a long way since the 1970s.

Entebbe airport had a large runway and an almost-complete, newly renovated terminal. However, there were only a few planes on the tarmac. The terminal is much smaller and less crowded than Jomo Kenyatta in Nairobi since Entebbe gets much less traffic. After passing through immigration, baggage claim, and customs, Wendy and I were picked up and driven to Kampala. The road out of the airport was very beautiful as it curved around Lake Victoria with its nicely landscaped median. I had been reading Lee Kwan Yew's book about the development of Singapore and how he had insisted on beautifying the road into the city from Changi airport so that visitors would have a good first impression. I was sure that Uganda's President Museveni had taken his advice. As we got farther along on the road into Kampala, it wasn't quite as beautiful as the initial stretch, but as we compared our surroundings to Kenya, everything looked just a little greener, brighter, newer, and cleaner. It was obviously still a developing country, but Wendy and I seemed to detect a difference.

Based on population statistics, Kampala is nearly half the size of Nairobi, but it is really a much smaller city. The small city center quickly gives way to residential neighborhoods and low-rise commercial areas that spread out for miles and miles. We observed that some of the neighborhoods were quite nice with large homes and groomed yards. Other areas looked like the poor commercial and residential areas in the smaller rural cities in Kenya. In Kenya, electrical power was a problem as it went off frequently, requiring every office and residential complex to have a generator. The same was true in Uganda, but the outages were even more frequent. Sometimes they lasted for hours, but usually they were quite short. However, the unreliable power would often wreak havoc with electronic equipment. Every time the power went off at our hotel, the Internet connection was lost, and the server had to be restarted. One time, I was talking to our daughter in the United States using the Internet, and I had to restart the call six times.

Our original plan had been to visit TechnoServe's current

Uganda project in the western part of the country and then to have several meetings with donors. However, our African experience had taught us to be very flexible. Erastus and his senior staff were working on a proposal with a very short deadline. Consequently, he had no time to go with us to the field, and it would have required two days of another person's time just to take us to the field and essentially give us a tour. Although Wendy and I really wanted to see the team and the activities in the field, this didn't seem like a productive use of resources, so we cancelled the field visit. The donor meetings fell through as well, so we spent our time, during the week, helping on the proposal and doing our Kenya work. The frequent power failures had damaged the server at our small hotel and there was no estimate on when it would get fixed, so we spent multiple days camped out and working in the luxurious business center of the Serena hotel in the city center.

At the end of the week, we felt we had helped as much as we could and were ready to take a few days off for touring. While we were primarily working to help the poor, we did want to take some personal advantage of our location. Our destination was Murchison Falls, Uganda's largest national park.

The roads north of Kampala toward Murchison Falls were not nearly as nice as the road in from Entebbe. Full of deep potholes, they were as bad as or worse than the roads in rural Kenya. As we drove for hours, my engineering mind kept trying to analyze the road problem. As I observed, the paved surface seemed to be quite thin with only compacted dirt below. Consequently, when a small hole developed, it exposed the dirt underneath to the rain. As the rain fell, it softened the dirt and undermined the paving at the rim of the hole. Since the edge of the paving surrounding the hole no longer had support from below, it would break off. The hole became larger and the cycle of decay would start again. So pretty quickly, any small hole got wider and wider and deeper and deeper until it became a pothole that could break an axle. The same process occurred at the edges of the roads. The paving surface was undermined and over time broke off in little pieces, which made the road edges look like they had been nibbled away by a giant invisible monster. Of course, over time the road narrowed with many sections being about one-and-a-half-lanes wide.

We had lots of time to observe the countryside. For most of the trip, the vegetation was very green and very lush. This meant that the soil was rich and rain was abundant. Unlike Kenya where only 20 percent of the land area is suitable for agriculture, much of Uganda is composed of very good farmland. So although many Ugandans don't have a significant cash income, they can at least grow enough food to feed their families.

Once inside Murchison Falls Park, we drove 80 km (50 miles) on a single-lane dirt road. It was very rough, but no worse than the pock-marked paving that we had just left. Along our drive through a densely forested region, we stopped to observe a tortoise crossing the road. As we stopped, the car was immediately filled with a giant swarm of tsetse flies. They seemed to be instantly everywhere, filling the space inside the car and attacking us. Our driver, Dominic, immediately grabbed a magazine and started furiously swatting and trying to swish the flies out of the windows with one hand as he started the Land Cruiser with the other. Simultaneously, I grabbed the insect repellant and chivalrously gave it to Wendy who began bathing every exposed piece of flesh. Then I did the same, a little more judiciously while concurrently swatting and swishing. Dominic started the car and began to drive as we opened all of the windows. We all continued waving our arms wildly. Within a short time, we were able to either kill the flies or get them to leave the vehicle. No one had been bitten, but the intensity and speed of the attack had been startling. Tsetse fly bites are painful, and they do carry sleeping sickness.

Our first destination in the park was a point above Murchison Falls. As we learned, Murchison Falls is not a high graceful waterfall; it is a thundering cataract where the full flow of the (White) Nile River is forced through a narrow canyon and over multiple cascades. Approaching the falls we heard a constant load roar from the water as it accelerated through the canyon and bounced against the rock walls. As we got even closer, the whole earth seemed to pulsate under our feet from the force of the water.

After viewing the powerful falls from above, we quickly drove 35 km downriver to the ferry that we would take to cross the Nile and get to our lodge. Because the ferry only runs every hour, and we were going to be close for catching the five o'clock ferry, Dominic drove aggressively on the dirt roads and got us to the dock by four-fifty. However, someone had decided that there would be no five o'clock ferry that day. We would have to wait until 6:00 p.m. We smiled, got out of the car, and began to casually walk around. TIA; we'd learned to adapt, but sometimes it would help if they served cocktails.

At 6:00 p.m., Dominic maneuvered the Land Cruiser on to the ferry, essentially a barge with two large rotating drive engines. We walked on and rode across. Our lodge was perched on a small hill very close to the river. This proximity allowed us to be continuously serenaded by the rumbling bass grunts and roars of the hippos that populated the river. At dinner we got another treat when a family of elephants invaded the pool area, just below the second floor dining porch. One elephant came close enough that his trunk could nearly reach us. Maybe he wanted to sample our dinner, but it was just out of reach. The staff attempted to shoo the elephants away, but the elephants were in no hurry to leave. The staff was no match for the elephants, so they gave up and after a while the elephants left when they were ready.

Having seen Murchison Falls from above, the next day we

wanted to see it from the river below. The lodge ran boat trips up the Nile to just below the falls, and on this day the trip was so popular that a small boat was being used in addition to the large launch. Based on our prior experience on the Zambezi River above Victoria Falls, we chose the smaller boat because it could maneuver closer to shore and provide more intimate views of animals by the river. The smaller boat didn't have a bar, but Wendy and I weren't interested in cocktails in the middle of the day. However, we discovered that, under certain conditions, the smaller boat had other disadvantages. As we motored up the river, the skies darkened, and it began to rain. The wind picked up just as the thunder and lightning began. Unlike on the large, fully covered launch with roll-down side shades, the weather was a problem for our little boat which had only a partial roof and no side protection. The rain was pelting us at a forty-five-degree angle from a constantly shifting direction. I had an umbrella and tried to manipulate it against the wind in a progressively losing battle until the roof began to drain onto my seat when I totally gave up and just got as wet as nature wanted to make me. Our captain got a little worried about being the highest point on the river as the lightning increased, so he pulled the boat against the shore of a small island. The surrounding high ground and trees provided some protection from the lightning, but he warned us to be vigilant for crocodiles and hippos approaching the boat. After a while, the rain stopped, and we continued our journey up the river. We got a great view of the falls, and by the time we were back at the dock, our clothes were dry. Nylon backpacking clothes work great in Africa.

The next day as we drove back to Kampala, we made one important stop along the way. Another attraction within the Murchison Falls Park was a chimp sanctuary where we could view chimps in their natural habitat. This was not like a zoo with a viewing walkway and windows into the cages. In this sanctuary, the chimps generally stay within a five-mile radius, but each day the guides and the tourists must hike around until they find them in their wild natural habitat. Before Wendy and I started hiking with our guide, he explained the safety rules. Chimps are smaller than humans, typically less than four feet high and less than one hundred pounds, but they are about five times as strong. Because these wild chimps had not directly interacted with humans, they didn't know that they could easily overpower a human. Consequently, when humans entered their immediate territory, the chimps would hoot, holler, and jump up and down to intimidate the humans. We were to ignore this behavior, stand tall, and act very confident as we observed the chimps. If the chimps seemed like they were going to attack, we were to crouch down in a submissive position and pretend to be eating leaves. In no circumstance were we to run from the chimps. If we did, the chimps would chase us down and kill us. We got the message and followed our guide into the forest.

The forest was crisscrossed with trails and our guide seemed to be leading us in a random path looking for the chimps. After an hour and a half of hiking, Wendy and I began to wonder if he knew what he was doing, but he finally heard some chimp sounds so we set off in their direction. As we approached the chimps, they started making the anticipated noises. It was actually quite amusing because it sounded like the primate house at the zoo or a group of schoolchildren imitating a band of chimpanzees. We were shortly in the midst of a band of fifteen to twenty chimps spread throughout the surrounding trees above us. They kept their distance and expressed varying levels of displeasure with our presence. They were cute, yet fascinating and definitely scary. We saw a Colobus monkey enter their group, heard some terrible screaming, and then saw the chimps eating the monkey. Chimps are mankind's closest relatives and like us they are omnivores. Also like us, they can be very violent. After about a half hour of tense observation we hiked back to the Land Cruiser, reducing the stress level for both the chimps and ourselves. Our close encounter inspired both of us to read *Next of Kin* by Roger Fouts to see how really close we are to our genetic neighbors.

As Dominic drove us back to Kampala, he took the flying-over-potholes strategy versus the slowly, carefully avoiding them approach he used on the way to the park. It was a lot bumpier, but we got back in half the time. On the way back we still had lots of time to observe, but this time the focus was bicycles and their diverse, amazing loads, including a baby pig, two goats, one hundred pounds of banana leaves, twenty empty Gerry cans (for banana gin), eight banana bunches, six sacks of veggies, six stacked crates of empty soda bottles, three suitcases, three enormous charcoal sacks, two huge sacks of potatoes, a giant load of used clothes, a small hardware store's worth of household items including mops and brooms, a bundle of about thirty sugar canes about six feet long, and about thirty pieces of eight-foot-long lumber.

In addition to bicycles, Ugandans use lots of small motorized scooters that are equally overloaded with cargo or passengers. These small scooters are called "boda-bodas." We heard several varying stories on the origin of the name, but all the stories agreed that the original phrase was "border-to-border" and referred to the transportation of goods across borders. Evidently, in the past, large trucks would stop as they approached a border and unload their goods onto these small scooters for actual transport across the border. Whether the scooters were exploiting a loophole in tariffs, less likely to be stopped for inspection or being used for straightforward smuggling was never clear, but the name and the scooters persist.

Believe, Begin, Become in Kenya

*A*fter our trip to Uganda, we returned to our regular "routine" in Nairobi. Wendy split her time between Young Women in Enterprise and the Believe, Begin, Become business plan competition. I continued to support Fred, primarily acting as his deputy country director with a focus on strengthening our internal administrative processes. We had made significant progress, and I felt good about my contributions so far. In the finance arena, I had provided project managers with better reporting on their spending. Since financial reports from headquarters only came out quarterly and were often late, project managers didn't have up-to-date information on their spending. This often caused them to overspend or to be overly cautious and not fully spend their funds when they could have been especially useful. I became familiar with our local finance system, dug into the monthly numbers, and created timely financial reports on Excel spreadsheets. I gave these reports to all of the project managers to help them keep their spending more in line with budgets. I also monitored spending levels myself and sat down with several project managers when I noticed their rate of spending would exhaust their funds before the project was supposed to end. With more timely information, we avoided several potential overruns. I also instituted regular, formal project status reporting to keep Fred fully informed and to assure that projects were on track and getting results. A third important change was to establish local project files in distinctive "blue binders" to assure that all relevant documentation on each project could be readily accessed without having to request that it be sent from headquarters when there was a question. While I knew that these changes would improve the quality of project management and ultimately deliver more benefits to our clients, I also missed the direct contact I'd had helping small businesses in Swaziland where my impact was more direct and tangible.

During this period, we lived on Rapta Road, and every morning on our way to work would pass the offices of IOM where there was always a queue of people waiting long before the offices opened. IOM stands for International Organization for Migration and among their goals is "to provide humanitarian assistance to migrants in need, including refugees and internally displaced people." We realized that the people in the queues must be refugees from Somalia where the turmoil was generating a constant flow of displaced people into Kenya. We never knew what happened to people after they got to IOM. We hoped that they got better lives, but it just pointed out to us how easy it was to ignore someone else's ongoing tragedy as we carried on with our normal life.

On a brighter note, we noticed that the government of Nairobi was progressing on their beautification of the city. There was a lot of planting going on. Borders of small flowering shrubs were popping up next to city sidewalks and in median strips (reducing the bare dirt index). To protect their investment and prevent pedestrians from trampling the vulnerable shrubs, the government had adopted a strategy that would never survive in the United States. Discreetly supported by wooden posts and strung throughout the shrubs were taut strands of barbed wire. Without the extreme fear of liability litigation that would typically result in the United States, the Nairobi government was determined not to let their beautification investment get wasted and destroyed by uncaring pedestrians.

Wendy's support of Believe, Begin, Become (BBB), TechnoServe's first business plan competition in Kenya was very different from what she did for the BBB in Swaziland. And the Kenya effort was on a vastly larger scale from any other TechnoServe business plan competition. TechnoServe had partnered with Kenya's Ministry of Youth Affairs (MOYA) to sponsor the competition, and it was receiving a much higher level of attention than in any other previous country. In previous countries, we had received up to six hundred entries, and in Kenya, we expected between five and ten thousand. We were also planning to provide over forty hours of training simultaneously in eight locations to the anticipated three hundred semi-finalists. MOYA wanted a high-profile way to support young people (into their thirties) in a country where their unemployment rate was approximately 40 percent. They also wanted to make the program very geographically fair and attract entrants from every area of Kenya, not just the larger cities. With her extensive marketing background and since she had participated in the BBB program in Swaziland, Wendy was perfectly positioned to provide broad marketing support to the team including writing press releases, developing marketing materials, and creating the training for the initial recruiting sessions.

Because of her marketing role, Wendy was able to tag along to the formal presentation of simulated donation checks to TechnoServe, hosted by Kenya's vice president at his office! She shook hands with the VP as well as the minister and permanent secretary (PS) of MOYA. Besides the TechnoServe representatives, there were several senior executives from private sector companies including: managing director of Lenovo for eastern and southern Africa, the chairman of the Kenya Pipeline Company, and one of the board of directors from Kenya Commercial Bank. TechnoServe was receiving dummy checks for forty-five million Kenyan Shillings from MOYA, seven million from Lenovo, and one million from Kenya Commercial Bank (70 Ksh = U.S. $1). The press snapped photos while the ministry recorded the speeches.

Wendy was on a roll. Within two weeks, she had accompanied TechnoServe colleagues to meetings with Kenya's vice president, the minister of Youth Affairs and permanent secretaries of both Youth Affairs and the Education Ministries. She had been seen on Kenyan TV twice! In her meetings, she was particularly impressed by both the vice president and the PS of the Youth Affairs Ministry. She told me that the PS of Youth Affairs was very knowledgeable and quick-thinking when responding to questions from the press. Wendy also said that he gave the impression of a venerable African chieftain who truly wanted the best for his people and was very accessible. She predicted he would have a long and successful political career.

Because BBB was such a large endeavor for our office, it wasn't long before I got involved as well. To aggressively promote BBB, we were doing awareness days throughout the country. In the larger venues, these sessions consisted of stage shows that alternated singing, dancing, and other entertainment with short inspirational talks on business. In the more remote areas, the gatherings were smaller and focused totally on business learning rather than entertainment. Wendy and I went to a midsized city, Nyeri, where the event was presented on a temporary stage that had been erected in an open field that apparently was a city park. It had rained heavily the night before, so the field, which didn't have much grass, was an oozing plain of mud. Despite the conditions, the firm that had been hired to promote the event was able to attract nearly two thousand people by driving around the city with a loudspeaker truck. The people who came seemed very interested and stayed around for hours paying close attention. There were a lot of young people who seemed intrigued.

Wendy and I stood behind the table in the TechnoServe booth, handed out application forms with the training brochure she had developed. We also answered questions when the questioner spoke English. Many of the teenagers seemed to want to engage us in conversation just because we were obviously foreigners. We were the only Wazungu (white people) to be seen in the area, and while most of the teenagers would have seen white people before, they had probably never had a chance to interact with them. The young children were even cuter and very amusing as they seemed to want to just shake our hands and look closely at our white skin. It was a very warm experience; I felt I was making a very personal global connection just by being there.

Wendy's work in the booth was interrupted when the emcee of the show called her up to the stage to participate in the dancing. She did a credible job, but in a later discussion with colleagues was very self-effacing and repeated the cliché that white people can't dance. Her Kenyan colleague reaffirmed the perception saying, "I've noticed that. Even in the discos. Why is that?" Wendy muttered a vague answer about being something cultural and not being as exposed to music as children. After a long day, we rode back for hours over potholed roads, but both of us felt very good inside.

Over the next week, Wendy and I both anticipated our upcoming visit to the exclusive Muthaiga Country Club, made famous by *White Mischief*. We had each read the book about the rich colonialists of the 1930s who lived in Nairobi and farther north around Lake Naivasha where they owned large plantations. The management of the plantations and households was typically delegated to trustworthy local employees, so the owners had little work to occupy themselves. They filled their time primarily with their social lives, which featured heavy drinking, some drugs, and extensive sexual encounters with each other's spouses. The Muthaiga Country Club, which is still a prestigious country club on the northern edge of Nairobi, was at the center of these activities. Wendy had been dying to visit it since reading the book, but we didn't know any members.

Eventually, some new friends invited us to the club to hear a recital by a pianist touring from the United States. It was interesting to me that a country club would have sponsored this type of event. Perhaps the club maintains an old tradition of bringing culture to the hinterlands or perhaps just wants to demonstrate that they are not the Muthaiga Club of old. I was already convinced that there had been change since the first person I saw when entering the club was an African woman, presumably a member, at the bar casually having a drink. There were also a number of Africans attending the recital. We asked our friends about the legends of *White Mischief.*" They said the culture still exists, and that although not so overt, the activities still go on. It would not have been obvious from the mostly geriatric audience at the recital, but who knows; maybe they're really carrying on the old traditions.

Nairobi streets and sidewalks are congested with entrepreneurial sellers of all sorts of common goods, such as pictured here, second-hand shoes.

Next door to our first Nairobi apartment, a building looked as though it was constructed of tree branches, which actually comprised the scaffolding for pouring concrete.

In the TechnoServe Kenya office in Nairobi, Wendy poses with some colleagues who worked with her on the Young Women in Enterprise and Upscaling programs.

Wendy and colleagues judge participants in one of Young Women in Enterprise's regional business plan competitions in Juja, a small town northeast of Nairobi near Thika. Since some girls only spoke Swahili, Wendy often could only take notes on their confidence and demeanor.

The banana program is a typical, well-run "value chain" in TechnoServe Kenya's portfolio. Senior Business Advisor Henry Kinyua explains to visitors how his team helps farmers grow high quality bananas, then sell and transport them to market.

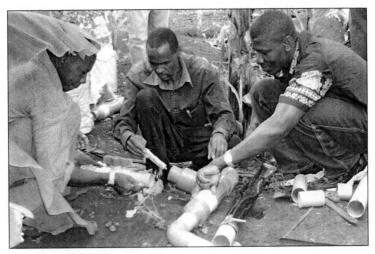

As part of TechnoServe Kenya's banana program, staffers teach farmers how to install valuable irrigation to improve harvest size and quality.

A female farmer in TechnoServe Kenya's banana program is guided on how to install drip irrigation, to plant the best seedlings, and optimally care for them to improve the crop yield.

TechnoServe Kenya staff teaches farmers how to sort the harvested bunches into quality and size groupings to get the best prices when they go to market.

Rick and Wendy visited several of TechnoServe Kenya's Upscaling program's clients including Aspen Orchards & Dairies that produced yogurt drinks, seen being hand-sealed and labeled, for local markets.

On our trip to the Outspan Hotel in Aberdare National Park in central Kenya, we briefly visited Nyala Dairy, another TechnoServe Kenya value-chain success.

One typical means of east African transportation is "boda boda"— often-overloaded taxi-motorcycles seen here on the outskirts of Kampala, Uganda. "Boda boda" is loosely translated from "border to border" since these vehicles transport lots of legal and other goods from borders of adjacent countries.

During Wendy & Rick's trip to Murchison Falls National Park, 300 km northwest of Kampala, Uganda, they had to wait for a not-always-timely ferry to cross the Nile River to their hotel.

Local villagers fish for Nile Perch along the Nile River in Murchison Falls National Park, Uganda.

TechnoServe partnered with Kenya's Ministry of Youth Affairs to send Believe, Begin, Become teams across Kenya in order to recruit thousands of youth to compete in regional business plan competitions. This was the crowded recruiting event in Nyeri in central Kenya.

Unexpectedly Wendy was called up to the stage to dance at the Believe, Begin, Become recruiting event in Nyeri, central Kenya. She proved once again that white people can't dance relative to native Africans.

Nakuru, Lamu, and Tsavo

*N*ot having a car made it inconvenient to get out of Nairobi for short excursions. However, we eventually got so restless that we resolved to rent a taxi for the day and visit nearby Lake Nakuru Park. We had heard that the park was especially attractive because of its abundant flamingoes, in addition to rhinos, buffalo, and the usual gazelles, etc. Although the park is only fifty miles north of Nairobi, it was a two-hour drive. That gives you an idea of the quality of the roads. Actually, the poor quality of the main road was even recognized in Kenya, and it was being reconstructed. This was great news for the future, but it didn't help us much. We did enjoy the short section of road that had been recently rebuilt. However, for the rest of the trip we alternated among bouncing along the old pot-holed road, cruising on the dirt shoulder, which had been widened to take cars around the construction, or creeping through a long detour on an acceptable, but slow, road through rural towns. I was glad our taxi driver, Steve, had the responsibility for contending with the roads, not me. Wendy and I just lounged in the back seat, absorbed the bumbs, and breathed the dust.

As we went through the small rural towns, poverty was clear and omnipresent. Commercial areas usually consisted of the African version of the strip mall, including a few concrete block buildings often brightly painted to advertise a national brand such as cell phone service, bottled water, or even paint. In front of the buildings was typically a large flat open space of bare dirt. In the United States, it would be the area for parking cars, but there were very few cars. It was often occupied by "kiosks," roughly constructed stalls where mostly women sold fruits, vegetables, and sometimes a variety of other goods. In some areas, there was activity only on market days. In other locales, the activity was daily. In either case, we saw a lot of people moving around in a small area, but it was never clear how much money was actually changing hands. Coming into and out of these areas were donkey carts, hand-drawn carts, bicycles, and an occasional truck, all loaded with various supplies or produce.

The markets seemed to be working, but at a very low level. People weren't starving, but they were barely getting by. Roughly half of the people in Kenya lived on less than a dollar per day. As we told our friends about our experiences in Africa, we tried to make sure that we didn't just describe the beautiful scenery and the fascinating wildlife. We wanted to give them a total, clear picture.

After driving through the town of Nakuru, we arrived at the park and began our journey through the forested and open areas surrounding the lake. At first we saw just a few relatively unimpressive animals. As we approached the southern end of the lake, we saw a herd of rhinos, more than we had ever seen together, just grazing in a field of grass. We knew enough about African game to see that these were white rhinos. We learned that they had recently been reintroduced to the park from South Africa.

After lingering to watch the rhinos, we proceeded around the lake to the western shore where, in the distance, we saw a pale pink blur blanketing the edge of the lake. We weren't sure if we were seeing mineral deposits or some pervasive plant life. As we got closer, however, we began to make out the individual bodies of flamingoes. The number of flamingoes was astonishing, probably more than a million, densely packed together just feeding and preening. Occasionally, one would run around the crowd seemingly very purposeful but headed to do who knows what. More amazing was the sight of a few flamingoes taking flight. Seeing them standing in the water, it's hard to imagine how such an ungainly creature could actually fly.

After observing the flamingoes from the mudflats that form the lake shore, Steve suggested that he drive us up to the bluffs that overlook the whole park for an expansive and impressive view. As we drove up the road with a sign to Baboon Cliffs, Steve said he would stop at the viewing point. Driving up to the heights, we occasionally glimpsed the fantastic panorama. Unfortunately Steve had only been to the park one time before and consequently we missed the viewing point and the turnoff back to the park entrance. When we eventually got to an intersection, we realized that we were in the far southern end of the park, having gone about twenty kilometers out of our way. Fortunately, the route to the exit was clearly marked, and we followed it. The trip back to Nairobi was bumpy but uneventful. Overall, we had enjoyed a great experience.

As we got out of the car, we noticed how dusty it was. We then realized that it wasn't just the car that was dusty. Wendy and I were both covered from head to toe with a layer of fine red grit. As I showered later, the tub ran a rusty red as the water flowed away from my body.

Later in the evening, Wendy was lamenting the fact that Kenya didn't have the wonderful frog sounds that had been a near constant evening refrain in Swaziland. The intensity varied by season, but there always seemed to be background croaking for any nighttime outdoor activities. Once, during frog mating season we had gone to dinner at Finesse, a restaurant beside the Mbabane River, and we had to yell across the dinner table to be heard above the frogs seeking mates. Wendy loved the frog sounds so much that she made them the ring tone on her cell phone. Strangely, just as she was complaining, we heard some faint frog sounds in the distance and Wendy smiled. She felt she was back in her element. The frog sounds stopped, but they came back for a while later in the evening and then stopped again. The next day we got an e-mail from our daughter saying, "I called your cell phone twice last night, but you didn't answer." Needless to say, Wendy became more attuned to her cell phone ring tone.

After finally getting outside of Nairobi, we decided to do it again for a weekend. We wanted to see the Kenyan coast, and friends had recommended Lamu, an island only a mile offshore. Lamu is a well-known, yet uncrowded, vacation spot. It doesn't have large full-service resorts that cater to families and honeymooners, which is why it's so peaceful and pleasant to visit.

For the Lamu trip, our fun started at the domestic terminal of Nairobi's Jomo Kenyatta airport. As with many airports, the terminal for short, domestic flights in small planes is much more low-key than the ones for large jets. Wendy and I went to the airline counter, and after viewing our identification, the clerk wrote out our flight tickets to Lamu by hand and pointed us to the one gate for all of their flights. There were no signs announcing departures or arrivals, but since the departure lounge was small, the airline employees just yelled out the departures as the planes were ready. At the time when our flight to Lamu was supposed to take off, the attendants were calling out for the flight to Malindi. We were curious but just assumed that flights were backed up and our flight would be next. Finally, the gate attendant called out the last call for Malindi. Then she said, "That means all of the rest of you are going to Mombasa, right?" We quickly ran up and said that we were waiting for the flight to Lamu. She said, "Oh, the flight to Malindi continues on to Lamu." No one had mentioned this previously. We scampered out to the plane.

After briefly stopping in Malindi, our flight continued up the coast to the Lamu airport, which is actually on Manda Island. Although we've landed on smaller and more primitive airstrips, Lamu Airport remains the smallest and least developed airport, with regularly scheduled flights, that we have ever visited (definitely less developed than Matsapha in Swaziland). At Lamu, the departure lounge is a concrete slab with a thatched roof, supported by four poles at the corners of the slab. Blocks of concrete serve as benches for waiting passengers. There is no arrival lounge. Arriving passengers just wait at a particular spot on the dirt to identify their luggage so that it can be loaded into hand carts to be hauled the two hundred yards to the dock. At the dock, luggage is loaded on to one of several small boats that take passengers to their destinations on Lamu Island.

Wendy and I stayed in Shela, about two miles from the larger Lamu Town. It was nearly the end of their tourist season. With the long rains starting soon, all tourist accommodations would close for two months. Because the tourist traffic was low, we were able to get a very nice suite at a reasonable price. Our beachside suite had a bedroom upstairs and a sitting room on the ground floor. Our upstairs bedroom flowed into an enclosed balcony overlooking the bay between Lamu and Manda. The architecture was very much like the Moorish style we had seen in southern Spain, except for the very distinctive front door. Traditional doors on Lamu are carved wood with a large latch and padlock on the outside. The whole ambiance seemed very exotic.

After we arrived and unpacked, our first thought was for lunch, so we walked across the guesthouse courtyard to the dining room. As we walked, we heard a strange noise and noticed two large (approximately two foot long) turtles copulating. It captivated my attention, and I went back to the room to get the camera for a picture. Since turtles are slow at everything, I had plenty of time to get the camera and take pictures. Then we had a nice leisurely lunch. As we walked back, the turtles were still at it!

Lamu Island has no buses or taxis, so from a dock near our guesthouse, we took the short boat ride to Lamu town rather than walk two miles on the road in the blazing sun. Disembarking at Lamu town, we climbed an old staircase, crossed the wide, open, and busy walkway along the waterfront and immediately inserted ourselves into the narrow passageways that threaded through the town. Walking in the town felt as if we were in a rabbit warren or a maze. Fortunately, the town was built mostly on a grid. I was able to remember how many times we'd turned and in which direction, so we kept our orientation and found our way around. We still had to avoid the omnipresent donkeys, which were the trucks of Lamu.

Lamu was unique in many ways. The Kenyan coast was known for the Swahili culture, a mixture of African and Arabian traditions, dress, food, etc., which originated from the Arabian traders who sailed the east coast of Africa for thousands of years. Lamu was the best example of well-preserved traditional Swahili culture. In Lamu, the Swahili language was dominant; there were more Muslims and people of mixed-raced backgrounds, and it wasn't uncommon to see black African women in full, traditional Muslim dress.

In fact, Lamu town, on Lamu Island, seemed like a two-hundred-year-old town from the Middle East. Houses were mostly built from stone and dead coral, harvested from local waters. Many houses were multistory and built facing each other across footpaths barely wide enough for two people to pass. The major thoroughfares were wide enough for two loaded donkeys to pass, but their saddlebags would brush against each other. No streets were accessible to cars, but that was not a problem since the only car on the island belonged to the district commissioner.

In addition to a tour of Lamu town, the other compulsory tourist activity was to take a sundowner cruise on a dhow. Dhows are the sailing boats that Arabian traders have used for over a thousand years along the coast of Africa. They look like the pictures in history books of ancient sailing ships on the Mediterranean. I wasn't that interested in a slow sail around the harbor, but Wendy twisted my arm, and so I agreed. The first part of the sail was uneventful. We saw the sunset, had our cocktails, took pictures, then we set sail to go back to our hotel. Of the two crew members handling our dhow, the younger one now took charge of the sailing. Because of the direction of the wind, the boat set off toward a point up the coast from our hotel. I assumed that at some point, it would tack back in the other direction. I was wrong. Our junior captain headed us straight into the beach about a mile from our hotel. When he realized what was happening, it was too late. We ran aground on the beach. With help from his crewmate who jumped into the shallow water and pushed, he was able to get us freed from the sand. However, the wind was blowing directly onshore, making it impossible to sail the boat. The young crew member began poling from the deck and the other stayed in the water and pushed. After about an hour of this activity, we came upon a dock only a quarter mile from our hotel. We jumped out on the dock and walked the rest of the way. We had a great time, but a message from the U.S. embassy, later in the summer, made us think twice about going back.

Warden Message: Alleged Threat to Kidnap American Citizens Inside Kenya

U.S. Embassy Nairobi has received information that Islamic extremists in southern Somalia may be planning kidnapping operations inside of Kenya. There are indications that Islamic extremists based in Somalia may be planning to target Westerners, especially American citizens, in the Kiwayu Island tourist area and other beach sites frequented by Western travelers on the northeast coast near Somalia. All U.S. citizens in these areas should exercise extreme caution and remain vigilant at all times.

Lamu Island is in the area referred to in the communication. We hadn't been planning another trip there, but this made it certain. Lamu is a wonderful vacation spot, but I didn't want an extended vacation in Somalia.

Later in the summer we had another great experience spending a long weekend with a small group of acquaintances in Tsavo National Park. Someone had discovered that the Kenya Wildlife Service had excess residences within national parks that rented out for nominal fees and had made the reservation for our group. We stayed in the old warden's house, a large, reasonably comfortable but spare facility. It was fine; we weren't expecting a five star.

Tsavo is located southeast of Nairobi on the road to Mombasa, Kenya's major port. The long ride gave us an opportunity to make a number of observations. Since it's one of the most heavily traveled roads in Kenya, one might assume that the Nairobi-Mombasa Road would be well maintained. That would be a bad assumption. There were sections of highway in the middle of the journey that were not bad and allowed driving at the speed limit. There were even sections of four-lane dual carriageway (divided highway). Evidently, the entire highway was supposed to have been dual-carriageway, but for some reason, the money disappeared before the project was completed. Things like that seemed to happen a lot. Often the situation was just ignored. Sometimes the perpetrators were publicly exposed with accompanying outrage, but then things would just blow over and there would be no consequences, even when there was significant evidence of criminal activity by politicians. For example, read *It's Our Turn to Eat: The Story of a Kenyan Whistle-Blower* by Michela Wrong.

In contrast to the reasonably good stretches of road farther away, the sections near Nairobi were terrible. In addition to the standard broken pavement and potholes, another phenomenon could be observed. In cross-section, the rutted pavement looked like two capital letter *U*s side by side, connected by a convex curve in the middle. This pattern had obviously been generated by overloaded trucks and an underconstructed highway. Someone probably made money on underbuilding the highway, and someone else was probably continuing to make money by allowing overloaded trucks to travel it. Without even careful observation, it was obvious that Kenya imported heavier goods (machinery, vehicles, and equipment) than it exported (flowers, coffee, tea). The road ruts were much deeper on the highway coming into Nairobi (sometimes a foot deep) than they were going out to Mombasa.

Despite the road, we were looking forward to visiting Tsavo, which is a large but lesser visited game park. It was made somewhat famous by the movie *The Ghost and the Darkness* with Michael Douglas and Val Kilmer. The very scary movie, based on the book *The Man-eaters of Tsavo*, tells the true story of a pair of lions at the turn of the twentieth century who sought out humans to kill and eat. During this period when the Trans-Kenyan Railway was being built, these lions killed over one hundred people. Since the period described in the movie, the lions from Tsavo have been involved in numerous other killings. Some people have speculated that these lions are a different and more aggressive subspecies. Studies have supposedly shown that the Tsavo lions have shorter manes and a higher level of testosterone than lions found elsewhere. We didn't know how much was real and how much was hype for the tourists, but we were going to be careful.

The warden's house was spacious with lots of beds for the eight of us. Wendy and I got lucky and slept in the master bedroom. Despite being in the middle of nowhere, the house came with comforts. The caretaker was our cook, and he had a stove that ran on bottled gas. The diesel generator ran when we needed light. There was even a hot water heater that consisted of two recycled steel drums with a fire pit underneath. When we wanted to take a hot shower, we just asked the caretaker to build a fire.

The major attraction of the house was a porch with viewing deck above, which faced a waterhole. We looked forward to seeing the game in close proximity, but based on experience, we knew that came with potential downsides. We asked the care-taker if it was necessary to close all the windows at night to keep out baboons. He said baboons weren't a problem but not to go out after 11:00 p.m. because that's when lions often came to the watering hole. Every night, we were all safely locked inside the house well before 11:00 p.m.

After settling into our rooms and having a nice "sund-owner" gin and tonic on the viewing deck, we all sat down to dinner on the front porch. Only one couple knew everyone in the group. The rest of us felt like we were part of a group that had been assembled for some auspicious (or suspicious) activity that was about to unfold. It was like the opening scene in one of those movies where someone in the group gets murdered in the middle of the night and the rest of the group is trapped and can't leave.

As we ate and drank, the mood lightened up, and we became fascinated by the geckos climbing on the brick wall next to the dining table. Five geckos were congregating around the light-bulb, which naturally was attracting large moths and other insects. The geckos were like a group of teenage males out for a Friday night adventure. They were hanging out together but competing at the same time. We became fascinated as they would carefully stalk the moths so as to not scare them off and then pounce when they got just close enough. The competitive stakes were high because the gecko that captured each moth got to eat it all. All of the geckos were incredibly fast, but there was one who outshone the rest and got to eat a lot more moths. Another was very clever and was able to catch a cricket. As the alcohol flowed, we became more and more engaged and entertained by the details of the digestion as well as the capture. The geckos invariably caught the moths by the tail and then proceeded to devour them like a snake swallowing a pig. The moths continued to wriggle around and flap their wings as if to escape, but none ever did. Once they were caught by the geckos, the end was inevitable.

The waterhole adjacent to the house did not disappoint. During the day, various animals wandered up to have a drink or a splash and then wandered away. We saw impala, waterbucks, and warthogs. But the real action was at night. In addition to the smaller game, a family of elephants visited both nights; and on Saturday night, we were visited by a herd of fifty buffalo.

Elephants and buffalo weren't our only night visitors. During dinner, one of our fellow guests used the bathroom off our bedroom. Shortly after emerging, he stated that there was a "monster in our bathroom sink." I went in to check and everyone on the veranda heard when I yelled out a two-word expletive. In the sink was what appeared to be a very sturdy spider more than six inches in diameter. Upon further observation, it might have been an insect since it seemed to walk on only six legs. But then there were the two additional forelimbs that ended in menacing pincers, certainly for grasping and conveying prey to its mouth. It could have easily been a model for those movie creatures that come from outer space to take over the world. Thank goodness the light was on.

I didn't know if this creature was poisonous or would bite, but I didn't want to find out. Before doing anything, I had to get a picture, but then I planned to smash it with my heavy shoe. I was shocked when one of the women in our party intervened. She knew that it couldn't stay in the sink, but she didn't want it killed. Being braver than I, she managed to trap the creature in a covered plastic bowl and deposited it outside at a safe distance from the house. I showed the picture to the rest of our party, but Wendy didn't want to have nightmares (who knows, it might have had a mate lurking nearby) so she didn't even look at the photo until several days later back in Nairobi.

The next day, we discovered that the other bathroom had more but less threatening visitors, tiny frogs hiding in the corners and crevices of the sink, tub, and toilet. The poor fellow, who had discovered the creature in our sink the night before, also discovered the first frogs. He was doing his business when apparently a frog leaped out at him as he flushed the toilet. We don't know who was more frightened. Upon more careful inspection, approximately twelve tiny frogs were discovered. From then on, most of the women were a little nervous about sitting down.

A Quick Visit to the United States

And Going Home to Nairobi

In June, our daughter, Diana, graduated from Ross University Medical School, an event not to be missed. The ceremony was held in Lincoln Center in New York City. Wendy left Nairobi earlier than I because she wanted to visit friends in California and my mother in Washington DC. I flew straight to New York. Wendy had numerous travel problems with weather and mismanaged luggage by a now-merged airline (whose nickname was north-worst), but after a last-minute $100 round-trip taxi ride from Manhattan to Newark to pick up luggage, we were all safely in New York with our clothes.

The graduation ceremony was wonderful! Avery Fisher Hall at Lincoln Center is an elegant and prestigious venue for a graduation, and the graduates looked so impressive in their caps and gowns. Following the ceremony, we took lots of pictures with Lincoln Center providing many great backgrounds. Then we headed for a late lunch with friends and family at a nearby restaurant, the first of a number of celebrations over the next two days. On Saturday, we had the main party. It was a late afternoon cocktail reception. We had commandeered the bar area of an uptown restaurant, which was packed with relatives and friends, some who had known Diana for twenty-five years and some who had known Wendy for nearly forty. It was wonderful to share the occasion, and everyone who came was greeted by Sallie Mae, Diana's recently acquired and appropriately named five-foot-high stuffed animal giraffe.

For those who didn't already know, we recounted the story behind Sallie Mae. It started during a family visit to New York when Diana was eight years old. One of the sights we saw was the famous FAO Schwartz toy store with its collection of unique and amazing toys. Among the especially attention-grabbing items was an eight-foot-high toy giraffe, priced at about $2,500. Diana had asked me to buy it for her. I told her that I would buy it for her when she graduated from medical school since Diana already knew she wanted to be a doctor. My answer got me off the hook at the time, but I really meant it. I never forgot my promise and neither did Diana.

Some months before graduation, Diana let me know that she remembered my commitment but that she was releasing me from it because she wouldn't have enough room in an apartment, and it would be an excessive amount of money to spend. However, I still wanted to remember the commitment with a symbolic gesture. I searched online for various types of toy giraffes. I looked at many small toys at varying prices, and then I found the one I had to have. It was a five-foot-high stuffed animal with a cute face and a reasonable price, shipping included! Several days later, Diana got back to her apartment just as the UPS delivery man arrived with a large box. Diana was frequently accepting packages for her neighbor, so she assumed this was just another. She was very surprised when the UPS man said it was addressed to her. She muscled the box inside and opened it carefully. When she opened it up, she smiled widely and felt a lump grow in her throat. She immediately called me to say thank you because without reading the card, she knew where it had come from. Then she began to think of names. She finally settled on Sallie Mae to represent the government loans that had helped to pay for her medical school tuition.

After my very short trip to the United States, I arrived back in Nairobi. It was very strange to be on vacation in the United States and go back to Nairobi to live. The Nairobi weather was very different from what we had left just two weeks earlier. It had gotten overcast, gray and cool (less than 70 degrees F). The locals called this cold and had been warning us that it would come in July. Occasionally it got "really cold" (almost down to 60 degrees F). It was amusing to see the locals bundled up in their heavy parkas and wool hats.

As I jumped back into my daily routine starting with walking to work, some things were very familiar, such as inhaling the smoke of open trash fires and the sooty exhaust from diesel trucks, which probably combined to equal the harmful effects of smoking a pack a day. Other things seemed new as I saw them in more depth, such as the terrain over which I walked to work every day. In some places, I walked on real, raised, concrete sidewalks. In other areas, the sidewalks were at street level but protected with steel posts that prevented cars from running over pedestrians. Some places once had sidewalks but were now covered with intermittent concrete and broken rubble over bare dirt. Along some roads, broad dirt shoulders substituted for sidewalks, but matatus cruised onto these reck-lessly to disgorge their passengers and zip away. In some places, the dirt shoulders were below the road surface and only wide enough for a narrow footpath with a deep drainage ditch on the other side. Along other roads, the only choice was walking on the roadway, facing traffic as we were taught as children (except that in Kenya, it meant walking on the right instead of the left). Usually this was safe, except when drivers made extra lanes to pass cars they didn't feel were going fast enough. Even this was usually safe because you could see the cars speeding toward you and squeeze to the edge of the road as they passed. Unfortunately, that didn't cover every situation, as we learned one morning when we walked out our apartment gate, turned right to face the traffic, and were nearly hit from behind by a matatu speeding down the wrong side of the road. He didn't want to wait in the line of cars backed up at the stop sign. Welcome back to Nairobi.

As I became more attentive to the details of my walking, I planned my route more carefully to safely navigate the traffic, and I developed two important new safety rules. My first rule, opposite of what we were taught as children, was to cross only in the middle of the block, not at intersections. In the middle of the block, traffic is only coming at you from two directions. In the middle of the block, you can see cars from a distance, judge their speed, and calculate when to bolt across the street. At an intersection, there are no controls (or they're ignored); traffic can come at you from at least four directions; and cars are unpredictable as they jockey for position, trying to outmaneuver their competitors. My second rule applied to actually crossing the street. Before crossing, look back and forth continuously. First, because the situation is constantly changing in unpredictable ways; and second, because if you grew up in the United States where the traffic drives on the right you will instinctively look the wrong way for oncoming traffic and then step in front of a speeding truck. Obviously, few people make this mistake more than once.

Of course, sometimes you can't avoid crossing at intersections. At one place on my way to work there was a traffic circle with multiple streets coming together. At this point I just had to follow rule number two and seize the opportunities as they came. These opportunities usually came when cross traffic provided blocking, but I still had to be watchful for crossing cars that decided to turn, without signaling of course. It was exciting every day.

Matooke in Uganda

Genocide Memories in Rwanda

Wendy and I flew to Kampala again to work with Erastus as he built up the Uganda TechnoServe program. Our flight was supposed to arrive at 2:00 p.m., so I thought I would have plenty of time to get to the TechnoServe office and get on a conference call by four. I say "office" because I had heard that TechnoServe would have a working office by the date of our arrival. Our flight arrived a bit late and immediately after another plane, so the lines were long at immigration. When the TechnoServe driver picked us up, we were told that an office had been rented, but it did not have furniture, telephone service, etc. We went to our hotel, and with traffic, arrived right at 4:00 p.m. I asked to go quickly to our room so that I could get on the call, using my cell phone. At about 4:10, I dialed into the call. After beeping a number of times for no apparent reason throughout the call, my cell phone cut me off after about forty minutes.

I didn't know why the cell phone was no longer working, but I thought I might be able to get back on the call using Skype. So I went to reception to see how to get on to the Internet. Their process to get on to the Internet was to sell access codes that were good for a fixed period of time. I agreed to buy some codes, but they were out. The woman at reception promised to call the

246

service provider and then send someone to my room with the codes. A half hour later, someone came to the room with the access codes. I tried them, but couldn't get on. I called reception, and they said they would send someone up to check on my problem. About fifteen minutes later, a very pleasant young woman came to our room carrying a laptop. After looking at my computer and then trying a few things on her own laptop, she apologized that the wireless wasn't receiving in our room. She indicated that it was working in the corridor and garden area, just outside my room. At this point, I was certain that the conference call had finished and decided it was time for cocktail hour. C'est L'Afrique!

The next morning, Friday, Wendy and I were working on our computers in the small garden area outside of our room where the wireless network was working. We were waiting to go to a meeting with a potential donor. Erastus arrived and told us our meeting had been pushed out to the following week and so we had nothing scheduled for the day. We had planned to go to the field to observe the TechnoServe matooke project on Monday, but now the logistics would work better to leave right away. Matooke (ma-toke-kay) is a member of the banana family, called a starch banana, that is boiled when green and eaten almost like mashed potatoes. William, a project manager who reported to Erastus, was already planning to take Payson Bullard (son of the TechnoServe founder) to the field to document our success on this project, and this way, we could all go together. So we quickly packed up some clothes and set off from Kampala toward Mbarara (hum the *M*, but longer than in Swaziland, bah-rahr-rah) in the southwest corner of Uganda, near the DRC (Democratic Republic of Congo), which gave Wendy some pause, but we headed out anyway.

During this time period, the eastern region of the DRC continued to experience unrest due to the multiple factions asserting their power against the weak central government.

Some of these factions were guerilla groups left over from the 1994 "troubles" in Rwanda and the resulting migration, and some were more modern criminal gangs engaged in illegal mining. Often the lines were blurred, but there were periodic flare-ups in the conflict, which usually resulted in thousands of refugees fleeing across the border into Uganda.

For much of the drive, the road was incredibly good compared to what we had previously experienced in Africa. It was like a two-lane rural road in California. It would be interesting to know the history of various roads, as to when they were built and who built them because there was such diversity in the quality. We heard that President Museveni had originally come from southwest Uganda, so the roads leading to his home territory were especially good.

Our drive reminded me of my impressions from our previous trip. Uganda was green everywhere. Some people would say verdant. Practically the whole country gets enough rain for good agriculture. As we drove through farmland, my favorite view was overlooking the hills covered with tea plants. As it's growing, tea is very dense. The low shrubs are very bushy and planted close together. From a distance, the overall effect is of a thick-pile green carpet covering the hills. I wanted to reach out and feel its dense softness.

About halfway through our trip for the day, we stopped for lunch in Mubende (Moo-ben-day) at a café William knew. We parked in a dirt lot in front of a nondescript concrete-block building. We walked inside where it was dark because there were few windows and no lights. The only electricity was being used for two soft drink coolers. William ordered food for all of us, and we walked outside to sit on the porch and wait for our food. The porch seemed to be the place to eat because there were several sets of turquoise, molded plastic tables and chairs, all with dark blue, oilcloth tablecloths imprinted with beer advertising. There were no other customers, but it was past normal lunchtime.

When lunch came, it was our first introduction to the typical diet in southwestern Uganda: nearly 100 percent carbo-hydrates! We had large helpings of rice, Irish (white) potatoes, sweet potatoes, and matooke. There was some peanut sauce to go on the matooke, which would have provided some protein and fat, but it was burned so we didn't eat it. There were also two small pieces of chicken to share amongst the four of us. It didn't look that appealing, so Wendy and I deferred to William and Payson who gladly devoured it with just a few bites. Later, when we reached our hotel, Wendy had an attack of hypogly-cemia, and she had to be very careful over the next few days to get some protein with her meals.

Since the next day was Saturday, we decided to visit Queen Elizabeth Park. We couldn't get reservations at the lodge inside the park, so we stayed in the town of Kasese (Kuh-say-say), just a few miles north. To quote the Lonely Planet Guide to East Africa, "Kasese is a boom-and-bust town that tasted glory during the copper years...but generally seems to have passed its use-by-date. It's a small, hot, dusty, quiet town in a relatively infertile and lightly populated area, and it wears an air of per-manent torpor." I thought it was a perfect description. We were among the few guests at the best hotel in town. The accom-modations were Spartan but adequate, and the modest dining room had a diverse menu with some very tasty meals, especially for $7 apiece.

On Saturday, William, Wendy, Payson, and I visited Queen Elizabeth Park, bordered on the north by the Rwenzori (*Rw* as in Rwanda-en-zoree) Mountains (also called the Mountains of the Moon) and on the west by Lake Edward (its outflow is ultimately a tributary of the Nile) that is shared with the Democratic Republic of the Congo. The park contains Lake

George, which flows into Lake Edward through the Kazinga Channel. The many bodies of water encourage the varied species of animals and particularly birds that are found in the park, and the number one tourist activity is to take a cruise on the Kazinga Channel to see the wildlife.

On our cruise, we saw the expected crocodiles and hippos, as well as lots of buffalo and a few elephants. However, the more interesting aspect was the bird life. Queen Elizabeth Park is purportedly home to six hundred species of birds, and we saw many of the most interesting ones. We had seen the majestic fish eagles and giant goliath herons before, but here we saw many new species including the wonderfully colored saddle-billed stork. This tall elegant bird, with its primarily black and white coloring, is initially reminiscent of a conservative waiter in a tuxedo, but the bright red and yellow highlights on its beak quickly establish it as a rakish dandy.

As we cruised the Kazinga Channel, our guide pointed out the small fishing village where he grew up, which is still allowed to remain within the park's boundaries. He also recounted several stories that highlighted the unique dangers of living in rural Africa. The most memorable was from his early teen years when he and two friends were walking home one night after playing games at another friend's home. A lion had come into their village and was watching in the dark as the three boys approached. Our guide and one friend walked by the lion, but the lion attacked their other friend. The first two boys ran and escaped, but in the morning, the villagers found remains of the other boy's clothes and skeleton. Several other people in the village had been killed by lions in the intervening years. As if to drive the point home about the unique dangers of living in rural Africa, that evening we heard that earlier in the day a speeding bus on the nearby highway had hit a wandering hippopotamus. Several passengers on the bus, along with the hippo, had been killed. At times it was easy to get comfortable and complacent about living in Africa, like being a tourist and only experiencing the interesting highlights. But then, a story like these would wake us up and remind us how different our life was from those around us.

We spent the next few nights in Mbarara as we visited the matooke farmers that TechnoServe was supporting. Again, we stayed in the best hotel in town, which was slightly better than Kasese, but outside of major cities, there was no understanding of the quality of accommodations and service expected by Westerners. The employees were very friendly, but things just didn't work. The accommodations were adequate, but all of the rooms had holes in the window screens and bare bulbs for light. Also, in our room, the hot water in the bathroom sink didn't work. We mentioned the hot water problem, but no one seemed to particularly care and no attempt was made to fix it. TIA once again.

I still don't know if the hotel staff thought they couldn't do anything or thought it wasn't their job to do anything or if they just didn't understand that something needed to be done. I'm sure the behavior was learned over many years and probably generations. Maybe it started with paternalistic colonialism. Maybe it starts over again with every individual facing so many challenges that she feels overwhelmed and powerless to make change. It's always easier to conform than to fight the system, and I think that's what most people do to get by. I often did it myself.

However, there were times when I could take action and change my situation. As we settled into our room, I sat down on my bed. My butt seemed to sink almost to the floor. The middle of my bed had no support for the mattress. I didn't want to change rooms, so being an engineer by training, a problem fixer by nature and knowing how difficult it would be to get someone else to do anything, I attacked the problem myself. I took the mattress off the bed to reveal the support structure.

The mattress was supposed to fit into a frame and be supported by a series of slats that fit into the frame. A few of the slats were broken and many were just lying loose on the floor. I set to work. I moved the broken slats to the foot of the frame, where there would be less weight, and placed the best slats from the floor under the center where they would support my butt. To remove or replace a slat, it had to be bowed and then maneuvered into or out of a slot in the frame, so this exercise was physical as well as mental. However, when I finished, my bed was well supported, and I could sleep just fine. This was Africa, but I could still fight back.

On Monday, William, Wendy, Payson, and I visited the matooke farmers whom TechnoServe had been assisting. Beyond helping them adopt good agricultural practices, TechnoServe's primary support had been in organizing the farmers into groups to aggregate their produce and to connect them with buyers. TechnoServe had organized "markets" where farmers would deliver their matooke for buyers to purchase and load onto trucks. This is a simple but critical innovation in many TechnoServe programs and always the one that farmers appreciate most. It provides farmers with a reliable market for their produce and buyers with a reliable supply of matooke. Most importantly, the market can sustain itself when TechnoServe leaves.

As we talked with the matooke farmers, they were very thankful for their increased incomes resulting from TechnoServe's support. They talked about being able to send their children to school, to purchase irrigation equipment, and in some cases, to buy a cell phone. After Payson had finished asking them questions, we offered to answer questions from the farmers. Although they asked several general questions, they primarily wanted to know if we were capable of increasing the market for matooke in the United States. They were very disappointed to hear that no one in the United States had ever heard of matooke, much less ate it.

As I have visited farmers and other small entrepreneurs, it never ceases to amaze me how creative some people can become when given the opportunity to participate in capitalism. In addition to matooke farming, many of the group members were beginning to get into other commercial activities, including matooke trading. One member was buying produce from his neighbors, renting trucks for transporting it and selling it in Entebbe. The most interesting group was the one who had noticed what they thought was a good opportunity to make a profit in beans. They noticed that beans always sold for a low price at harvest time and a higher price later when the supply had diminished. To take advantage of this, they pooled some of their matooke profits, borrowed a little more money, and bought beans when the price was low at harvest time. They were holding the beans to sell at a higher price. In essence, they had independently discovered leveraged commodity trading. I expect next year they'll have a hedge fund and be trading derivatives.

After only a few weeks back in Nairobi, I left again to attend the TechnoServe East African senior staff meeting in Kigali, Rwanda. It was my first time in Rwanda. I was only there for a few days, and I never got outside of Kigali, but Rwanda looked like a beautiful country. It was so hard to imagine what had happened there.

Kigali was like a smaller version of Kampala, without the paralyzing traffic. Built on green hills, Kigali presented continuously attractive vistas in every direction. Driving through the city, it was hard not to immediately notice how nice the main roads were. They appeared newly constructed and were flanked by a myriad of new buildings with more under construction. Even outside the commercial and government areas, the mostly brick and terracotta houses looked relatively new and well-kept although modest and aligned along dirt roads. I was sure that much of the new construction was being financed by major companies and countries with guilty consciences. I just hoped that it would contribute to sustainable growth in Rwanda's economy. I firmly believe that if there are enough good jobs and business opportunities that everyone will live together peacefully.

With limited free time, I went to the memorial center, which is focused on genocides, primarily of the twentieth century. Surrounded by beautiful but understated memorial gardens, the center is built on a mass burial site containing the remains of 250,000 people. The memorial building itself contains exhibits explaining the various genocides of the last century, ultimately leading up to the events in 1994 in Rwanda. The exhibits were excellent, combining scholarly descriptions with displays that evoked powerful emotions. It immediately reminded me of the Holocaust Museum in Washington DC as well as what I knew about the holocaust itself. Confronted with incomprehensible events like these, I often try to achieve some understanding by putting them into frameworks, comparing and contrasting them to other things I know. I couldn't help myself. My mind had to start processing these horrific events.

Compared to the "troubles" (as they refer to it) in Rwanda, the Holocaust was bigger, more well-organized, and mechanized. It was carried out by a highly structured and controlled society. Many of the people involved excused themselves by saying, "I didn't know what was happening," or "I was just doing my job." All of this was possible during the Holocaust because most of the killing wasn't up close and personal, and most Germans could ignore what was going on and go about their daily business. In Rwanda, genocide was very visible, and a large proportion of society was directly involved. In Rwanda, fewer people were killed, but it happened in a shorter period of time and most of the killing was very personal. There were no railroad cars, concentration camps, or gas chambers. People died, often at the hand of their neighbors, from individual bullets or more often a blow from a machete, and the dead bodies were very visible.

The thought occurred to me that in mathematics most people understand infinity as one concept, but mathematicians who study the concept in detail actually define different types of infinities. I wondered if there are different types of infinite evil.

While the "troubles" in Rwanda have long since passed, and the world has moved on, not everyone is living happily ever after. The consequences of 1994 live on today. While some of the major perpetrators of the genocide have been tried and convicted by the International Court in Arusha, Tanzania, many who were not caught continue to pursue their evil aims across the border in the Democratic Republic of Congo where they fled in 1994. Although inside Rwanda things have been mostly peaceful since 1994, just across the border, there have been multiple wars and almost continuous sporadic fighting. Once the genie of racial hatred leaves the bottle, it is incredibly difficult to put back.

Sometime later, back in Nairobi, I read *Shake Hands with the Devil* by Romeo Allaire, the Canadian general in charge of the small United Nations peacekeeping mission in Rwanda when the killing started. It is an excellent but very depressing book about his frustration at not being able to stop the killing because no one would listen to him seriously and supply the necessary resources when they could have helped. During the day, I tried to put the Rwanda story out of my mind, but I continued to read in the evenings, and my weekly mefloquine nightmares took a very dark turn.

An Inspiring Visit

Shortly after arriving back in Nairobi, Wendy discovered that she would be hosting a representative from the Nike Foundation, which was sponsoring TechnoServe's Young Women in Enterprise (YWE) program. Although I had previously visited a YWE site in a rural area, most of the YWE work was in the slums of Nairobi.

As Wendy described the visit in her blog:

We drove 30 minutes out of downtown Nairobi into the large Mukuru slum. All Nairobi slums actually consist of multiple villages, though as an outsider I couldn't tell where one ended and another began.

Led by TechnoServe's Young Women in Enterprise team and alumna Cecilia, we entered one slum village where Cecilia worked and lived. There were hundreds of rows of hundreds of one-room, tin-roofed-and-walled huts, most windowless, with dirt floors and cloth as doors when the solid doors were open to the streets. The streets consisted of mud with a liberal coating of trash and garbage, often split by running water, the source of which I didn't want to consider.

Due to these conditions, the main 3 modes of transportation are walking, pull-carts, and bicycles (all Dutch according to our Nike guest who lived 5 yrs. in Amsterdam). We did have to move out of the way once for a small pickup and once for an older Mercedes sedan, probably a landlord. All the slum lands are owned privately and tenants pay rent to the landlords. Water is shared from a single faucet on most streets. Electricity is usually pirated from the few paying customers. Most often, shops are the "store-fronts" of people's living quarters that line the main streets where people walk, children play, and the sewage system runs. After a few minutes of getting our balance on the slippery road surface, we crossed a bridge over a river which just seemed like another branch of the sewage system. As we entered the "main" area of the slum village, I made several observations: how cleanly dressed most people are, despite their homes and streets; most children and adults wear flip-flops everywhere, even when warmly dressed in hoods and sweaters; and like kids anywhere, large groups play together then run up to anyone with a camera so they can be immortalized while being silly.

Despite the environment, the Mukuru visit was very uplifting because the tour was coordinated by Cecilia (more below) with a few of her friends from the Young Women in Enterprise program. We were invited into the home of one of the YWE Club young women, where on the tarp-covered wall above the mother's head was the plaque her daughter had won at the Young Women in Enterprise business plan competitions. This older mother had 7 daughters and 1 son. The parents (read, father) decided to educate the son and not the daughters. Unfortunately, the young man was electrocuted and the father disappeared, leaving

257

the minimally-schooled mother and daughters to fend for themselves. Five sisters still live with their mom in the one-room homestead. Nearby one daughter, the YWE alumna, runs a small kiosk where passers-by can purchase hot or cold milk in mugs (which she washes and re-uses). We visited another YWE alumna's shop selling sweets. This single young mother of 2 had been divorced, though her ex-husband was in the shop when we arrived, now attracted by her earning a living . . .

Our final Mukuru stop was at the home of our tour guide, Cecilia, who won the YWE regional first prize for her knitted clothes' business and was a speaker at the YWE final competition. A good entrepreneur, she brought product samples and sold a number to the judges and guests, including me, at the competition. I ordered 5 scarves in Kenyan colors, gave her my business card and asked her to call me when they were ready. A week later she called to ask when she could deliver them. Since I was in Uganda, I requested she come to the office on Wednesday the following week. When I asked how much the scarves were she said Ksh. 500 (~ U.S. $7)—I assumed per scarf. The next Tuesday night she text messaged me (SMS is the local term) to confirm I would be in the office Wednesday afternoon. She arrived on time, wearing one of her colorful scarves on her head. I paid Ksh. 500 for all 5 scarves—her pricing. I then told her that she could get much higher price in Nairobi proper and if she would come back to me with her competitive research, I would buy many more scarves at the higher price. Two weeks later, she called to say that she hadn't had the time to do the research, so we discussed meeting in July after I returned from the U.S. to research together.

In her Mukuru home on July 4th, she showed the

Nike guest her products and knitting machine. He bought a baby outfit and scarf. Cecilia explained how she almost had enough money to buy a more compact knitting machine for herself. Then she would hire and train another girl to use the current device, thus expanding her business capacity by 100 percent.

It is people like Cecilia who are the hope for Africa, especially African women. Her smile and enthusiasm are contagious. She is a natural leader, organizing her Mukuru YWE alumnae and friends to build better businesses through improved record-keeping, stock purchasing, etc. I fully expect that in 10 years or less, with her entrepreneurial savvy, she will run a very successful business with multiple employees and locations. With her leadership skills, I predict she will someday be a Kenya Member of Parliament.

A woman selling used clothes and other goods at a typical market on the outskirts of Nairobi at this typical "kiosk" which can be seen anywhere outside the main office districts of Nairobi.

Lake Nakuru National Park, located in central Kenya, is home to many thousands of flamingoes which love the plankton that grow extensively in the alkaline Lake Nakuru and similar nearby lakes.

Peponi Hotel is the premier place to stay on the tiny island of Lamu off the coast north of Mombasa, Kenya, known for its mixed Arab-African aka Swahili culture.

The traditional buildings on Lamu Island off the coast north of Mombasa, Kenya, are constructed with "bricks" containing local shells, as seen from the top of one building in Lamu Town.

Along the Kenyan coast and around Lamu Island, a key form of transportation is the "Dhow" boat—viewed from our hotel. Typically used by old Arab traders, they still move most of the island's goods, local folks, and tourists to and from the mainland.

"Matooke" are starch-bananas (vs. our typical, sweet banana), which are a staple in most of Uganda. TechnoServe Uganda advisors, seen here, work with Matooke farmers to improve their livelihoods by increasing harvests, providing market connections, and helping diversify their crops.

Ugandan smallholder "Matooke" farmers often transport their harvest by bicycle to their local co-op on market day.

Matooke bunches are consolidated at regional co-op sites to be trucked to larger Ugandan markets like Kampala.

Advised by TechnoServe Uganda staff, some Matooke farmers have diversified their crops with other produce like potatoes, seen here with a woman farmer.

Some Matooke farmers, seen in central Uganda, have added dairy cows to supplement their income.

Based on TechnoServe Uganda advisors' recommendations, some Matooke farmers have diversified their income with goats, for their milk, and chickens, for their meat.

To memorialize the estimated 500,000 to 1 million Tutsis and moderate Hutu tribespeople slaughtered during 100 days in mid-1994, Rwanda constructed a garden and museum for viewing by both Rwandans and foreign visitors.

The Grand Prize Winner of the Young Women in Enterprise (YWE) Business Plan Competition in 2007 was Cecilia Katungwa from the Mukuru slum in Nairobi. Besides a new mobile phone she won the equivalent of several hundred dollars to expand her successful but small knitted-clothes business.

Wendy accompanied her Young Women in Enterprise (YWE) colleagues in giving a tour of the Mukuru slum in Nairobi to the visiting Nike Foundation representative. Entering the slum required crossing over the "river."

The purpose of touring Nairobi's Mukuru slum with the Nike Foundation representative (the major program donor) was to visit a few Young Women in Enterprise (YWE) members, requiring us to walk down typical streets there.

One YWE program manager, Esta Kamau, led us toward Cecilia Katungwa's and other YWE club members' businesses down a side street through Nairobi's Mukuru slum, when we were visiting there with the Nike Foundation representative.

One YWE club member's business in Nairobi's Mukuru slum was a milk kiosk where the young woman owner provided healthy boiled milk in clean cups to the local residents, like the children seen here.

Managing Budgets and Donors

$\mathcal{A}$s with many companies and non-profit organizations, in TechnoServe, fall is the time for planning and budgeting for the upcoming year. In every organization, matching expenses with revenues is a challenge. There are always too many good ways to spend money to improve performance than can be justified by existing or planned revenues. Hopeful managers who submit prospective budgets are almost always disappointed as their superiors are forced to cut back their anticipated expenses. Although I had gone through this many times in the commercial sector, I had to learn some new twists common to nonprofit development organizations. As with most other similar organizations, TechnoServe's revenues come primarily from project awards. Government agencies, such as USAID, corporations, and large foundations provide TechnoServe with a fixed amount of money for a particular period of time to accomplish specific goals. For example, USAID might provide TechnoServe with a three-year grant to increase the incomes of cashew farmers in a particular area by 50 percent. Since most projects last several years, the majority of the next year's funding is already committed when the annual budget has to be created. However, the abrupt starts and stops of project funding make it very difficult to create a consistent level of funding and a smooth budget.

The idea of programs with fixed budgets, specific objectives, and limited timeframes is a good one for accountability; but it generates challenges for the organizations receiving the grants. As anyone who has worked in a project-based organization knows, there is always a challenge of matching resources (primarily people) to a changing workload as projects come and go. It was a particularly challenging year for the Kenya office since a big project was ending, meaning that a lot of people would be available but would not immediately have work. We had proposed a number of new projects but hadn't heard back yet from the potential donors. For some organizations, this would not have been a problem because they hire people to do a specific project and immediately let them go when the project finishes. TechnoServe believes that it can produce a greater impact by having a longer-term commitment to its employees and continuity in its ongoing development operations in the countries where it has its offices. They try to maintain a portfolio of development projects and balance resources to meet the requirements.

Usually TechnoServe was able to maintain a core of highly experienced employees in all of the country offices, but there were fluctuations in employment levels as programs came and went. Some practices in the donor community make this situation harder for all development organizations. First is the project orientation of nearly all donors. This is a manageable challenge when the projects are long enough (minimum three years) and the donors' priorities don't change too radically over time. Some donors are very good about establishing and maintaining their direction; others jump around to the "cause du jour," making it difficult for their grantees to have any continuity in their programs. Another challenge is that donors want their recipients to spend exactly what they have been granted, no more and no less. In the private sector, it is usually good to come in under budget on projects. In the development community, donors want you to spend all of the money they gave you to do exactly what you said you would do. They don't want you to shift their money to other programs or to give it back to them. And of course, they are not willing to pay for overruns. Under-budget projects are usually handled through "no cost extensions" that allow the projects to continue a little longer than planned and help a few more people.

A third challenge to nonprofit organizations is donors' previously mentioned aversion to anything called overhead or administration. Donors justifiably want as much money as possible to be spent directly on the intended beneficiaries in the field and not on people doing administration in offices. However, someone has to answer the phone and greet people at the office door; someone has to keep track of the money being spent and someone has to be developing a proposal for the next project. Donors recognize the necessity for all of these; they just don't want to pay for them. They want these expenses to be paid from some other source of funds. One of the consequences of all of these practices is that organizations like TechnoServe cannot afford to have employees without immediate project assignments. That is the reason we were so concerned as we prepared our budgets.

Along with the budgets, Fred had a number of people in the office preparing concept papers for potential new projects. A concept paper is a three-to-five-page document describing a potential project, its costs, and its benefits. These are used to begin a discussion with a donor who may be interested in funding the project. If a donor is interested, a detailed proposal is developed. Wendy and I became the reviewers and editors for all of the concept papers. Although we had no experience as English teachers or professional editors, our skills in English and mine in finance were critical.

Although all of our office colleagues spoke English very well, we discovered that for most of them, it was their third language. Typically, their first language had been the local tribal language for the area where they were born. Their second language had usually been Swahili. Finally, at some point in school, they had begun to learn English, and they developed their proficiency throughout their further education and business careers. English was the language of business, but most people in Nairobi felt more comfortable speaking Swahili in social settings. On top of this, most of our colleagues were skilled in consulting with smallholder farmers or small business owners. Their skills were not in proposal writing or cost-benefit analysis. For a while, Wendy and I felt like teachers correcting compositions. Although many of the ideas for new projects were good, they were often not well presented in a well-structured and logical manner. And some were not financially justifiable. We reviewed, edited, and commented on the papers and then returned them to their authors for rewriting and more review. After several rounds, we got a number of concept papers into very good shape and sent them on to headquarters for donor discussions.

Finals of the Business Plan Competition

$\mathcal{K}$enya's business plan competition (Believe, Begin, Become—BBB) had progressed through several phases as contestants' business ideas were turned into business plans while the contestants advanced through several rounds of competition. After the first judging, the remaining contestants got training in business concepts and the necessary components of a business plan. As they reached the finals, contestants received individual mentoring to refine their business plans for presentation to judges selected from the local business community. The top prizes were cash grants to establish or grow a business. Secondary prizes consisted of further professional coaching on establishing a business.

Although TechnoServe had previously run these competitions in numerous countries, the participation and competition in Kenya was at a level we had never seen before. The Kenya BBB got nearly six thousand entries. The TechnoServe BBB team had carefully developed the logistics and recruited volunteers from the United States, Europe, and Korea to handle the anticipated large number of entries, but it was still a huge challenge. It was also very exciting, both inside and outside of TechnoServe, to watch the contestants make progress as they were narrowed down. Wendy and I were excited and booked our return flight to the United States so that we could watch the final awards presentation.

The final ceremony was held in the Jomo Kenyatta Convention Center in downtown Nairobi, an impressive venue that stands out on the Nairobi skyline. The main hall is arranged as a circular amphitheater with tiered seating, somewhat like a smaller version of the UN General Assembly Hall. The atmosphere was charged as well-dressed finalists and their supporters arrived from provinces throughout Kenya. Bright lights glared as sponsors and government officials were interviewed and videotaped. The proceedings began with speeches praising the contestants as well as extolling the importance of the competition and its value to the Kenyan economy. Attendees listened politely, but everyone was waiting for the announcement of the prizes.

As the various prizes were awarded, there were cheers from the supporters of the winners, but these winners also knew that they had not won the grand prize. This was to be the last announcement. When the grand prize winner was announced, the applause was thunderous. Many of the other contestants, sponsors, and TechnoServe employees had met the winner and knew her fantastic story.

Two weeks prior to the awards ceremony, the final judging process had occurred. All of the final contestants had been taken to a one-week offsite retreat. Early in the week, the contestants had been given training in presentation skills and coaching on turning their business plans into presentations to be judged. Later in the week, the contestants made their presentations to the judges and the winners were chosen but not announced. Unfortunately, on the second night, a young woman contestant, Jacqui, was taken to the hospital with acute appendicitis and had her appendix removed. Like the successful entrepreneurs I had observed in Silicon Valley, Jacqui was not going to be held back by this misfortune. She knew that the BBB was a great opportunity so she left the hospital two days later, and somewhat weak, with her mother and sister providing support, made her business presentation to the judges. I don't know if her determination had a major influence on the judges because she had a very thoughtful plan for the business that she had already started and was already demonstrating excellent growth. We had heard this amazing story and cheered loudly with the rest of the crowd when her name was announced as the grand prize winner.

It was an inspiring end to our time in Africa, and we felt good. We hadn't changed the world overnight, but we had helped to get some people out of poverty and on the road to more productive and satisfying lives. We had been able to utilize our business skills and experience and provide unique capabilities to help solve a variety of diverse challenges. On the personal side, we made amazing connections with our colleagues who came from entirely different backgrounds but were committed to the same goals, and many of them remain our friends. We also had a wonderful adventure exploring places, cultures, and environments very different from our typical routine in the United States. We were ready to go home, but our time in Africa had been a wonderful experience.

Coming Home

Arriving home was somewhat comfortable and somewhat surreal. Moving back into our house felt very familiar but at the same time abnormal. Some of the impact was the jet lag that didn't really wear off for over a week. Some of the strangeness was the fact that all of our clothes, kitchenware, utensils, bathroom sundries, etc., had been packed away in the garage while we were gone and needed to be unpacked. Being up at unusual hours and being tired during the middle of the day compounded the weird feelings as we set about moving back into our home.

After the initial few weeks, we became comfortable seeing friends and reestablishing old patterns of activity. It now all seemed very familiar and easy, and Africa seemed farther and farther away. We missed our friends in Africa and the sense of purpose we had every day getting up for work. We missed the excitement, but we knew it was time to come home to the United States, to our family, and to our long-time friends.

After a while in the United States, Africa often seemed like a magical dream, but we knew it wasn't and that the wonderful experiences we had there would influence us for the rest of our lives. We hadn't changed the world overnight, but we felt good about the work we had done and believed it would have long-term benefits. Maybe we had made changes in Africa, but certainly Africa had changed us. Any time a news story on Africa appears—in any media format—our ears perk up; we read about it then discuss it as it fits or contrasts with our experiences. Plus we have traveled back to Africa on business and pleasure six times since returning to California at the end of our time in Nairobi. Africa had also given us a greater appreciation for how billions of people spend their whole lives just trying to survive. Africa had made us want to continue to contribute.

Specifically, I have taken a part-time position as a senior advisor at TechnoServe so that I can continue to do meaningful work throughout this period in my life. I could have pursued a full-time executive role, but that's not what I want at this stage. I still believe in the cause and the organization and will still work hard part-time to contribute. Wendy has done several projects for TechnoServe, but mostly she has focused on marketing projects for local businesses and returned to JA of Silicon Valley as a member of the board of directors. Our current activities and lifestyle align reasonably well with our goals for this phase in our lives. We want to continue to contribute and give back, but we still want time for fun and personal travel, particularly to visit family and friends. We want to be good people, but we don't need to be heroes.

Your Turn

*W*hile we hope you've enjoyed reading about our adventures in Africa, our success won't be complete unless we've inspired you to embark on your own journey to find purpose and adventure. As you contemplate the next chapter in your life, we'd like to offer just a few recommendations:

First of all, do something that will excite you. It's a new time in your life. Don't be constrained by the old rules that limited you during your primary career. You probably don't have all of the familial responsibilities you had earlier in your life, e.g., supporting young children. Without these pressures, you don't have to commit to the most practical and stable job. You don't even have to choose something that will offer a long-term position. You can be flexible. You can experiment and try different things. If you've always had a wild dream in the back of your mind, now is the time to go for it. Have an adventure. I'm not saying to go crazy and take unreasonable risks. Limit your risk, but then be naive and open to new and different experiences. Stretch out of your comfort zone, even as an experiment. Think of a new adventure even just in terms of days or weeks—as a short pilot program. And it doesn't have to be in a developing country. It can be in your own state or region where there are still plenty of needs to fill. Who knows where these short-term efforts might lead? During my research phase, I spent two weeks in Peru and two weeks in Nepal doing small volunteer projects. Before we embarked on our full-scale journey, we limited our risks with Wendy's rules of compulsory hot showers and flush toilets, no flying bullets, and no countries ending in "stan." We also limited our first commitment to six months. However, we had no idea where we'd be deployed, and when we were, we knew nothing about Swaziland. But that was okay.

My second recommendation is to use your skills, but in a different way or a different environment. Stretch your brain. Learn new things. Gerontologists say that this is a way to keep your brain functioning well. Even if you go into a new environment, you will be surprised as to how effective you can be with the basic skills that you take for granted. You probably have thirty to forty years of experience and most people in the world don't have your level of knowledge and skill. Whether it's basic business, technology, healthcare, construction, teaching, or just how to solve problems and get things done, you'd be amazed at how valuable your skills can be to people who don't have them.

When I first started thinking about what I wanted to do in this stage in my life, I thought about becoming a paramedic and working in disaster areas around the world. As I thought about it, I turned away from this idea because it would take me a year to learn to be a rookie paramedic, and I realized that I already had valuable skills and many years of experience that could be useful in developing countries.

Although in Africa I wasn't consulting to high-growth, high-tech companies, most of the basic principles still applied, and my clients were very appreciative. I learned about the banana and pig businesses and the challenges of managing an international NGO, but I was helping my clients with basic business analysis and consulting skills as I learned the specifics of each enterprise. Wendy directly applied her skills from Junior Achievement to start up JA Swaziland and to support Young Women in Enterprise in Kenya. She also utilized her marketing communication, sales training, and start-up experience across a broad set of projects and other support activities.

My third recommendation is to do something that makes you feel good about yourself. At this point in our lives, we've already achieved most of our career success and made most of the money we're going to make. It's at this time that most people start thinking about other aspects of their lives. Many people ask themselves questions such as, "Have I lived a good life? Am I proud of what I've done?" After thinking about these questions, people who have been fortunate in their lives often want to give back something to society. There are many ways that you can do this and feel good about yourself. It does feel good to directly see the impact of your work or have someone thank you for your help, so you should consider these things as you choose your path. However, in the end, it's not important what other people say or think about you. What's most important to you is what you think about yourself. Do something that makes you internally proud of yourself.

My fourth recommendation is, "Don't get discouraged with failure." If you're pursuing a wild idea or trying to change the world, it may not happen overnight. It may not happen at all or at least in the way you envisioned. If you have a background in the culture of Silicon Valley, this may be easier to accept. In Silicon Valley, we try to do amazing things all the time. Sometimes they work out. A lot of times they don't, and we move on to try something else. Bad things will happen; obstacles will get in your way, but you will make a difference. Sometimes platitudes really do apply. Accept what you can't control. Move on and do your best. It's better to light one candle than curse the darkness.

A number of my consulting clients in Swaziland were not

successful. Wendy's track record was much better. Her youth program ultimately became an international chapter of Junior Achievement, but it still struggled at times during the years that followed. Overall, we didn't change the world, but we were able to help some people and feel good inside about what we'd done.

My last message is, "You don't have to be a hero or a martyr." You can do good work and at the same time enjoy the opportunities. Wendy and I did a lot of travel and saw a lot of local sites when we were in Africa. Take advantage and don't feel guilty.

In the end, what are you waiting for? Start planning, and when you're ready, just do it!

Epilogue

What's Happened Since leaving Africa?

Since returning to the United States, I've continued to work with TechnoServe, on a part-time basis, primarily leading internal operations improvement projects as the organization has continued its rapid growth. In addition to keeping me occupied with interesting and worthwhile activities, my association with TechnoServe has allowed me to partially monitor the ongoing progress of the clients and projects that we worked on in Swaziland and Kenya.

In Swaziland, the Junior Achievement (JA) Program that Wendy coestablished has been one of the ongoing success stories. From 2008 through 2012 over fifteen thousand students participated in the entrepreneurship courses taught by JA. Among these courses is the *JA Company* program in which participants establish actual small companies to produce and sell products. The most successful of these companies compete on a local, regional, and continental basis. In 2011 and 2012, the winning company from Swaziland also won the all-Africa title. This is a hopeful sign for a country that sorely needs entrepreneurs.

Another entrepreneurship initiative with sustainable impact has been the BBB (Believe, Begin, Become) Business Plan Competition and its "aftercare." When few new businesses were set up even by the winners of the first business plan competition, TechnoServe established an "aftercare" program to continue to coach the winning entrepreneurs through the challenges of the start-up process. TechnoServe also created a self-help organization for the non-winning graduates to allow them to share experiences and provide mutual support. The combination of these two initiatives has significantly increased the number of new businesses emerging from the business plan competitions. Further, as TechnoServe anticipated the end of the business plan competitions in Swaziland and the related support, they packaged their training materials into an entrepreneurship train-the-trainer course and shared it with other business development organizations for their use on an ongoing basis.

As for my clients, MPE Timbers seemed to pull away from contact with TechnoServe after Wendy and I left Swaziland. However, colleagues in the TechnoServe office heard that MPE got funding and began to build the drying kiln necessary to process large poles. When TechnoServe attempted to discover more about their progress, MPE became evasive and did not want to share information. No one from TechnoServe ever heard about a thriving pole treatment business, so we assume that they were not successful in actually starting the business.

As for Phiwa and Tasty Meals, it was obvious before we left Swaziland that the prospects for Tasty Meals were not good. Phiwa shut down the business and took an engineering job in South Africa to make as much money as he could to pay off his debts.

Despite all the efforts of the Dairy Board and its motivated leader, the smallholder dairy industry in Swaziland continues to struggle and has not been a source of significant economic growth. Unfortunately, neither has pork. With further analysis, Mkhululi discovered that Swaziland's large quantity of pork imports, which he hoped to replace with domestic production, were primarily processed pork and Swaziland did not have sufficient processing to make a large addition to domestic pork production viable, although some small pork farmers were helped to be successful.

Organic cotton was also a short-lived initiative, but with increasing world prices, nonorganic cotton has become a very viable crop for Swaziland. TechnoServe has worked with the government to revitalize Swaziland's once-thriving cotton sector with very positive results to date.

The horticulture sector has also been a success story. The entrepreneur, Sdemane Farming, who lost a crop to the hailstorm, has been very successful with TechnoServe's comprehensive support in production, marketing, and financing. Sdemane continues to grow premium baby vegetables for the European export market. TechnoServe has had a number of additional successes in the horticulture segment including a project to grow chili peppers for a famous producer of hot sauce.

Although it's a small industry in a small country, TechnoServe was also successful in building the honey sector in Swaziland. Honey gave TechnoServe an opportunity to use its full value chain approach as they provided technical assistance to hundreds of beekeepers, built the capacity of the local honey processor ESKH, and promoted the establishment of the National Honey Council.

Perhaps the most impactful TechnoServe Swaziland initiative has been in handcrafts, a sector with opportunity that had not yet been identified when Wendy and I were in Swaziland. Once again, TechnoServe utilized a comprehensive value chain approach, working with thirteen individual handcraft companies, as well as the industry as a whole. At the individual company level, TechnoServe improved the focus and profitability of the firms by teaching them how to use return on investment analysis along with other business tools. With improved business focus and support in product design and marketing,

TechnoServe assisted many of these companies to access the export market for their products. At the industry level, TechnoServe was instrumental in creating the collective marketing platform Pure Swazi, and in building the capacity of SWIFT, the Swaziland Fair Trade organization. An internal evaluation of the program estimated the impact at $1.7 million in incremental revenue to the local industry. This directly improved the lives of 2,500 formal sector workers and perhaps an additional fifteen to twenty thousand rural handcrafters.

TechnoServe in Kenya has also been very successful in the past five years. At the end of our 2007 stay, the TechnoServe Kenya office was facing the prospect of significant downsizing as a large project came to a close. Fortunately, two large proposals at the time were successful, resulting in the hiring of many more employees to staff them. One of these projects was in the dairy sector and followed in the footsteps of Nyala Dairy and other similar TechnoServe projects in Kenya. Thousands of smallholder dairy farmers were organized into cooperatives or similar business groups around chilling plants where they could deliver their milk for bulking and ongoing transport to major milk processors. These solutions increased the farmers' incomes as well as providing them access to credit and critical supplies for their farms. This project was replicated in Uganda and Rwanda.

The other successful proposal was for the largest project that TechnoServe had ever performed. Now in its second phase, this project focuses on improving the growing and processing of coffee across East Africa and has increased incomes for hundreds of thousands of coffee farmers. Because of its proximity to the equator, its altitude, and its soil conditions, East Africa has some of the best coffee-growing land in the world. This meant that East African farmers had the potential to grow outstanding coffee for the expanding specialty coffee market represented by Starbucks and other premium coffee sellers. However, due to their agronomic and processing practices, many farmers were only able to sell their coffee into the mediocre commodity market, losing the potential for large increases in the selling price of their coffee. TechnoServe again took a comprehensive value chain approach and assisted individual farmers with their practices in the field, farmer groups with their processing mills, and the industry in general as they campaigned for better regulations and laws. TechnoServe also worked with the farmer business groups and cooperatives to improve their business practices and promote openness to members on the details of their finances and operations, occasionally exposing corruption.

TechnoServe Kenya has also begun new projects in horticulture and youth entrepreneurship training. The office now has more than one hundred employees.

On the individual front, Jacqui was the winner of Kenya's BBB business plan competition who defied doctors' orders after her emergency appendectomy to deliver her final presentation. Her company, Language Solutions, has continued to expand and now offers foreign and local language training, translation of written documents, and simultaneous interpretation services for live meetings. When last contacted, she had approximately twenty employees and had used her prize money to develop her online services and to reach out to international clients. She had been frequently featured in the Kenya media as a role model.

Cecilia, the regional winner of the Young Women in Enterprise (YWE) competition, has continued to overcome adversity while growing her successful business. Around the time we left Kenya, Cecilia acquired a new knitting machine as well as a contract to produce sweaters for school uniforms. This combination allowed her to hire several part-time workers. Shortly thereafter, she acquired enough retail and wholesale knitting clients to open a store at Nairobi's Kenyatta Market. However, as her business grew, a tragedy near her home in the Mukuru slums generated a serious but temporary setback. A neighbor couple was arguing about the husband's infidelity. When the argument became physical, the couple's cooking fire started a blaze that destroyed Cecilia's home and inventory. Cecilia found a new location to live and operate her store. She successfully reestablished her business and expanded her school-based clients, which allowed her to continue supporting her two siblings.

Unfortunately, fate intervened again. In late 2011, the City Council of Nairobi decided to raze the area of Kiagomb'e in which she was living and working. Fortunately, Cecilia was able to retrieve most of her personal effects and her inventory before the bulldozers flattened her neighborhood. So in late 2011, Cecilia moved her home and shop to Cabanas, another step up from her Mukuru origins. Business was not good at Cabanas and her premises were too small to house both her business and her residence. Not to be defeated, in February 2012, Cecilia and her Kacece Creations moved again, this time to Kayole, a definite improvement from her prior facilities with a concrete-walled home (unlikely to succumb to fire!), running water, and electricity—most of the time—as well as a toilet and shower. Her shop was near the corner of an open area from where her sign could be seen, which she hoped would increase foot traffic. However, in early 2013, she was not getting much foot traffic and was experiencing competition from Asian imports. She evaluated her situation and decided that additional education that could lead to a career offered a better opportunity than remaining a small entrepreneur. So with the support of some former TechnoServe volcons, she has returned to high school to finish her diploma. Despite these many years of incredible challenges, Cecilia remains upbeat, supported by her determination, religious faith, and belief in herself.

NOTE: To read more success stories, please visit: www.walleigh.com.

Postscript

Is There Any Hope for Africa? Yes!

*O*ne month after we returned to the United States, Kenya had a very close presidential election with sufficient voting fraud to have swayed the outcome. Violence erupted around the country, and by the time it was put down, over a thousand people had been killed and hundreds of thousands displaced. This was a tremendous shock to anyone at all familiar with Kenya. Everyone thought that Kenya was a well-established country with citizens who generally respected the rule of law. No one thought that Kenya was a replica of the United States. It still had significant corruption and was primarily controlled by a group of old politicians who had grown up in the Jomo Kenyatta and Daniel Arap Moi era, but to have this level of violence bordering on insurrection and a potential civil war was unthinkable. But it did happen, and the events were broadcast globally on the evening news.

As we discussed these events and our recent African experience with our friends, we repeatedly got the question, "Is there any hope for Africa?" As we have told our friends, the answer is absolutely there is hope. Overall, Africa is moving in a very positive direction, and we should help those who are trying to improve their countries. Of course, in getting to an "overall," many serious problems are averaged out by many success stories, and much progress comes in the form of three steps forward, two back. But this is progress, and it does continue. More and more African countries are becoming democratic. Many African countries are experiencing economic growth rates well above the developed countries. New generations are moving into the halls of power in both commerce and politics, and these younger people are not tainted by the cold war, a belief in Marxism, or alliances with old political machines. They have new visions for their countries that include true representative democracies and true market-oriented economies.

Because they are starting so far behind in per capita income, African countries will not soon be at parity with the west, but they are making great progress, and we should help and encourage the good ones. We should also chastise and apply pressure when countries slip into old patterns of corruption, favoritism, manipulated markets, and oppression of minorities. We must be very careful with our aid directly to governments because it can be seen as a "prize" for corrupt administrators to pursue. Even our support given directly to the people has to be carefully administered to prevent a culture of dependency.

African growth and development will come primarily from the efforts of Africans, but we can and should influence and accelerate their economic growth and development of democracy. We should not give up hope when we hear stories of corruption. One only has to go back a hundred years (or much less) in the history of the United States to read stories about pervasive corruption and oppression of minorities. Yet we have survived and thrived. So will Africa.

CPSIA information can be obtained at www.ICGtesting.com
Printed in the USA
BVOW05s2351020415

394361BV00002BD/16/P

9 781627 871853